THE
Ultimate
DOG
BOOK

THE
Ultimate
DOG
BOOK

DAVID TAYLOR

CONSULTING EDITOR
CONNIE VANACORE

COMMISSIONED PHOTOGRAPHY BY
DAVE KING • JANE BURTON

SIMON AND SCHUSTER

New York London Toronto Sydney Tokyo Singapore

A DORLING KINDERSLEY BOOK

SIMON AND SCHUSTER
Simon & Schuster Building
Rockefeller Center
1230 Avenue of the Americas
New York, New York 10020

Simultaneously published in Great Britain
by Dorling Kindersley Ltd.
9 Henrietta Street, London WC2E 8PS

Project Editors
Sharon Lucas, Maria Pal

Project Art Editor
Gillian Shaw

Editor
Richard Williams

Designer
Sally Ann Hibbard

Managing Editor
Vicky Davenport

Managing Art Editor
Colin Walton

Typeset on Aldus Pagemaker
Reproduced by Colourscan, Singapore
Printed in Italy by A. Mondadori, Verona

1 3 5 7 9 10 8 6 4 2

Library of Congress Cataloging in Publication Data
Taylor, David, 1934-
    The ultimate dog book / David Taylor ; commissioned photography by
Dave King, Jane Burton.
        p. cm.
    "A Dorling Kindersley book"—T.p. verso.
    ISBN 0-671-70988-7
    1. Dogs.   2. Dog breeds.   3. Dogs—Pictorial works.   I. Title.
SF426.T38 1990
636.7—dc20   90-32242
                                                                  CIP

Contents

The Essential Dog

Breeds

Keeping a Dog

Reproduction

The Essential Dog

The most popular pet worldwide is the domestic dog, *Canis familiaris*. It holds a quite unique position in human society. The relationship between dog and man is that of two more or less carnivorous mammals that have shared shelter, food, weather, and fortune; exploited, quarreled with, and fawned over one another; worked, played, and endured together for a hundred centuries. Not even the horse has been so intimately involved in recent human evolution.

Man has employed dogs in a rich variety of ways – as guards, guides, hunters, war-machines, rodent controllers, draft animals, and foot-warmers, as well as providers of hair and meat. Today, around six million dogs are kept as pets in Britain and at least fifty million in the US. There are about 400 breeds. Although their sizes and shapes vary enormously, all dogs are essentially the same design of animal, not far removed from their primitive ancestors. They are resilient and adaptable creatures, and the process of evolution hasn't found it necessary to alter them much.

The number of different breeds means that there will always be one just right for you, no matter what your taste, fitness, accommodation, or purse. And whatever you choose, giant or Toy, purebred or mongrel, athlete or lap-dog, you can be sure that, if treated with care and intelligence, it will repay your kindness a hundredfold in companionship and affection. It may even become your best friend.

Origins and Domestication

About sixty million years ago, a small mammal rather like a weasel or polecat clambered through the primeval forests. Its name was *Miacis* and it was the ancestor of the group of animals that we call canids: the dog, jackal, wolf, and fox family.

Unlike modern dogs that walk on their toes, *Miacis* was flat-footed. It had a carnivore's teeth and a smallish brain, but was more intelligent than its contemporaries, the creodonts, another group of primitive meat-eaters. The creodonts were much more common than *Miacis*, but gradually became extinct, the last one dying out around twenty million years ago.

Canine ancestors

By around thirty-five million years ago, *Miacis* had given rise to a variety of early canids. We know of over forty types, some like bears, some like hyenas, and some like cats. Some, however, were like dogs: *Cynodictis*, for example, resembled a primitive Cardigan Welsh Corgi. These dog-like canids were the only ones to survive the evolutionary process, and some of them provided the basis for the domestic dog.

Dogs as we know them first came on the scene in Eurasia between 12,000 and 14,000 years ago. From what kind of animal did they directly spring? It was originally thought that their ancestor was a form of jackal or jackal/wolf cross. Scientists now believe, however, that it was the smaller southern strain of the gray wolf (*Canis lupus pallipes*) still to be found in India. During the period in question the gray wolf (despite its name, an animal with a wide variety of coat colors) was distributed throughout Europe, Asia, and North America.

Other possible dog ancestors include the woolly wolf of northern India and Tibet and the desert wolf of the Middle East. It is, however, certain that all domestic dogs sprang from one of these sources (or possibly more than one, in parallel development), and that they are not genetically connected with any other species.

ANCIENT DOG BREEDS

The Saluki shares common ancestry with the Greyhound, and originated in the area now known as Syria at least 4000 years ago.

The Mexican Hairless Dog found in South America has much in common with the Chinese Crested Dog of mainland Asia, and they may be related.

The African Wild Dog is an endangered species, having been hunted to extinction by man because of its success as a predator.

THE EARLIEST TYPES OF DOG

Five distinct types of dog have been identified from fossil remains dating from the beginning of the Bronze Age, c.4500 BC:
- Mastiffs
- wolf-like dogs
- Greyhounds
- Pointer-type dogs
- sheepdogs

These basic types proliferated by selective breeding and natural genetic mutation to produce the hundreds of breeds we know today.

Canis familiaris inostranzevi
Mastiff-type dogs from Tibet were domesticated in the Stone Age, and later used in battle by the Babylonians, Assyrians, Persians, and Greeks.

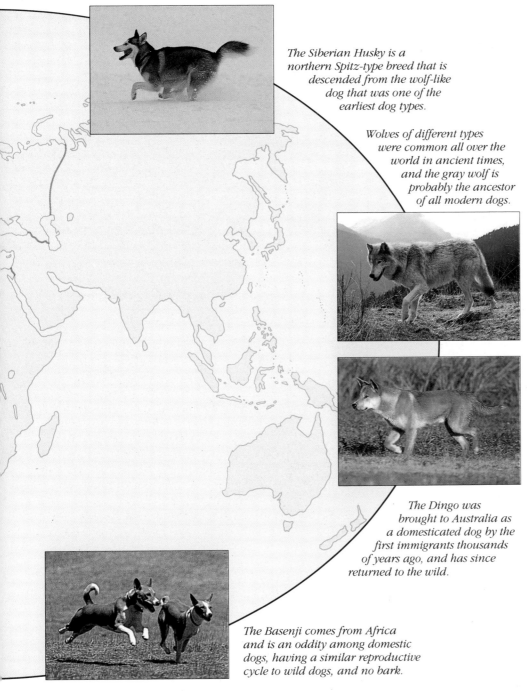

The Siberian Husky is a northern Spitz-type breed that is descended from the wolf-like dog that was one of the earliest dog types.

Wolves of different types were common all over the world in ancient times, and the gray wolf is probably the ancestor of all modern dogs.

The Dingo was brought to Australia as a domesticated dog by the first immigrants thousands of years ago, and has since returned to the wild.

The Basenji comes from Africa and is an oddity among domestic dogs, having a similar reproductive cycle to wild dogs, and no bark.

Dog diversification

Because of their intelligence, versatility, and use of social co-operation within the pack, wild dogs spread quickly all over the world. The Dingo, however, which many believe was the basic type of *Canis* from which the modern dog evolved, was already domesticated when it was introduced to Australia thousands of years ago by the first immigrants. Wild dogs were probably domesticated in different ways in different parts of the world; some while scavenging for food around human settlements, others when early man hunted dogs for food and took litters of puppies back to the homestead for fattening up.

From bones and fossils found around the world and dated back to about 6500 years ago, we can say that at that period there were five different types of dogs: Mastiffs, wolf-like dogs, Greyhounds, Pointer-type dogs, and sheepdogs. Since then, thousands of breeds have been developed by both artificial and natural selection. But over the centuries many have been lost, and only about 400 remain today.

When the Europeans first arrived in North and South America in the fifteenth and sixteenth centuries, for example, they found at least twenty distinct dog breeds: now the Mexican Hairless, Eskimo Dog, and Peruvian and Chilean Wild Dogs are among the few surviving natives. Other ancient breeds include the Basenji, native to Africa, and, from the Middle East, the equally venerable Saluki and Afghan.

Canis familiaris palustris
Wolf-like dog similar to Spitz-type dogs such as the Elkhound (above), Siberian Husky, Keeshond, and Eskimo Dog.

Canis familiaris leineri
The Greyhound is one of the oldest types, identified from drawings on Mesopotamian pottery dating back 8000 years.

Canis familiaris intermedius
Pointer-type dogs were probably developed from Greyhounds for the purpose of hunting small game.

Canis familiaris metris optimae
Sheepdogs have been used to guard flocks from predators for thousands of years, and probably originated in Europe.

Design and Anatomy

The dog is essentially an animal of the chase: enduring, patient, intelligent, and fleet of foot. Above all it is a sociable beast, with none of the aloof, lordly, go-it-alone attitudes of the cat family. This is clearly seen in the behavior of packs of wild dogs, which not only co-operate in setting up group ambushes, but also make sure that unattached adults contribute to the community by acting as baby-sitters while parents go hunting.

The dog family, which includes foxes, jackals, and wolves, is not highly specialized biologically. In fact, its broad adaptability and multipurpose form have been major factors in its survival worldwide. Nevertheless, it is important to consider some of the dog's systems which contribute to its ability to survive and which are generally common to Dingo and Dachshund, Chihuahua and Cocker Spaniel.

A leaping dog is a study in grace and power. The spring comes from the powerful hindquarters, and the tail is used to balance the dog while it is in the air.

Locomotion

It is a well-known fact that the cheetah is the world's fastest land mammal, achieving speeds of possibly up to 80mph (129km/h) over short distances. The fleetest members of the dog family are not in the same league, although wolves can achieve speeds of around 35mph (56km/h), and Salukis and Greyhounds bred specially for racing can approach 43mph (70km/h).

But hunting in the animal world is often carried out over long distances. Here is where the stamina of the dog family pays dividends. African Wild Dogs will pace one another, some loping behind for a while as others race ahead. When the leaders tire, the lopers move to the front and keep up the relentless pace of the vanguard. After a long chase this species may actually run down and kill lions.

In the water the dog is generally a no more than adequate swimmer, employing the paddle stroke named after it. One canine, however, really is an excellent swimmer and diver. This is the wild Raccoon Dog of China, Japan, and Siberia. An expert at fishing, the Raccoon Dog can stay underwater for several minutes when in pursuit of prey.

SENSES

A dog has the same senses as a human, but they differ markedly in power. This is because of the different needs of our respective ancestors.

Smell

Dogs have a very powerful sense of smell. Although it varies from breed to breed and among individuals in any one breed, their olfactory ability is outstanding and far superior to our

Left: Dogs are essentially long-distance runners. They can sprint in short bursts, but owe their success as hunters to their easy, loping gait, and their great stamina.

Right: Despite the powerful build of the average dog, they are surprisingly agile creatures that can jump many times their own height.

filter smells from the incoming air. To accommodate such a structure, dogs have developed long noses (with some exceptions among the recent "artificial" breeds). There are also many more sensory cells in the dog's olfactory

own – in fact about one million times better. Only eels are notably better smellers than dogs, while butterflies have a sense of smell approximately equal in sensitivity, but can use it at much longer distances. Dogs are used in France and Italy to find the truffle fungus, which grows up to 12in (30cm) underground, and in Holland and Denmark to detect gas leaks. They are more sensitive than the most advanced of odor-measuring machines, and are used all over the world to search for explosives, drugs, and people. How do they do it?

Smells consist of molecules of particular chemicals floating in the air. When these molecules land on the special olfactory membrane inside a nose, nerve impulses convey the "smell information" to a particular part of the brain. This olfactory center is highly developed in the dog and far larger than in man. The olfactory area in the adult human nose is about $\frac{1}{2}$ sq. in (3cm²), whereas in the average canine nose it covers almost 20 sq. in (130cm²), being arranged in folds in order to

membrane than there are in the human's. We have five million sensory cells. A Dachshund has 125 million, a Fox Terrier 147 million, and a German Shepherd 220 million.

A wet nose helps in smelling: it dissolves molecules floating in the air, bringing them into contact with the olfactory membrane, and clears old smells away. Pigment helps too, but how this works is not understood. The pigment is not in the sensory cells but

nearby: the nasal membranes of the dog are dark, and the black pigment in the nose pad may also play some part in improving the dog's sense of smell.

Tracker dogs take advantage of the fact that the sweat of every individual human is as unique to him as his fingerprints. A dog can recognize the "scent image" of a person and make deductions from the evaporation of various ingredients of the smell with time. This allows it to run along a trail for a few yards, register the change in the image, and thus even determine which way the person was going.

Taste
The dog's sense of taste is relatively poorly developed, compared with man's. This is probably because, unlike man's ancestors, vegetarian primates that can select from a range of foods in front of them, dogs are carnivores that spot their prey at a distance, and have to eat what they can catch.

The strong muscles of the shoulders take most of the strain on landing, and the pads of the forefeet ensure a good grip.

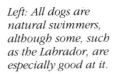

Left: All dogs are natural swimmers, although some, such as the Labrador, are especially good at it.

Right: The sight of dogs being used as draft animals to pull carts is now rare. Spitz-type dogs are well adapted for this work, however, and in cold regions they continue to pull sleds as they have done for centuries.

DOGS' EYES

field of
vision
200°

field of
binocular vision

field of
vision
270°

Boston Terrier

Greyhound

The dog has a wider field of vision than man because its eyes are set further towards the sides of its head. The field of vision ranges from 200° in flat-nosed breeds to 270° in long-nosed breeds, compared to 100° in man. Dogs are not as good as man at focusing on objects at close range or at judging distance, however, because of their smaller field of binocular vision.

Vision

A dog's sight is well adapted to hunting small, fast-moving animals. Most species do not hunt primarily by sight, however, and often miss creatures that stand still. Certainly dogs are not sensitive to color, and see mainly in black, white, and shades of gray.

Hearing

This is something else at which dogs are excellent. Although some breeds have better hearing than others, most dogs are equipped with large external ears that are served by seventeen muscles, and can prick and swivel these sound receivers to focus on the source of any noise. They can register sounds of 35,000 vibrations per second (compared to 20,000 per second in man and 25,000 per second in the cat), which means that they can detect noises well beyond the range of the human ear. They are also sensitive enough to tell the difference between, for example, two metronomes, one ticking at a hundred, and the other at ninety-six beats per minute. Dogs can also shut off their inner ear so as to filter from the general din those sounds on which they want to concentrate. (This gift makes them ideal guests at cocktail parties!)

POINTS OF THE DOG

The height of a dog is measured from the withers to the ground.

The length is measured from point of shoulder to point of buttock.

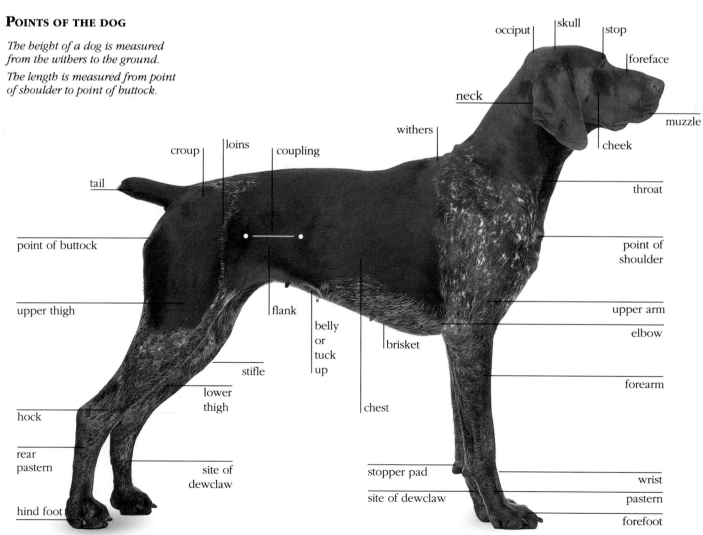

occiput | skull | stop

foreface

neck

muzzle

cheek

withers

throat

croup | loins | coupling

tail

point of buttock

point of shoulder

upper thigh

flank

belly or tuck up

brisket

upper arm

elbow

stifle

chest

forearm

lower thigh

hock

rear pastern

site of dewclaw

stopper pad

site of dewclaw

wrist

pastern

hind foot

forefoot

Other abilities

Like cats, dogs are very sensitive to vibrations and will give warning of earth tremors some considerable time, and occasionally even days, before humans are aware of any movement. The curious thing is that dogs react like this only to the imminence of true earthquakes; somehow they can tell the difference between advance tremors of the real thing and the 150,000 other harmless vibrations of the earth's crust that occur each year and do not alarm them.

The dog is equipped with one efficient weapons system – its teeth. The powerful jaw muscles provide a hefty bite if required. A 44lb (20kg) mongrel has been found to exert a bite of 363lb (165kg) pressure. The average human adult can gnaw no harder than 45-65lb (20-29kg), and the strongest of men under special training can only manage 160lb (73kg).

Finally, what about extrasensory perception in dogs? Repeated testing under apparently stringent conditions has produced evidence to suggest that certain canines possess psychic/telepathic abilities: what is usually referred to in humans as a "sixth sense". This is how your dog knows you're going for a walk even before you've decided yourself!

Bloodhound

German Shepherd

DOGS' EARS

Dogs vary in the sensitivity of their hearing: those with erect ears such as the German Shepherd can swivel them to improve reception and determine the direction of a sound; those with long, floppy ears such as the Bloodhound do not have this ability. The purpose of long ears remains unclear: they may have been bred into dogs used to hunt in thick undergrowth in order to prevent foreign bodies falling into the ear canal. Another suggestion is that they help to channel scents to the nose as they brush along the ground.

COAT COLORS

The following specialist terms are used in the canine world to describe the colors and markings of dogs' coats:

Blue merle Marbled mixture of black, blue, and gray hairs.

Particolor (or pied) Marked in patches of two colors.

Saddle Marking on the back in the shape or position of a saddle.

Wheaten The color of ripening wheat, pale yellow to fawn.

Tricolor A coat in three colors; black, white, and tan, for example.

Roan Fine mixture of colored and white hairs.

Sable Black-tipped hairs on a background of gray, fawn, tan, gold, or silver.

Brindle Streaked effect caused by black hairs on a light-colored background.

Grizzle Mixture of bluish-gray, red, and black.

Behavior and Intelligence

"Playmouthing" is a feature of dog behavior that probably derives from food-begging.

Dogs stand higher in the IQ league than cats, canaries, or ponies. They are excellent learners with good powers of association. As social animals they are adept at interpreting subtle signals conveyed by other individuals – canine or human. Together, these traits enable the dog to "understand" people and to establish friendships with them.

Scent and visual signaling

Signaling plays an important part in a dog's life. Many messages involve smell: dogs mark territory by frequent urination, and by scratching the ground to leave scent from sweat glands in the paws. They also roll in grass and more pungent substances such as manure in order to enhance (to a dog's nose at least) their body odor.

Visual signaling by body language is highly developed too. A varied repertoire of body postures, facial expressions, and tail signals transmits information that other dogs, other animals, and humans can interpret. There is also a wide range of sound signals that includes aggressive growls and snarls, whines, howls, "yips" (from hounds while hunting), and a variety of barks.

The importance of play

Puppies love to play, and their play is more than just *joie de vivre*. Its purpose can be traced back to their wild relatives. Not only is it a substitute for hunting, prompted by the instinct of the pack-hunter, but it also provides valuable physical exercise for the growing animal. The puppy learns about the world as it investigates everything with its senses, and meanwhile it develops the social skills so important to such a gregarious species. Even more than kittens, which inherit a self-reliant, rather solitary way of life, puppies need lots of contact with their peers and human friends in order to grow up

THE BODY LANGUAGE OF DOGS

Faced with a dominant adult, this puppy is lying down exposing its belly, in a posture of extreme submissiveness.

The standing dog is showing aggressive dominance, with tail raised, the hair bristling on its back, and teeth bared in a snarl.

During play, this dog is practicing the position of extreme dominance by placing its paws on a rival's back.

In this confrontation the Border Collie is averting its gaze in order not to arouse the aggression of the Poodle, which is dominant.

SCENT-MARKING

Dog 1 makes his mark on a grass stem...

Dog 2 sniffs and marks the same stem ...

and Dog 3 sniffs the stem before marking.

into well-adjusted adults. Puppies deprived of contact with other dogs during the crucial period from three to ten weeks, when they are at their most playful, will not develop correct social responses. What is lost during this vital period cannot be instilled later. Such individuals become neurotic, with a tendency to be antisocial and unable to form normal relationships with other dogs.

For adult dogs, play is mainly fun and exercise, although in their wild cousins it may also serve to remind each animal of its position in the social pecking order. This helps to reduce the risk of serious fighting.

Playful wrestling can turn in an instant into something more serious, with growls and snarls as one of the puppies tries to assert dominance over the other.

The bowing stance (left) is an unmistakable invitation to play.

Antisocial behavior

Understandably with such a complex and intelligent species, things do go wrong, and dogs can sometimes present behavioral, psychological problems. These can range from the "problem puppy" that will not house-train, to serious biters, barkers, leg-mounters, and dogs with specific phobias.

Very rarely is a dog truly psychotic – behaving totally irrationally. In almost every case, its behavior can be explained by an examination of the fundamental nature of *Canis familiaris*. The fact that the dog is descended from social hunting animals, and an individual has had a deficient up-bringing, usually explains everything.

The good owner must study and understand his or her dog's essential character. If antisocial behavior does arise, the vet should be consulted, and then perhaps an animal behaviorist or "dog psychologist".

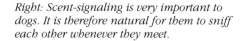

The abandon with which this Great Dane is rolling suggests that it is scratching its back. Dogs covering themselves in muck to enhance their odor use a more businesslike technique.

Right: Scent-signaling is very important to dogs. It is therefore natural for them to sniff each other whenever they meet.

Breeds

There are more than two hundred distinct breeds of domesticated dog in the world today, and although it is generally believed that the wolf is the ancestor of all of them, we do not know many details of the ancient family tree. Certainly it seems that man's first association with the wolf-dog that was to become his companion and collaborator changed its body form in fundamental ways, partly perhaps through primitive selective breeding, and also because life close to man altered the wolf-dog's lifestyle in ways that were gradually reflected in its anatomy.

By the Bronze Age there were at least five clearly differentiated types of dog, two of them originating from the large wolves of the sub-arctic regions. One of these was the ancestor of the Spitz breeds, the other of the mastiffs. Three further types, sheepdogs, pointers, and Greyhounds, are thought to have descended from the small wolves of India and the Middle East, and an early intermediate form may be represented today by the Australian dingo and the Pariah dog of Asia. However, although we can identify from archaeological remains, paintings, and sculpture, dogs that are similar to those we know today, most modern breeds were established no more than about a hundred years ago.

Dog breeds have been gathered into a system of groups since the late 1800s to provide a convenient framework for judging at shows. There are six groups in most countries, and the English-speaking world uses the same terminology on the whole, but with the odd variation. The group called "Non-Sporting" in the US and Canada is termed "Utility" in Britain, and what the US and Canada call "Sporting Dogs" go under the name of "Gundogs" in Britain and Australia.

Hounds

Athleticism and a wonderful sense of smell are the two great features of this group of dogs, and a breed of hound may possess one or both of them. Hounds were the earliest hunting dogs used by man; they provided the speed that the two-legged homo sapiens lacked when in hot pursuit of high-protein sources of

Norwegian Elkhound

Greyhound, were swift, silent sprinters that relied mainly on good eyesight in the chase. They were, and are, the canine equivalent of human one-hundred meter champions: generally tall individuals with a long stride.

Basset Hound

Scent hounds
Several centuries later, hounds that tracked game by ground scents were developed in Europe. Typically, these scent hounds had, like their present-day counterparts, strong, sturdy legs, long heads, pendulous ears, and muzzles with a remarkable sense of smell up to one million times better than a human being's. Today, there are also specialist scent hounds that have long bodies and short legs. In general, scent hounds display great stamina in wearing down their quarry, rather than relying on brief bursts of high speed.

food. It is therefore not surprising that hounds have featured more than any other kind of dog in writing and literature over the centuries.

Irish Wolfhound

Sight hounds
As with other aspects of the remarkable history of the domestic dog, it all began in the Middle East, where sleek and leggy animals that had long, flexible, muscular trunks, were selected for the chase of game in open desert country. We have proof of this from excavated pottery shards dated to the Assyria and Persia of six thousand years BC, which are decorated with greyhound-like dogs that are in pursuit of gazelle. "Sight hounds" or "gaze hounds" of this kind, whose modern descendants are such breeds as the Afghan, Saluki and

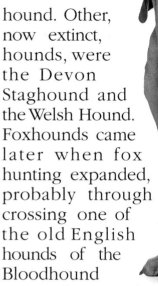

European breeds

Before 1066 there was at least one hound type, the St Hubert, in France, and it seems likely that William the Conqueror imported examples into Britain, introducing blood lines that still persist in modern breeds. From the St Hubert, the Bloodhound, the now-extinct Talbot, and the old English Staghound were derived. In tenth-century Wales the statutes of Prince Howel Dda refer to large

Dachshund

dun-colored hounds, Greyhounds, and Buckhounds or Coverthounds. A King's Buckhound was valued at one pound and a Greyhound at half that.

Breed development

During the Middle Ages it was the landed gentry who were responsible for the development of hound breeds. Long before fox hunting became popular they hunted deer and hare, using a large hound for the deer and, as their name indicates, harriers, along with Beagles, for the hare. In addition, there were other hounds around during the same period, including the Northern, a heavy solid type, and the Southern, a more light and fast

hound. Other, now extinct, hounds, were the Devon Staghound and the Welsh Hound. Foxhounds came later when fox hunting expanded, probably through crossing one of the old English hounds of the Bloodhound type with a Greyhound to give speed.

Segugio Italiano

Other distinctive breeds

Some scent hounds were trained to kill their quarry, whereas others, of which the Elkhound is an example, kept the prey cornered and then summoned the huntsman by "giving tongue" or baying. The long-bodied, short-legged hounds, such as the Dachshund, also have a long history, as ancient Egyptian wall carvings bear witness. Although the breed is nowadays rarely used for the underground hunting for which it is designed, it was popular in the fifteenth and sixteenth centuries in England, Germany, and Italy for the pursuit of foxes and rabbits, as well as badgers. In modern times, the Dachshund and Beagle are the two most popular hound breeds in the US, the former as an amiable house pet, and the latter as a keen hunter of rabbits.

Bloodhound

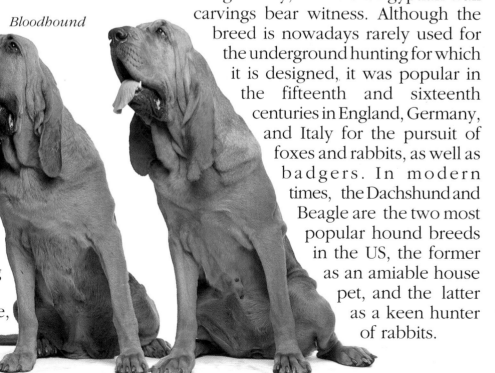

Afghan Hound

T HIS CHIC, MAJESTIC BREED should not be judged merely by its elegant appearance. As well as stunning good looks, the Afghan Hound possesses remarkable agility and a hardy constitution, enabling it to cope with the most rugged terrain.

History

Sometimes also known as the Kabul Dog, this ancient breed was depicted in four-thousand-year-old Afghan paint drawings, and on a Greek tapestry dating back to the sixth century BC. Originating probably in the Middle East, the Afghan spread along the trade routes to Afghanistan, and was used for the hunting of antelope, gazelle, wolves and snow-leopards. The first Afghans to reach Britain arrived in 1886, but were not introduced into the US until 1926.

Temperament

Afghan Hounds have an independent, lively, amicable yet sensitive temperament. Although tough, they will pine if they are deprived of attention. At one time, the breed had a reputation for being untrustworthy, but that has now been replaced by a character that, while still spirited, is said to be more amenable to training and discipline.

The Afghan delights in the comforts of the modern home.

BODY
Tall, with a trunk of moderate length, a level muscular back, and a deep chest.

COAT
Very long and silky, except along the back and face where it is short and close. All colors are acceptable, but white markings, especially on the head, are an undesirable feature. The coat should not be clipped or trimmed.

SIZE
Ideal height: dogs 27-29in (68-74cm); bitches 23-28in (61-68cm).

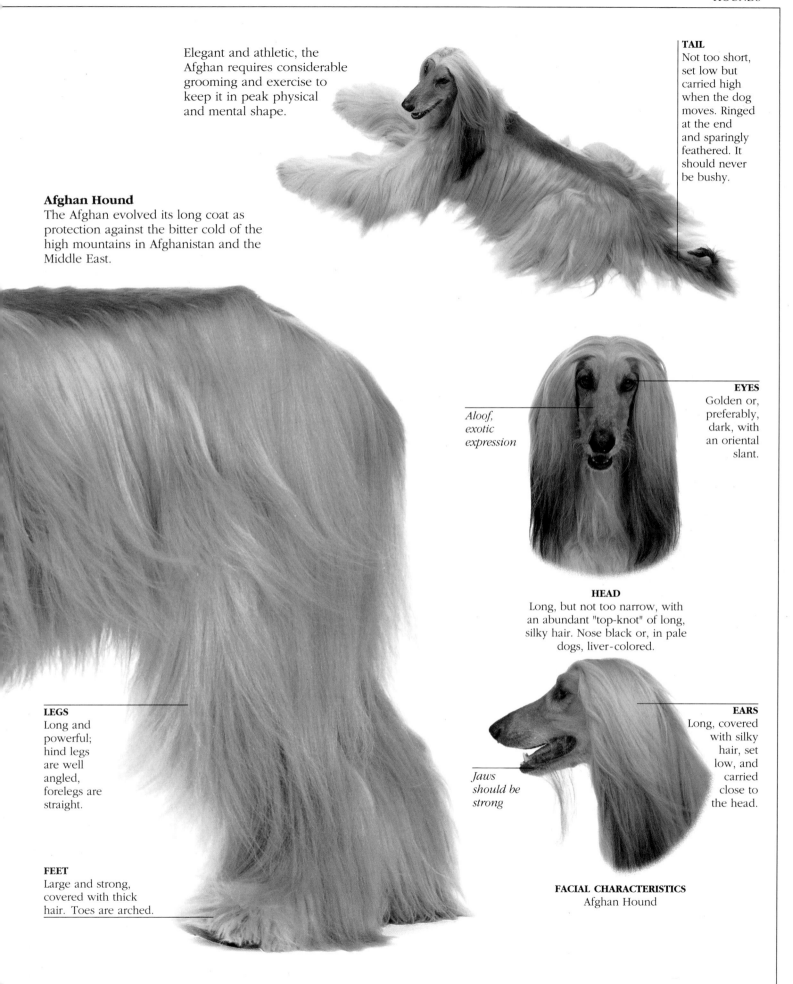

Elegant and athletic, the Afghan requires considerable grooming and exercise to keep it in peak physical and mental shape.

TAIL
Not too short, set low but carried high when the dog moves. Ringed at the end and sparingly feathered. It should never be bushy.

Afghan Hound
The Afghan evolved its long coat as protection against the bitter cold of the high mountains in Afghanistan and the Middle East.

Aloof, exotic expression

EYES
Golden or, preferably, dark, with an oriental slant.

HEAD
Long, but not too narrow, with an abundant "top-knot" of long, silky hair. Nose black or, in pale dogs, liver-colored.

LEGS
Long and powerful; hind legs are well angled, forelegs are straight.

Jaws should be strong

EARS
Long, covered with silky hair, set low, and carried close to the head.

FEET
Large and strong, covered with thick hair. Toes are arched.

FACIAL CHARACTERISTICS
Afghan Hound

Basenji

THIS IS A TRULY REMARKABLE DOG – it trots like a horse, keeps itself clean by fastidious licking, and "yodels" rather than barks! It derives its name from the Bantu word *Basenji* meaning "native" (of the bush), and is also sometimes known as the Congo Dog. In Africa it is used as a hunter, tracker, and watchdog.

History
Its ancestors were probably around at the time of the ancient Egyptians, for carvings of dogs resembling the Basenji have been found in many Pharaohs' tombs. Basenjis were discovered by Westerners a little over one hundred years ago in Central Africa, where they were being used as pack hunting dogs. They arrived in Britain at the beginning of this century, but quickly succumbed to distemper, a disease to which they had no natural immunity. They were first bred in Britain in 1937 and in the US in 1941.

Temperament
Basenjis are cheerful, perky, and mischievous creatures. Although sometimes aloof with strangers, they are generally very good with people. If they have to live with other dogs, their pack-dog instincts will probably dominate family life for a while, so be well prepared for considerable scrapping and bickering until leadership is firmly established!

HEAD
Narrowing evenly from the eyes, and of medium length. Nose pad is preferably black.

Basenji
Although full of energy and curiosity, the Basenji is quite content to laze around the house.

COAT
Loose skin carrying short, silky hair. Colors are black, tan, white, black and white, red and white, black, tan and white, with tan melon pips (points) and mask. White is preferably on feet, chest, and tail tips.

LEGS
Strong, muscular, and shapely.

SIZE
Ideal height: dogs 17in (43cm); bitches 16in (40cm).

FEET
Small and narrow, with prominently arched toes.

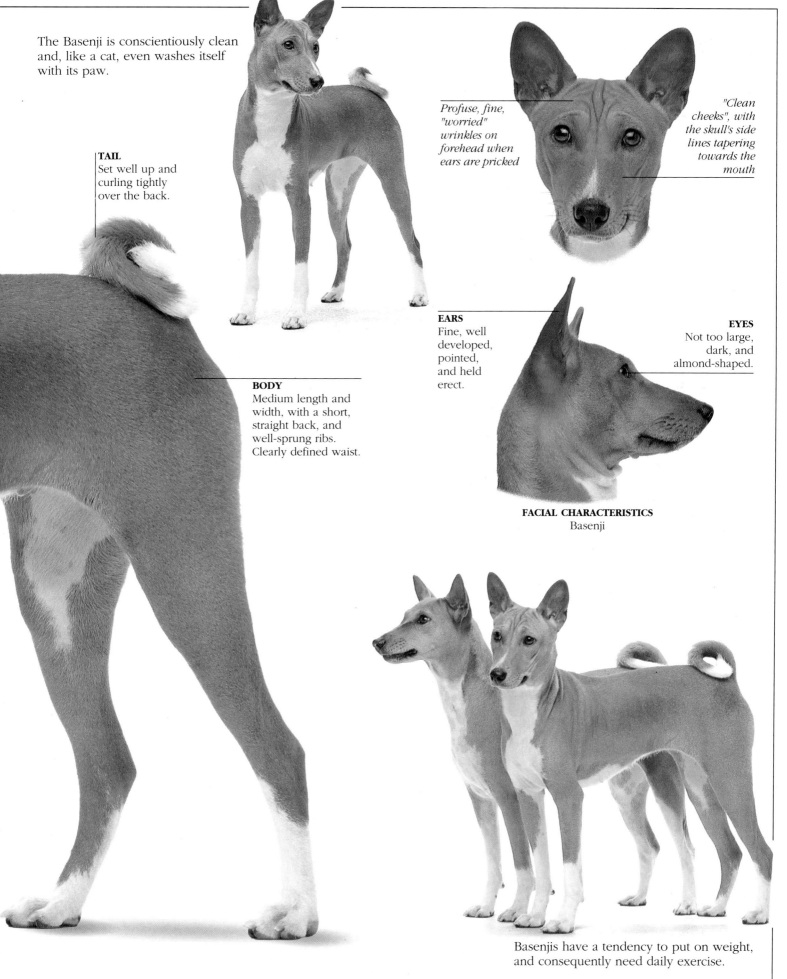

The Basenji is conscientiously clean and, like a cat, even washes itself with its paw.

Profuse, fine, "worried" wrinkles on forehead when ears are pricked

"Clean cheeks", with the skull's side lines tapering towards the mouth

TAIL
Set well up and curling tightly over the back.

BODY
Medium length and width, with a short, straight back, and well-sprung ribs. Clearly defined waist.

EARS
Fine, well developed, pointed, and held erect.

EYES
Not too large, dark, and almond-shaped.

FACIAL CHARACTERISTICS
Basenji

Basenjis have a tendency to put on weight, and consequently need daily exercise.

Basset Hound

R ATHER PLACID and with a tendency towards laziness, the Basset is nevertheless a most useful hunting dog. It is surprisingly agile and energetic, and can follow hares, rabbits, and pheasants by scent through the thickest undergrowth.

History

This breed originated in the late sixteenth century in France, the name "Basset" coming from the French word *bas*, meaning low. The general features of the Basset's head, and its acute sense of smell, suggest that the breed was produced from a dwarf mutation of the Bloodhound. The Basset was not introduced into Britain until the second half of the nineteenth century, and one appeared at the Wolverhampton Dog Show in 1875. The Basset Hound Club was formed in 1883. Queen Alexandra, wife of Edward VII, was a Basset enthusiast and regular exhibitor, and one of her dogs won at Cruft's in 1909.

Temperament

Though they look rather lugubrious, Bassets are lively, sociable, and good-natured characters. They need lots of exercise, and relish country walks where they can investigate hedgerows and thickets to their hearts' content. Kept as sedentary house-dogs, Bassets tend to become overweight and, as a consequence, can be arthritic in later life.

BODY
Broad, long, and barrel-shaped.

LEGS
Stocky, short, and sturdy, with loose, wrinkled skin.

SIZE
Ideal height: 13-15in (33-38cm).

FEET
Broad, heavy, and well knuckled, with tough, heavy pads.

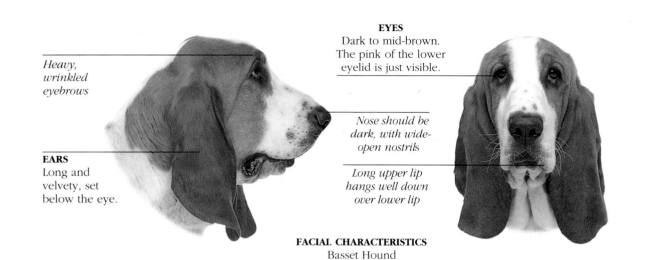

EYES
Dark to mid-brown.
The pink of the lower
eyelid is just visible.

*Heavy,
wrinkled
eyebrows*

*Nose should be
dark, with wide-
open nostrils*

EARS
Long and
velvety, set
below the eye.

*Long upper lip
hangs well down
over lower lip*

FACIAL CHARACTERISTICS
Basset Hound

Basset Hound

The Basset has a deep, bell-like bark;
the sound of a pack giving voice is a
stirring, memorable experience.

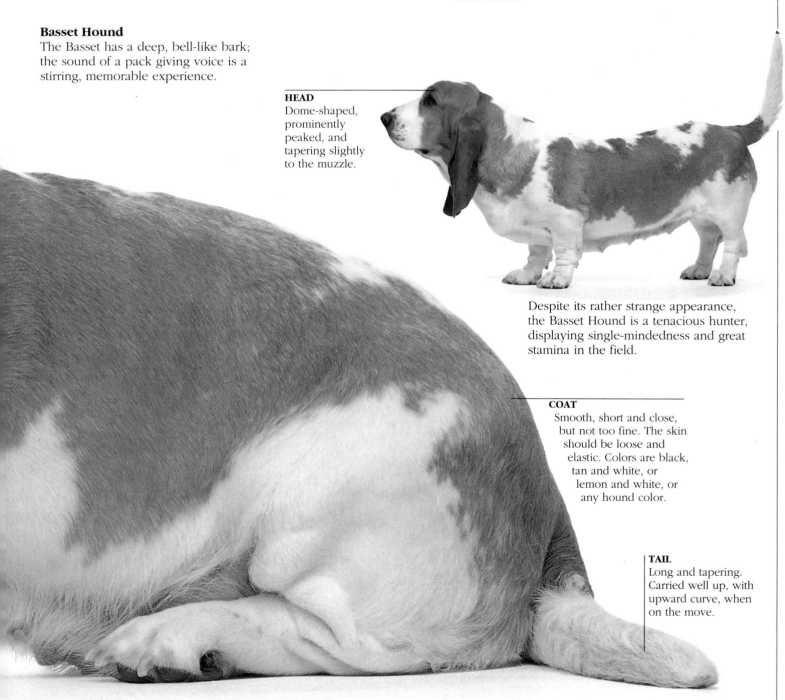

HEAD
Dome-shaped,
prominently
peaked, and
tapering slightly
to the muzzle.

Despite its rather strange appearance,
the Basset Hound is a tenacious hunter,
displaying single-mindedness and great
stamina in the field.

COAT
Smooth, short and close,
but not too fine. The skin
should be loose and
elastic. Colors are black,
tan and white, or
lemon and white, or
any hound color.

TAIL
Long and tapering.
Carried well up, with
upward curve, when
on the move.

Beagle

T HE FRENCH WORD *begueule,* meaning "gape throat", probably gave the Beagle its name, referring perhaps to the noisy clamor of the dogs when gathered into a pack. Equally content at the hunt or on the hearthrug, the Beagle makes an energetic and faithful companion.

History

These smallest of hounds perhaps go as far back as the ancient Greeks. Certainly the Norman French used Beagles for pursuing hare, and brought them to England in 1066. They were slightly smaller animals then, and were sometimes carried in saddle-bags, or even the pockets of mounted men. A mini-variety, the Pocket Beagle, was developed from such portable animals, but now no longer exists. One of several dogs associated with royalty, they have been owned by Elizabeth I, William III, and George IV, who hunted his pack on the Sussex downs near Brighton. The Beagle Club was established in the UK in 1895, and a few years later Beagles were exported to the US.

Temperament

Beagles are good natured, active, happy dogs, but can be wilful, and need firm handling.

SIZE
Height: 13-15in
(33-38cm).

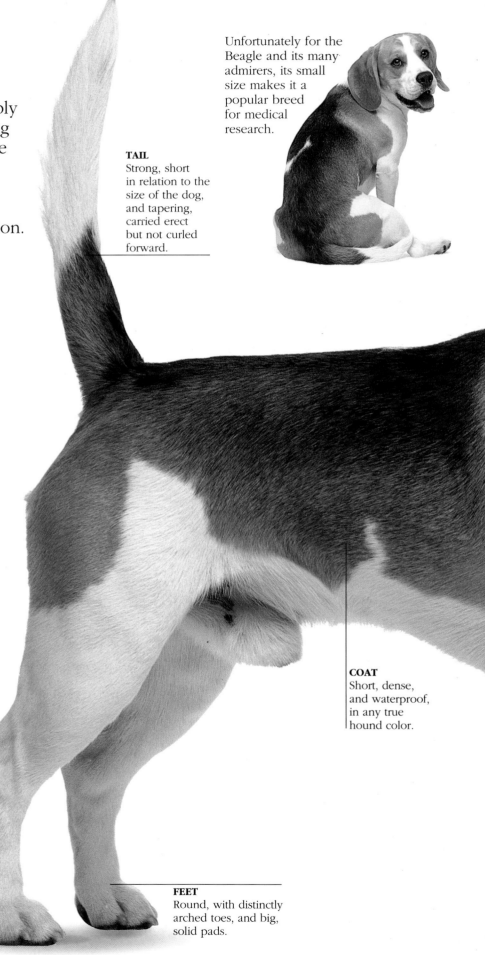

Unfortunately for the Beagle and its many admirers, its small size makes it a popular breed for medical research.

TAIL
Strong, short in relation to the size of the dog, and tapering, carried erect but not curled forward.

COAT
Short, dense, and waterproof, in any true hound color.

FEET
Round, with distinctly arched toes, and big, solid pads.

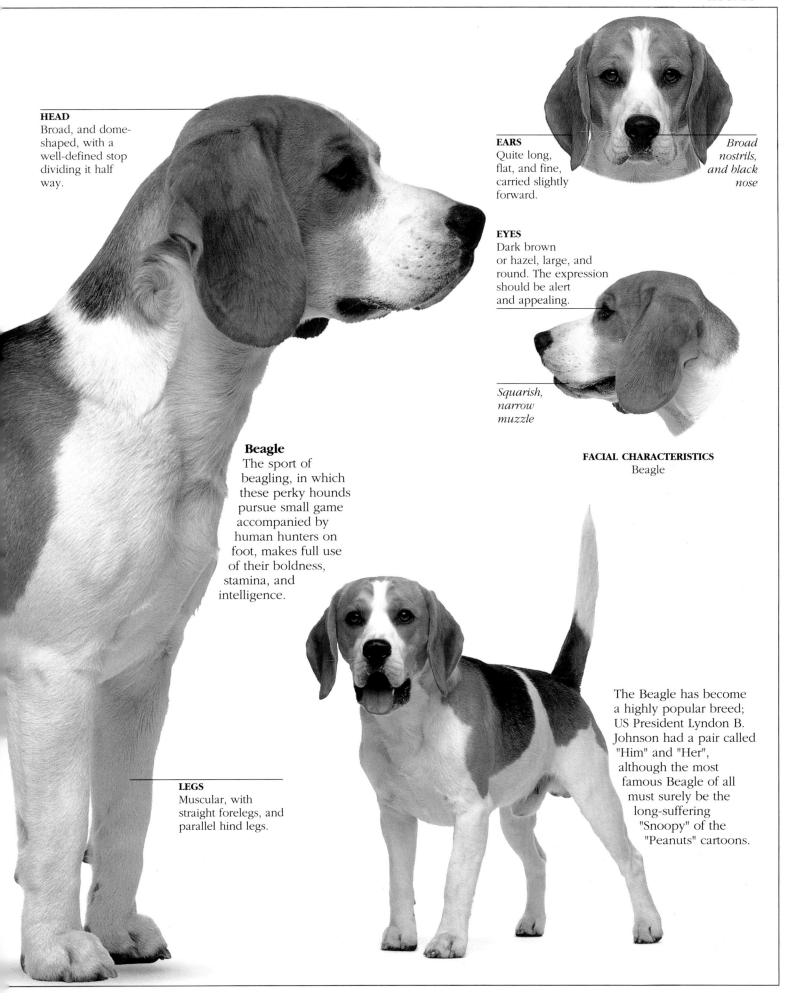

HEAD
Broad, and dome-shaped, with a well-defined stop dividing it half way.

EARS
Quite long, flat, and fine, carried slightly forward.

Broad nostrils, and black nose

EYES
Dark brown or hazel, large, and round. The expression should be alert and appealing.

Squarish, narrow muzzle

FACIAL CHARACTERISTICS
Beagle

Beagle
The sport of beagling, in which these perky hounds pursue small game accompanied by human hunters on foot, makes full use of their boldness, stamina, and intelligence.

LEGS
Muscular, with straight forelegs, and parallel hind legs.

The Beagle has become a highly popular breed; US President Lyndon B. Johnson had a pair called "Him" and "Her", although the most famous Beagle of all must surely be the long-suffering "Snoopy" of the "Peanuts" cartoons.

Bloodhound

THIS FAMOUS TRACKING HOUND of real and fictional criminology is pleasant, polite, and rather reserved. It probably derives its name from its amazing sense of smell in locating wounded (bleeding) game, or perhaps from belonging to a breed closely associated with the "blue blood" of the aristocracy.

HEAD
Big, long, and narrow, with slight tapering from temple to muzzle. Large, open nostrils.

History
As well as being among the purest of breeds, this lugubrious-looking creature is one of the oldest of hounds. Its origins can be traced back to eighth-century Belgium, in the Ardennes Forest, where St Hubert, the patron saint of hunting, kept a large pack of hounds (later to be known as St Huberts). They became a favorite breed of the French kings, and William the Conqueror brought them to England in 1066. Over the centuries, selective breeding in England refined the St Hubert into the Bloodhound as we know it today.

COAT
Short, dense hair on the body with softer, finer hair on the head and ears. Colors should be black and tan, liver and tan, or red. Any white should be on chest, feet, and tail-tip. The coat should be completely weatherproof.

Temperament
The Bloodhound is shy, gentle, and rather solemn. Once it has its nose down, it will be unable to pay attention to anything else, including the voice of its owner!

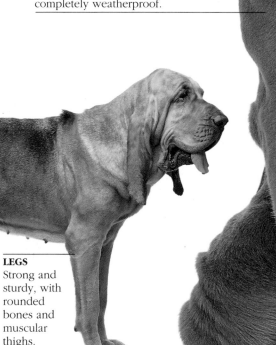

LEGS
Strong and sturdy, with rounded bones and muscular thighs.

Bloodhounds can make affectionate pets, and are popular with children, but will need plenty of space and exercise.

TAIL
Long, thick, and tapering. Set low.

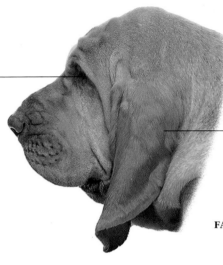

EYES
Dark brown or hazel in color, medium-sized and oval-shaped.

EARS
Very long, with a thin and silky texture. Set low.

Distinctive wrinkles on the forehead and side of the face

Scissor bite, with the upper teeth overlapping the lower teeth

FACIAL CHARACTERISTICS
Bloodhound

BODY
A broad, muscular back, deep chest, and powerful, solid loins.

The Bloodhound's dewlap, the loose, wrinkled fold of skin that hangs beneath its throat, is particularly pronounced.

Bloodhound
This breed is renowned for its inexhaustible enthusiasm for sniffing. Having found its quarry, the Bloodhound is unlikely to do it any harm, and will probably try to make friends instead!

SIZE
Dogs 25-27in (63-69cm) tall; bitches 23-25in (58-63cm).

FEET
Round, strong, and cat-like. Knuckles are well developed.

Borzoi

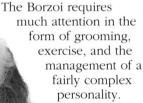

T HE RUSSIAN WORD for swift, *borzoi*, gave this slender and athletic dog its name. The tsars and aristocracy of pre-Revolutionary Russia used them in the ceremonial wolf-hunt. Also known as the Russian Wolfhound, the Borzoi is a speedy and impetuous chaser by nature, and in many cases needs obedience training to curb its instincts.

History

The Borzoi probably originated in the Middle East as a short-haired "gaze-hound" that hunted by sight. Taken to the northern lands, it was crossed with a long-legged Russian collie-type to give added hardiness and a long coat for the cold climate. It has many royal connections: as a traditional royal gift, Borzois were presented first to Queen Victoria in 1842, and then to Queen Alexandra (wife of Edward VII) by the tsars. Queen Alexandra's dogs were kept at the King's Sandringham estate in Norfolk, and bred with local collies to produce a new, refined Rough-Coated Collie, white in color, and with a long, elegant muzzle. Borzois were first exported to the US in 1889.

Temperament

Though they are often reserved and sometimes stubborn, Borzois are generally tranquil and affectionate with their friends.

COAT
Long, silky, and preferably curly or wavy. Any color, though usually white with darker markings. Short and smooth on head, ears, and front legs.

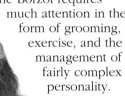

The Borzoi requires much attention in the form of grooming, exercise, and the management of a fairly complex personality.

SIZE
Minimum height: dogs 28in (71cm); bitches 26in (66cm).

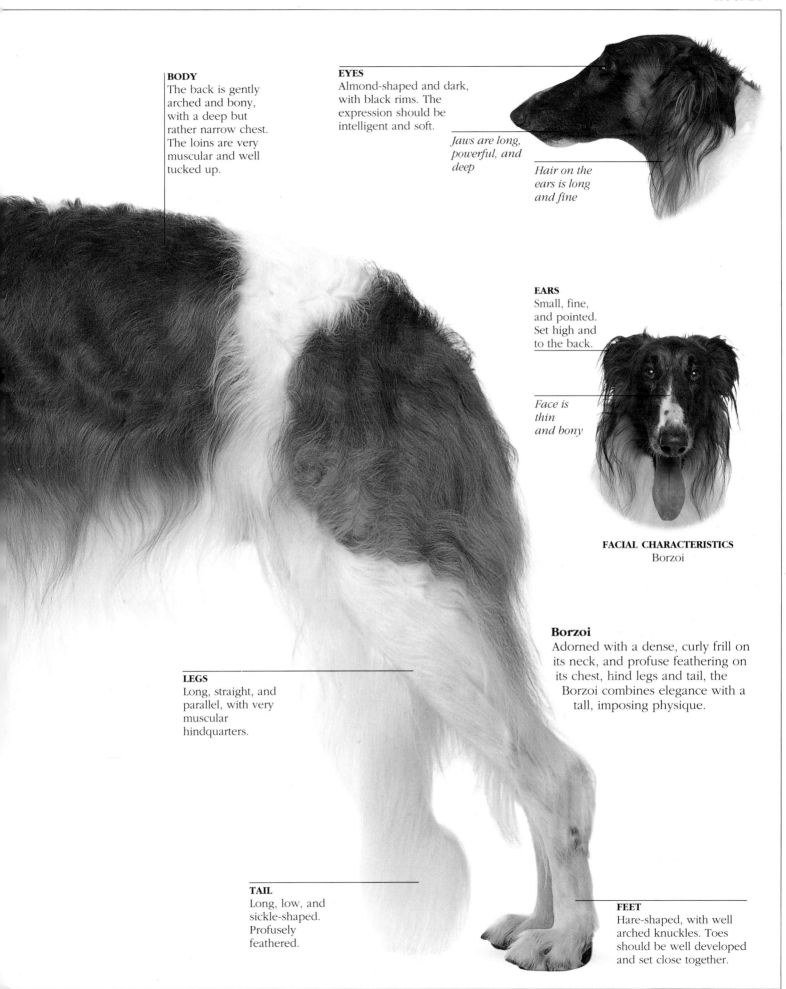

BODY
The back is gently arched and bony, with a deep but rather narrow chest. The loins are very muscular and well tucked up.

EYES
Almond-shaped and dark, with black rims. The expression should be intelligent and soft.

Jaws are long, powerful, and deep

Hair on the ears is long and fine

EARS
Small, fine, and pointed. Set high and to the back.

Face is thin and bony

FACIAL CHARACTERISTICS
Borzoi

Borzoi
Adorned with a dense, curly frill on its neck, and profuse feathering on its chest, hind legs and tail, the Borzoi combines elegance with a tall, imposing physique.

LEGS
Long, straight, and parallel, with very muscular hindquarters.

TAIL
Long, low, and sickle-shaped. Profusely feathered.

FEET
Hare-shaped, with well arched knuckles. Toes should be well developed and set close together.

Dachshunds

RATHER MALIGNED as a "sausage dog", the Dachshund is actually a spirited and plucky creature, bred for hunting, which will display immense tenacity and stamina when in pursuit of its prey. In German, *Dachshund* means badger dog (not badger hound), and although it has a good nose, it seems to be more of a natural terrier than a hound, happy to go underground to confront rabbits, foxes, and predictably, badgers.

Wire-haired Dachshund
This affectionate, rather cocky character sports a short, straight, harsh coat, except for on its ears, eyebrows, jaw, and chin. It has a beard, a dense undercoat, bushy eyebrows, and prominent ridges over its eyes.

History
Dogs with long bodies and little legs are depicted on the walls of ancient Egyptian temples, and stone and clay models of Dachshund-like dogs have been found in Mexico, Greece, Peru, and China. Some believe the breed to be purely Teutonic, for remains resembling the Dachshund have been excavated in several Roman settlements in Germany. There are six separate Dachshund varieties: smooth-haired, long-haired, and wire-haired, in standard and miniature sizes. The basic features of all six are the same and they differ only in size and coat-type. The early miniatures, the Kaninchenteckels, were created by crossing terriers and Pinschers with the smallest and lightest Dachshunds.

Temperament
All Dachshunds are lively and intelligent, but can sometimes be a little fussy.

BODY
Long, well-ribbed up, muscular, and sufficiently clear of the ground to allow unhindered movement.

COLOR
All colors. White should only be a small patch on the chest, or as even markings in Dapples.

LEGS
Hard muscles on forelegs. When viewed from behind, hindlegs are parallel.

Dachshunds have a brilliant sense of smell, and have been known to track a wounded wild boar for up to two days.

FEET
Full front feet, with smaller hind feet. The pads should be thick and firm.

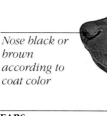

Nose black or brown according to coat color

HEAD
Long and tapering, with slightly arched muzzle.

Lips are well stretched, jaws are strong

EYES
Medium-sized, oval, and dark with a lively expression. In Dapples, one or both eyes can be partly or wholly light blue.

EARS
Mobile, fairly long, broad, and well rounded. They should be set high, with the forward edge just touching the cheek.

FACIAL CHARACTERISTICS
Dachshunds

Dachshunds make good watchdogs by dint of their alertness and a loud bark that belies their small size. They can make devoted and most affectionate pets.

COAT
Smooth-haired: short, dense coat, with loose, supple skin. Coarse hair on the underside of the tail.

COAT
Long-haired: soft, flat, and straight, or very slightly waved. Abundant feathering behind the legs.

Dachshunds
All Dachshunds are prone to "slipped disc" problems of the back, a tendency aggravated by their predisposition to overeat and become obese as they grow older. Although they do not need large amounts of exercise, regular romps and a controlled diet are essential in their healthy maintenance.

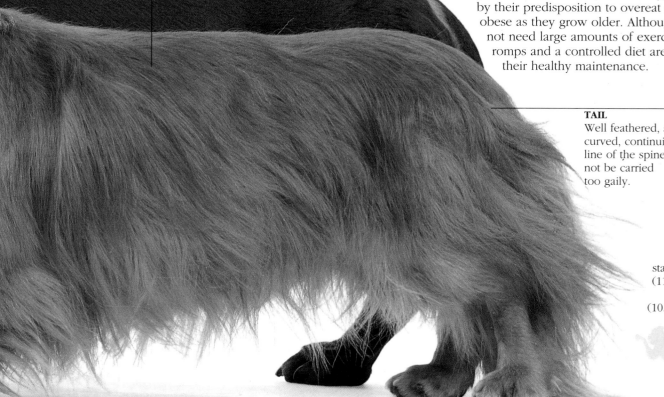

TAIL
Well feathered, slightly curved, continuing the line of the spine. It should not be carried too gaily.

SIZE
Ideal weight: standard dog 25lb (11.3kg), standard bitch 23lb (10.4kg); miniature 10lb (4.5kg).

Norwegian Elkhound

COLD WINDS, SNOW, AND ICE do not deter this most dogged of dogs, for it is Scandinavian through and through. The Norwegian Elkhound can be trained to pull sledges, and also makes a first-class household pet. A member of the Spitz family of dogs, it has remained essentially unchanged over thousands of years.

History

In Norway, ancient fossil skeletons of dogs have been found that are identical to the living Elkhound. It worked with Nordic hunters a thousand years before the time of Christ, and later accompanied the Viking raiders across the sea. Its traditional quarry ranged from rabbits and deer to lynx, bear, and elk. It arrived in Britain shortly after World War I, and was recognized by the American Kennel Club in 1935. Although it is not used as a hunting dog outside its native land, this Nordic creature is still used to catch prey in some parts of Scandinavia.

Temperament

It is an independent, civilized, and courageous breed. Norwegian Elkhounds are particularly determined dogs, for after cornering their prey they must stand their ground, and yet also avoid the deadly swipes of a bear's paw, or the powerful spear-thrusts of an elk's antlers.

SIZE
Dogs
20 1/2in (52cm) tall;
bitches 18-19in
(46-49cm).

The Elkhound relies on a highly developed sense of smell to track prey in silence.

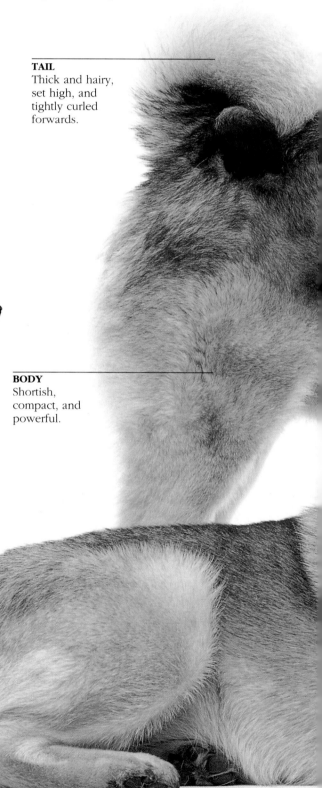

Norwegian Elkhound
This breed has a wide range of communication noises, from sighs, yelps, and yaps, to a variety of meaningful barks. On the hunt, the Elkhound informs its master that it has sighted its quarry by uttering a particular cry.

TAIL
Thick and hairy, set high, and tightly curled forwards.

BODY
Shortish, compact, and powerful.

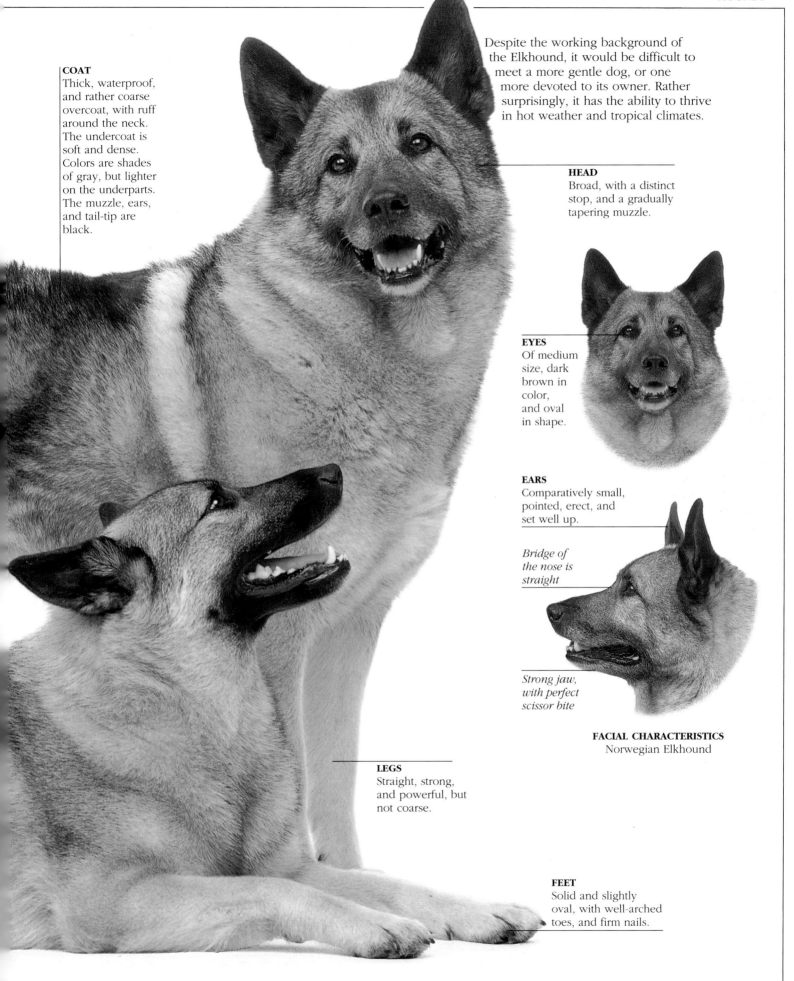

COAT
Thick, waterproof, and rather coarse overcoat, with ruff around the neck. The undercoat is soft and dense. Colors are shades of gray, but lighter on the underparts. The muzzle, ears, and tail-tip are black.

Despite the working background of the Elkhound, it would be difficult to meet a more gentle dog, or one more devoted to its owner. Rather surprisingly, it has the ability to thrive in hot weather and tropical climates.

HEAD
Broad, with a distinct stop, and a gradually tapering muzzle.

EYES
Of medium size, dark brown in color, and oval in shape.

EARS
Comparatively small, pointed, erect, and set well up.

Bridge of the nose is straight

Strong jaw, with perfect scissor bite

FACIAL CHARACTERISTICS
Norwegian Elkhound

LEGS
Straight, strong, and powerful, but not coarse.

FEET
Solid and slightly oval, with well-arched toes, and firm nails.

Foxhound

WHEN DESCRIBING THE FOXHOUND, who could be more poetic than Shakespeare? "My hounds are bred out of the Spartan kind, So flewed, so sanded; and their heads are hung with ears that sweep away the morning dew; crook-kneed, and dew-lapped like Thessalian bulls; slow in pursuit, but matched in mouth like bells." *A Midsummer Night's Dream*

American Foxhound
The American Foxhound is lighter, has a narrower chest, and carries longer ears than its English cousin. In the US the breed is used as a hunter, but is also seen in the show-ring.

History

The Foxhound's history can be traced back to the thirteenth century, when organized fox-hunting first became established in England. It seems likely that its lineage includes the now-extinct St Hubert (also ancestor of the Bloodhound), and Talbot Hound, together with terrier, Bulldog, and Greyhound blood. In the 1770s George Washington played a significant part in the creation of the distinct American Foxhound, by introducing French hounds into his pack of English Foxhounds. Later crossings with selected Irish and English hounds gradually refined the breed to produce the faster American type.

Temperament

Foxhounds are lively, friendly, and happy-go-lucky dogs, but they can be wilful and disobedient. Obedience training and firm handling are required, and they are not recommended as family pets, least of all for city dwellers.

BODY
Deep chest, long shoulders, and a very muscular, level back that runs smoothly into the loins.

FEET
Compact, round, and cat-like. Pads are well-developed, and toes are distinctly arched, with strong nails.

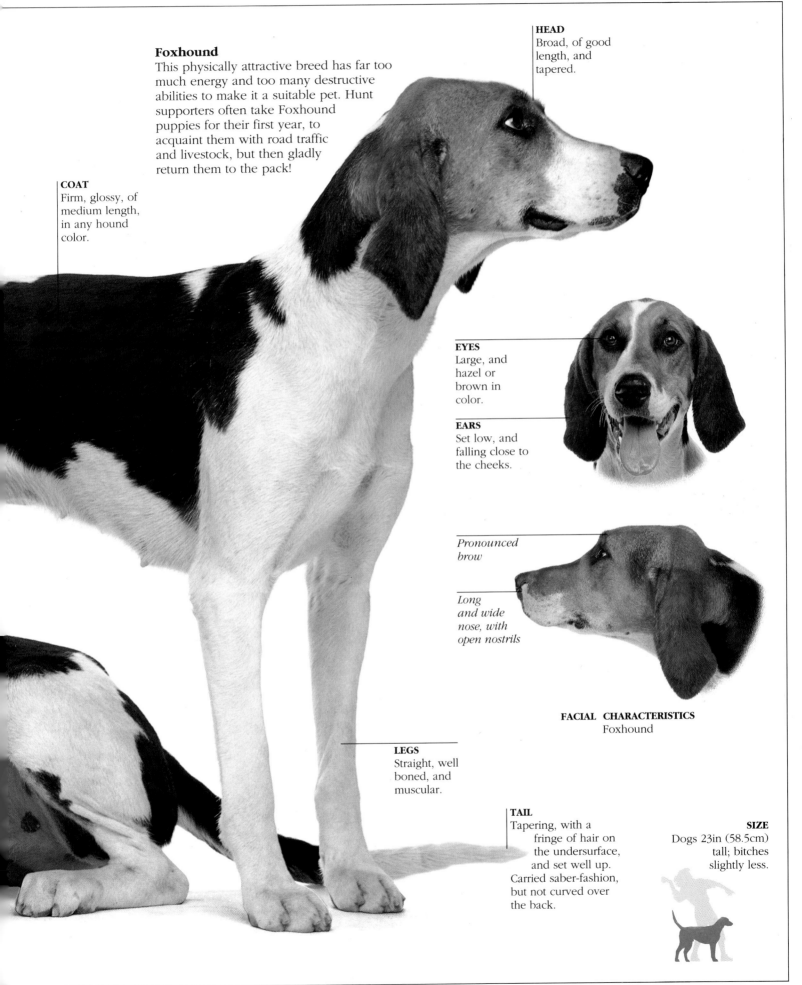

HEAD
Broad, of good length, and tapered.

Foxhound
This physically attractive breed has far too much energy and too many destructive abilities to make it a suitable pet. Hunt supporters often take Foxhound puppies for their first year, to acquaint them with road traffic and livestock, but then gladly return them to the pack!

COAT
Firm, glossy, of medium length, in any hound color.

EYES
Large, and hazel or brown in color.

EARS
Set low, and falling close to the cheeks.

Pronounced brow

Long and wide nose, with open nostrils

FACIAL CHARACTERISTICS
Foxhound

LEGS
Straight, well boned, and muscular.

TAIL
Tapering, with a fringe of hair on the undersurface, and set well up. Carried saber-fashion, but not curved over the back.

SIZE
Dogs 23in (58.5cm) tall; bitches slightly less.

Greyhound

ONE OF THE MOST ancient of breeds, Greyhounds are archetypes of the dogs that were first trained to hunt by sight, the "gaze-hounds". Although they are the fastest of dogs and can reach speeds of 43.5 mph (70 km/h), Greyhounds are basically rather lazy and adapt well to family life.

History
The breed probably has Middle Eastern origins, and it seems likely that it came to Europe with the first Phoenician trading ships. The Greyhound and its miniature version, the Italian Greyhound, became very popular in Europe in the Middle Ages, and were a favorite of royalty. Indeed, they are the most common heraldic dog, to be found in the coats of arms of Charles V of France and Henry VIII of England. Because of their excellent powers of acceleration, Greyhounds were tremendously successful hunters of small game, such as hare. These old adversaries face each other in the sport of greyhound racing, but today the hare is mechanical rather than flesh and blood!

Temperament
Greyhounds are sensitive, loving, well-behaved dogs. They are particularly good with children.

HEAD
Long and narrow but quite broad between the ears. The nose is black and pointed.

BODY
Broad, square back, and well-sprung ribs.

COAT
Close, fine, and silky. Any color is acceptable.

Chest is deep, providing adequate room for the heart

Segugio Italiano
The Segugio is another hunting dog that arose from crosses of Egyptian hounds and the mastiffs of classical Rome and Greece. Popular during the Renaissance, the breed was revived at the beginning of this century.

LEGS
Long and strong, with muscular, powerful thighs.

FEET
Fairly long, compact, well knuckled and rather hare-like, with strong pads.

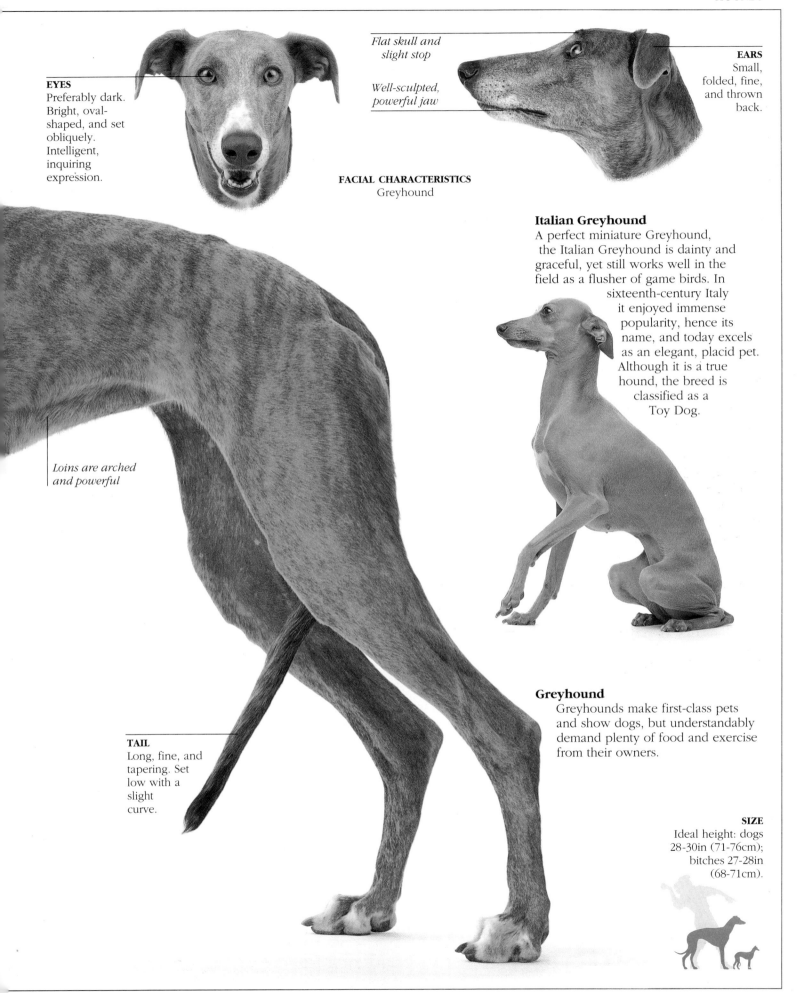

EYES
Preferably dark. Bright, oval-shaped, and set obliquely. Intelligent, inquiring expression.

Flat skull and slight stop

Well-sculpted, powerful jaw

EARS
Small, folded, fine, and thrown back.

FACIAL CHARACTERISTICS
Greyhound

Italian Greyhound
A perfect miniature Greyhound, the Italian Greyhound is dainty and graceful, yet still works well in the field as a flusher of game birds. In sixteenth-century Italy it enjoyed immense popularity, hence its name, and today excels as an elegant, placid pet. Although it is a true hound, the breed is classified as a Toy Dog.

Loins are arched and powerful

Greyhound
Greyhounds make first-class pets and show dogs, but understandably demand plenty of food and exercise from their owners.

TAIL
Long, fine, and tapering. Set low with a slight curve.

SIZE
Ideal height: dogs 28-30in (71-76cm); bitches 27-28in (68-71cm).

Irish Wolfhound

THIS STURDY CREATURE, frequently mentioned in legends, songs, and stories because of its gentleness and courage, almost became extinct in the nineteenth century, but after input from other breeds, particularly the Scottish Deerhound, its future was secured.

History

Its ancestor was the Cu, a massive shaggy-coated dog, used for the pursuit of wolves, elk, and wild boar. Irish Wolfhounds were often given as royal presents, and eventually became such popular gifts that Oliver Cromwell had to stop their export from Britain. With the last wolf in Scotland being killed in the early eighteenth century and the species disappearing from Ireland in 1766, the great dog that had hunted it likewise went into decline. The breed was revived in the second half of the nineteenth century, principally by a British army officer, Captain George Graham.

Temperament

The Irish Wolfhound is reliable, sweet-tempered, intelligent, and can be trusted with children.

COAT
Rough and wiry, especially over the eyes and beneath the jaw. Colors vary from white to brindle, and gray to black.

BODY
Fairly long back, deep chest, and arched loins.

This breed is the national dog of Ireland, and is also known as the Wolfdog, the Irish Greyhound, and the Great Dog of Ireland.

SIZE
Minimum height: dogs 32in (81cm); bitches 30in (76cm).

TAIL
Long, moderately thick, and slightly curved.

EARS
Set high, very mobile, and comparatively small. Preferably dark in color.

EYES
Dark and oval-shaped, with black eyelids.

Slightly tapering muzzle

Black nose and lips

FACIAL CHARACTERISTICS
Irish Wolfhound

Irish Wolfhound

These muscular, commanding creatures will need lots of space in which to gambol, but surprisingly, require no more exercise than the smaller breeds. Today's breeders are aiming to produce Wolfhounds of greater size and stature. Anything below 32in (81cm) in dogs and 30in (76cm) in bitches is to be faulted.

HEAD
Long but not too broad. Slightly raised frontal bones on the forehead.

LEGS
Forelegs are straight and strong; hind legs are long and muscular.

FEET
Big and round, with pronounced arching of the toes. Nails are very strong and curved.

Rhodesian Ridgeback

R ATHER SURPRISINGLY, the native land of this
shapely hound is South Africa, not
Rhodesia. "Ridgeback" refers to its unique
feature — the distinctive, dagger-shaped line
of hair running along its back, growing in
the opposite direction to the rest of its coat.

HEAD
Long, with strong,
level jaws, and a
flat skull.

History

In the sixteenth and seventeenth
centuries, European settlers took
breeds such as Bloodhounds,
Mastiffs, and various terriers to South
Africa. These dogs interbred with the
local stock, such as the half-wild
African Hottentot Hunting Dog, to
create the breed that we know
today. Ridgebacks make
excellent hunting dogs,
for they have great
stamina, can go without
water for more than 24
hours, and are able to
cope with the extreme
temperature changes of
the African bush. Used in
packs, they hunt leopard,
buffalo, and antelope, and
can pursue lion with such
success that the breed is now
also known as the Rhodesian
Lion Dog.

Rhodesian Ridgeback
The "dog with a snake on its back" is a
fierce, indomitable hunter, and, usually
working in a pack of three, will even
attack a pride of five lions.

BODY
Deep chested,
powerful, and
distinctly muscular.

Temperament

The Rhodesian Ridgeback is a
sharp-witted, friendly character
and makes a popular family pet.
Although a formidable fighter
when roused, essentially it
has a quiet temperament,
and rarely barks.

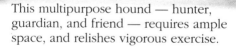

This multipurpose hound — hunter,
guardian, and friend — requires ample
space, and relishes vigorous exercise.

SIZE
Desirable height:
dogs 25-27in
(63-69cm); bitches
24-26in (6l-66cm).

COAT
Short, dense, sleek,
and glossy. Colors
are light wheaten to
red wheaten.
A small amount of
white on chest and
toes is permissible.

Black or brown nose, depending on eye color

Long, deep muzzle

EYES
Round, set wide apart, and dark brown or amber in color. The expression should be bright and sparkling.

EARS
Medium-sized, triangular in shape, set high, and carried close to the head.

FACIAL CHARACTERISTICS
Rhodesian Ridgeback

TAIL
Fairly long, tapering, and strong at the root. When active, carried with an upward curve.

LEGS
Strong and straight, with well-defined muscles.

FEET
Compact with well-arched toes. The pads should be tough and thick.

Saluki

T HIS SVELTE AND GRACEFUL dog is extremely fast and agile; the Bedouin of southern Arabia still use Salukis and falcons to capture prey such as gazelles and bustards. The Saluki hunts by sight, not by scent, and, with its blistering turn of speed, can run down virtually any game.

History
The Saluki's ancient origins lie in the Middle East, and it was named after the Arabian city of Saluk, now vanished beneath the sands. Used by various nomadic desert peoples, Salukis spread from the Caspian Sea to the Sahara Desert. Saluki-like dogs are depicted on Persian pottery dating from 4200 BC. The pharaohs reputedly hunted with hawks on their wrists and Salukis on leads, and mummified Saluki remains have been found in Egyptian tombs. Medieval Muslim huntsmen called the breed "the sacred gift of Allah". This religious connection made it permissible for Muslims to eat the game run down by the dog, which would otherwise be considered unclean. The Saluki is also known as the Gazelle Hound, Arabian Hound, or Persian Greyhound, and, as its appearance suggests, it is probably quite closely related to another ancient breed, the Afghan Hound.

Temperament
The Saluki is an even-tempered, loyal, and sensitive dog, with an aristocratic air. It may require obedience training to keep its deep-rooted hunting instincts under control.

COAT
Soft, smooth, and delicate. Colors include white, cream, fawn, golden red, grizzle, black and tan, tricolor (white, black, and tan), and various combinations of these colors.

BODY
Fine, shapely, and muscular, with a broad back, and deep, rather narrow chest.

Saluki
There are two varieties of Saluki, the feathered and the smooth-haired. The feathered Saluki displays light, silky feathering on the backs of its legs and thighs. Both varieties have feathering on the underside and tail.

LEGS
Long and fine, with well-muscled thighs.

FEET
Moderately long, well arched and well feathered between the toes.

EARS
Long, covered with feathered, silky hair, and hanging down close to the face.

HEAD
Long, narrow head, but the skull is fairly wide between the ears.

EYES
Large, oval-shaped, and hazel to dark brown in color.

Nose is black or liver in color

Scissor bite: upper teeth closely overlap lower teeth

FACIAL CHARACTERISTICS
Saluki

There is an ancient tradition among some Muslim peoples that the Saluki is never sold, but only presented as a gift, or as a tribute to a superior.

TAIL
Long, gently curved, and feathered with long hair on the underside. Set low.

SIZE
Height: 23-28in (58.5-71cm).

Whippet

A S FINELY SCULPTED, elegant, and graceful as its ancestor the Greyhound, the Whippet also contains terrier blood, particularly that of the Bedlington and Manchester Terriers. Although it enjoys the excitement of the racing track, it is just as happy with a comfortable home life, and makes an excellent, reliable pet.

HEAD
Long and fine, with a flat top to the skull. Nose should be black.

History
In Victorian times, miners in the coalfields of northeast England crossed local terriers with small Greyhounds to use for "snap racing" (rabbit or hare coursing). On cruelty grounds, this "sport" was made illegal in Great Britain, and the early Whippets quickly switched to "rag racing". This legal sport had Whippets racing towards their owners at top speed, in response to a wave of a piece of cloth. As a consequence, Whippets became affectionately known as "rag dogs", and this form of racing is still a popular Sunday activity in the north of England.

Sleek and graceful outline

Bicolor brindle coat

Temperament
This is the nicest dog you could hope to meet — gentle, loving, and loyal. It is perfectly happy to live in a town house or apartment, but it does need plenty of daily exercise.

Whippet
Although the Whippet looks frail, it is surprisingly powerful for such a small creature, and possesses remarkable acceleration.

The Whippet's habit of shivering doesn't necessarily indicate that it is frightened or cold, though it will require some protection against poor weather, and shouldn't be exposed to drafts.

COAT
Very fine, short, and dense.

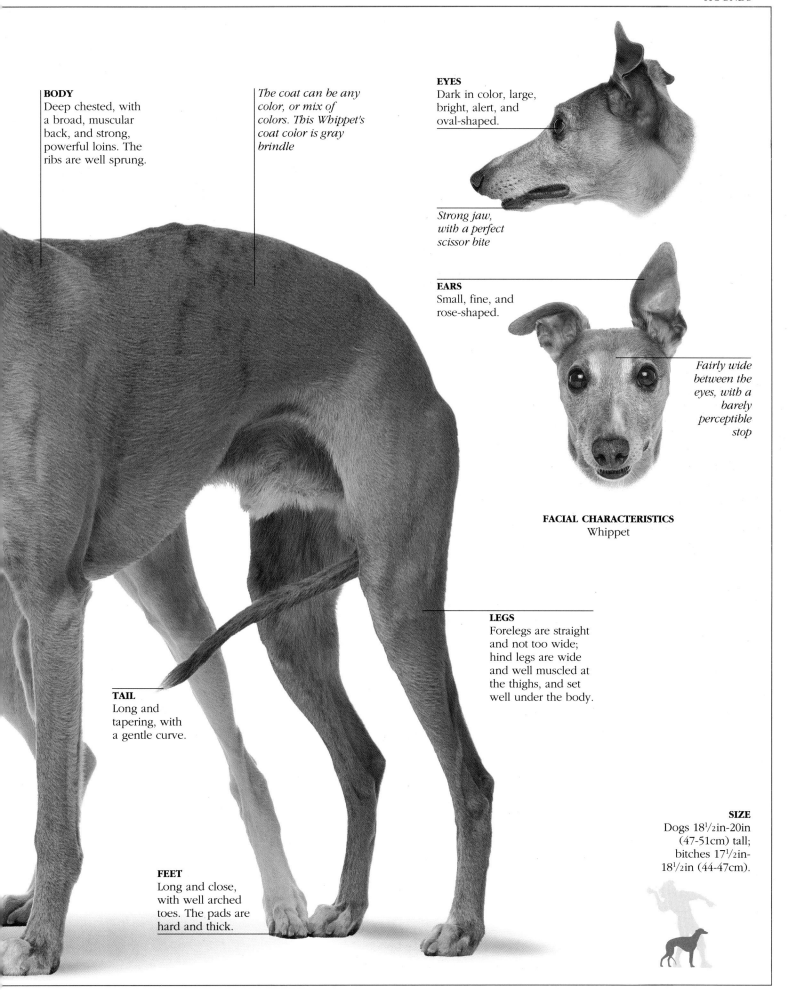

BODY
Deep chested, with a broad, muscular back, and strong, powerful loins. The ribs are well sprung.

The coat can be any color, or mix of colors. This Whippet's coat color is gray brindle

EYES
Dark in color, large, bright, alert, and oval-shaped.

Strong jaw, with a perfect scissor bite

EARS
Small, fine, and rose-shaped.

Fairly wide between the eyes, with a barely perceptible stop

FACIAL CHARACTERISTICS
Whippet

LEGS
Forelegs are straight and not too wide; hind legs are wide and well muscled at the thighs, and set well under the body.

TAIL
Long and tapering, with a gentle curve.

FEET
Long and close, with well arched toes. The pads are hard and thick.

SIZE
Dogs 18$\frac{1}{2}$in-20in (47-51cm) tall; bitches 17$\frac{1}{2}$in-18$\frac{1}{2}$in (44-47cm).

Sporting Dogs

The Sporting Dogs group, called Gundogs in Britain, comprises a wide variety of breeds, all of which were developed to act as hunters' assistants in some fashion, mainly by finding and retrieving game. They hunt principally by picking up scents carried in the air.

Spaniels

The largest sub-division of Sporting Dogs is the spaniel tribe. These dogs are intelligent, medium-sized, and stand not too high off the ground. They have a well-developed muzzle, a keen nose, and ears protected by long "flaps"; all sensible features for animals that must work in rough country. The word "spaniel" probably comes from the old French *espaignol,* meaning "Spanish dog", and some of the first users of spaniels, the Irish, are thought to have obtained their stock from the Iberian Peninsula. As early as the first century, mention is made in royal documents of Water Spaniels given to the King of Ireland as tribute.

German Short-haired Pointer

Spaniel breeds

Spaniels can be divided into those breeds that hunt and retrieve, those that retrieve only, and finally into Toy spaniels, which do not hunt and are nowadays included in the Toy Dogs category. Most of the sporting spaniels range over the ground ahead of the hunter but still stay relatively close to the gun, usually at a distance of between twenty-two and seventy yards (twenty and sixty-five meters) so that the charge from the shotgun can reach and kill the game that the dogs flush out. The reason for this is

Cocker Spaniels

that the spaniels give no warning, as the pointing dogs do, when they come upon their quarry, but instead flush it from cover at once, and then sit while their human companion takes aim. For such a dog, to chase flushed game would be very bad manners indeed. If the game is killed, the spaniel is sent after it to bring it back. They can also be trained to retrieve waterfowl from a shooting blind (a concealed enclosure), the Springer Spaniel being especially adept at such work.

Pointers and setters

The second sub-division of Sporting Dogs includes the pointers and setters, in general bigger dogs than spaniels with longer legs and, again, excellent noses and flapped ears. The athletic-looking pointers plainly show their close relationship to

Labrador Retriever

Italian Spinone

true hounds. Unlike the spaniels, these dogs move far ahead of the hunter and are often out of his sight. When they scent game, pointers don't immediately disturb the birds into flying, but stand rigidly with muzzle stretched (pointed) towards the quarry, usually with one forefoot raised. They remain in this position until the hunter flushes and shoots the birds. Like pointers, setters freeze when they find their target, but then "set" (drop to the ground). A well-trained dog will remain as mobile as a statue, if necessary for as long as an hour or more, awaiting the hunter's next command. Setters were in use by the sixteenth century, but the pointers are relatively recent breeds whose rise parallels the development of sporting guns. Shooting birds on the wing first became popular around the year 1700, and from then on "bird-dog" breeding and training flourished. Most of the pointer breeds were developed in Britain, with the first records of such types going back to 1650 when dogs used for pointing hares are mentioned.

Vizsla

Retrievers

The third Sporting Dogs group, the retrievers, are hunting specialists. Friendly, strong, well-built dogs, they are expert "finders and returners" of game, and were often used in conjunction with

Golden Retriever

"flushing" spaniels. The method was for spaniels to quarter the ground and "spring" the game, while the retrievers stayed close beside the guns. When the game was shot, the retrievers were sent out to bring it back. Powerful swimmers, they are also the commonest type of dog used in hunting waterfowl. In this type of hunting, the retrievers remain hidden in the shooting blind until the game is downed and then go splashing merrily off to retrieve it. Outside the three groups there are a few other Sporting Dogs, such as the Weimaraner, an all-rounder capable of tackling large and small game.

Pointers

THESE ARE AMONG THE OLDEST sporting dogs, and have been used for centuries to "point" game out to the hunter. The various types have different skills and specialities, but the common characteristic is the classic pointing stance, with tail and foreleg raised, and head extended towards the quarry.

History

The earliest pointers were used to help in netting birds, particularly quail and partridge. In the early eighteenth century, shooting game birds with shot pellets came into fashion, and the Spanish Pointer was introduced into England. This was a slow, heavy dog that kept its nose to the ground; to improve its speed and air-scenting abilities it was bred with the Greyhound and English Foxhound. The result was the English Pointer, which has since been introduced all over the world, and is now known simply as the Pointer. Another type of pointer was developed in Germany in the seventeenth century by crossing German hound stock with Spanish Pointers and Bloodhounds. This was a more substantial dog than the modern German Short-haired Pointer, which appeared in the nineteenth century when English Pointer blood was added to the breed.

Temperament

Pointers are generally kind and even-tempered, loyal, and obedient. They are also very energetic and always eager to work.

SIZE
Dogs 23-25in (58-64cm) tall; bitches 2l-23in (53-58cm).

German Wire-haired Pointer
Developed only at the turn of the century, the German Wire-haired Pointer combines the assets of the all-round gundog with the weather-resistant wiry coat of the terriers.

HEAD
Elegant and clean-cut, with broad, slightly rounded skull, with length of muzzle equal to the length of the skull.

BODY
Deep chest, with short, level back, and powerful loins.

LEGS
Forelegs straight, strong, and lean; hind legs muscular.

The German Short-haired Pointer is one of the most versatile of dogs. It is expert at hunting all sorts of game in the field, and also makes an excellent guard and house-dog.

EARS
Broad, set high, and hanging down close to head.

Large brown nose, with broad nostrils

Long, muscular neck, slightly arched

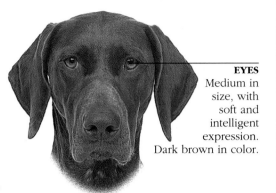

EYES
Medium in size, with soft and intelligent expression. Dark brown in color.

FACIAL CHARACTERISTICS
German Short-haired Pointer

TAIL
Set high, thick at base, and tapering. Customarily docked by two-fifths to half its length. Carried horizontally when the dog is on the move.

COAT
Short, coarse hairs giving dense, flat coat. Colors are solid liver or any combination of liver and white.

German Short-haired Pointer
This hardy athlete is among the most versatile of gundogs, tracking and pointing a wide variety of game, and retrieving on land or from water. Since its introduction in the 1920s, it has become very popular in the US.

Pointer
Also known as the English Pointer, this is a medium-sized, elegant gundog renowned for its speed, intelligence, and enthusiasm. Working best on land, it has legendary tracking and pointing skills, but is not usually expected to retrieve game.

FEET
Compact, round to oval in shape, with arched toes. Hard pads, with strong nails.

Bracco Italiano

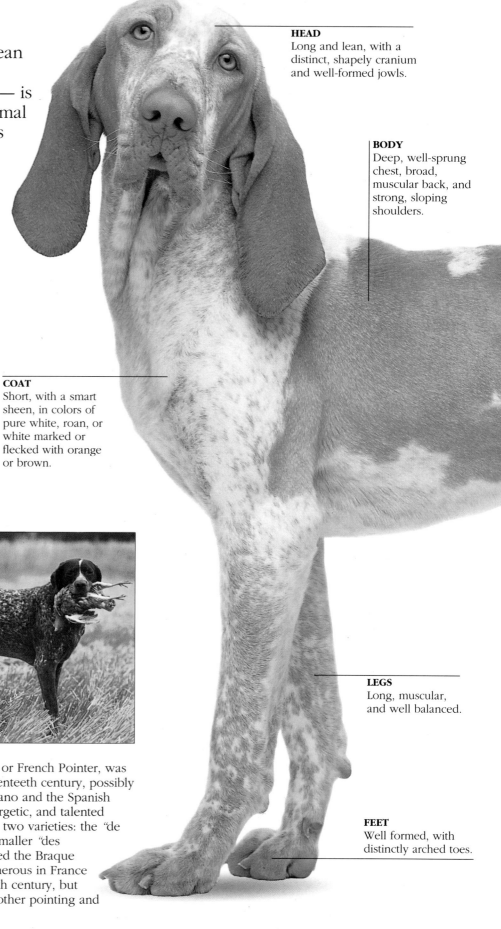

ARGUABLY THE OLDEST of European hunting breeds, the Bracco Italiano — or "Italian Hound" — is an athletic, open-air-loving animal whose character clearly reflects its rugged past.

History
Records show that the Bracco Italiano dates back to at least the fifth century BC. Developed at that time from the crossing of mastiffs that had originated in Mesopotamia (modern Iraq) with lighter, fleet-footed Egyptian coursing hounds, it is the breed from which, probably via the Spanish Pointer, all modern European pointers have sprung. It worked first with medieval net hunters and falconers, and later became the supreme gundog.

Temperament
Sensible almost to the point of over-seriousness, the Bracco is well mannered but still very friendly. Not a "townie" by nature, it demands wide-open spaces, lots of exercise and, principally because of its long, crinkly ears, plenty of loving attention from its owners.

HEAD
Long and lean, with a distinct, shapely cranium and well-formed jowls.

BODY
Deep, well-sprung chest, broad, muscular back, and strong, sloping shoulders.

COAT
Short, with a smart sheen, in colors of pure white, roan, or white marked or flecked with orange or brown.

LEGS
Long, muscular, and well balanced.

FEET
Well formed, with distinctly arched toes.

SIZE
Height: 21-26in (55-67cm).

Braque Français
The Braque Français, or French Pointer, was developed in the seventeeth century, possibly using the Bracco Italiano and the Spanish Pointer. A tough, energetic, and talented hunter, the breed has two varieties: the "de Gascogne", and the smaller "des Pyrénées". Often called the Braque Charles X, it was numerous in France up until the nineteenth century, but later gave ground to other pointing and setting breeds.

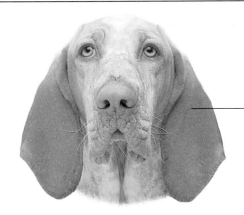

Nose can be straight or hooked slightly

EYES
Should be neither too deep nor too prominent. Yellow, orange, or brown in color.

EARS
Set back, well developed, and pendulous.

Ears are wrinkled and particularly sensitive to the touch

FACIAL CHARACTERISTICS
Bracco Italiano

TAIL
Thick and customarily docked.

Although European pointers have in recent times outdistanced the Bracco Italiano in popularity, the breed is still firmly lodged in more than a few hearts. It is extremely rare in the US.

Bracco Italiano
A breed that has always kept illustrious company, the Bracco is mentioned by Pliny and Dante, and was a feature of the French courts of Louis XII and Francis I.

Wire-haired Pointing Griffon
Often called the Korthals Griffon after the Dutch sportsman who, through selective breeding at the end of the nineteenth century, recreated the ancient Griffon hound, this is an all-weather, dedicated pointer and retriever of game. It carries the blood of setters, spaniels, Otter Hounds, and German Pointers, as well as that of the old Griffon.

Golden Retriever

H ARDY AND HARD-WORKING, the Golden Retriever was developed for wildfowl hunting, which explains why these dogs are always ready for a swim, whatever the weather. They are now popular family dogs, as well as continuing to be a favorite with sportsmen.

History

The exact origins of the Golden Retriever are still hotly disputed, but the breed may certainly be attributed to the efforts of Lord Tweedmouth in the mid-nineteenth century. Possibly starting with a mysterious dog called a "Russian Tracker", he then introduced some Flat-coated Retriever, Bloodhound, and Water Spaniel genes. The result was a dog with a natural retrieving instinct, and an acute sense of smell for tracking. It was recognized as a distinct breed in Great Britain in 1913 and in the US in 1925.

Temperament

This is a gentle-natured, confident, loyal dog. Extremely patient with children, the Golden Retriever is an ideal family dog, provided it is given ample exercise.

HEAD
Broad skull, with a well-defined stop, leading to a powerful muzzle wider at the stop than at the tip.

Golden Retriever
The Golden Retriever's ancestry makes it the perfect dog for working or playing in very wet, cold conditions.

Neck is strong, muscular, and of good length

COAT
Dense undercoat, with flat or wavy outer coat, which should be firm and water-resistant. Abundant feathering. Colors are rich, lustrous shades of gold. Lighter shadings are allowed. There may be a few white hairs, but only on the chest.

The Golden Retriever has been steadily increasing in popularity since its show debut in 1908, and is now a well-established favorite all over the world.

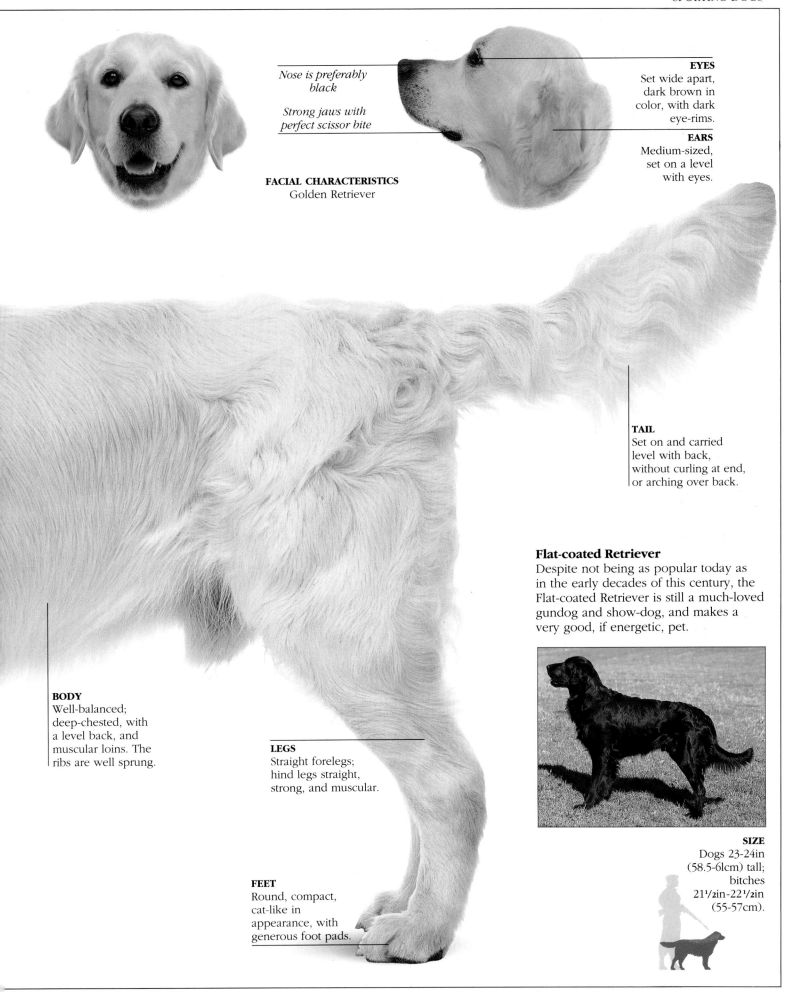

Nose is preferably black

Strong jaws with perfect scissor bite

FACIAL CHARACTERISTICS
Golden Retriever

EYES
Set wide apart, dark brown in color, with dark eye-rims.

EARS
Medium-sized, set on a level with eyes.

TAIL
Set on and carried level with back, without curling at end, or arching over back.

Flat-coated Retriever
Despite not being as popular today as in the early decades of this century, the Flat-coated Retriever is still a much-loved gundog and show-dog, and makes a very good, if energetic, pet.

BODY
Well-balanced; deep-chested, with a level back, and muscular loins. The ribs are well sprung.

LEGS
Straight forelegs; hind legs straight, strong, and muscular.

FEET
Round, compact, cat-like in appearance, with generous foot pads.

SIZE
Dogs 23-24in (58.5-6lcm) tall; bitches 21¹/₂in-22¹/₂in (55-57cm).

Basset Griffon Vendéen

Long popular in France, particularly in the Vendée, in the west of the country, the Basset Griffon Vendéen now comes in two sizes, the larger Grand, and the smaller Petit. Both are extremely energetic, sparkling, and affectionate animals that deserve a wider following than they have at present.

History

Ancient Gallic hunting hounds formed the root stock from which the Basset Griffon Vendéen was developed, and by the mid-nineteenth century the breed was, in essence, a rough-coated (griffon) form of the Basset Hound. The Grand was originally used for hunting wolves, and is still employed in wild boar hunts. It is one of the biggest of the French bassets, a group that includes the Basset Artésien Normand, the Basset Bleu de Gascogne, and the Basset Fauve de Bretagne. The Petit is simply a miniature version of the Grand, and is the only variety of the breed seen in the US.

Temperament

The Basset Griffon Vendéen is cheerful, sociable, loyal, and excellent with children. Both the Grand and the Petit must have plenty of exercise to burn off their abundant energy and are therefore not usually suitable for the confined life of a town apartment.

HEAD
Domed, but not too broad, with a distinct stop, a long muzzle, and a black nose.

BODY
Low-slung, compact, and well-balanced.

Italian Spinone
One of the most distinguished, and oldest, members of the Griffon family, the Italian Spinone is skilled as a hunter's companion on open tracts of land, as well as in water. It is regarded by many as one of the best pointing breeds of all.

FEET
Large and compact, with short, strong nails, and solid pads.

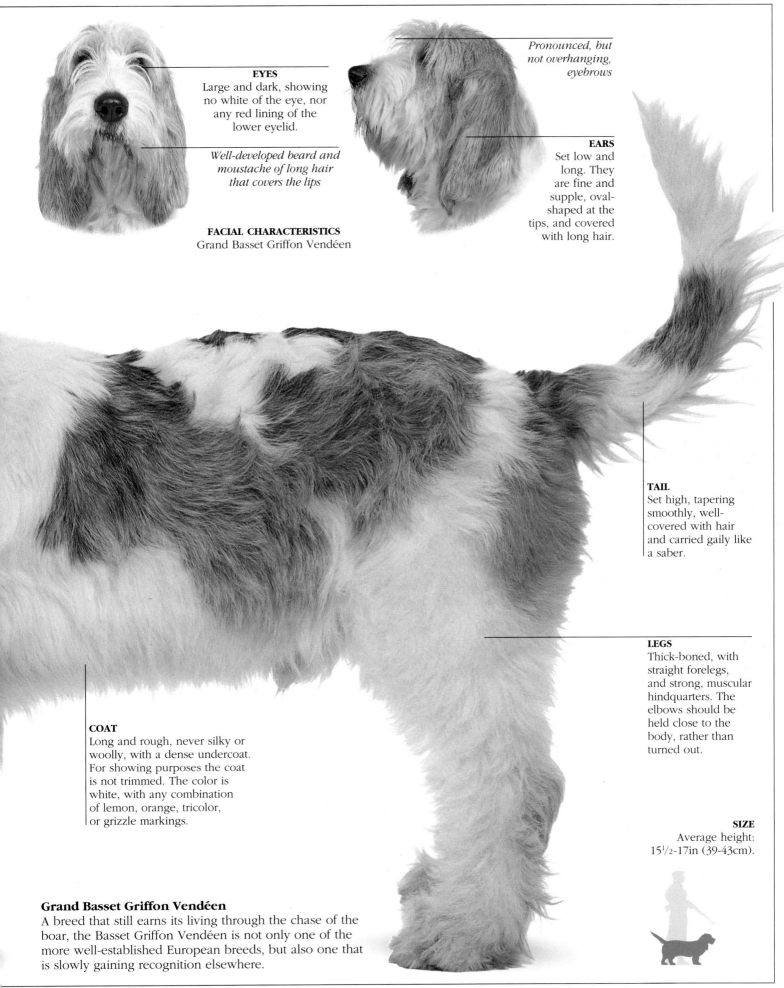

EYES
Large and dark, showing no white of the eye, nor any red lining of the lower eyelid.

Well-developed beard and moustache of long hair that covers the lips

Pronounced, but not overhanging, eyebrows

EARS
Set low and long. They are fine and supple, oval-shaped at the tips, and covered with long hair.

FACIAL CHARACTERISTICS
Grand Basset Griffon Vendéen

TAIL
Set high, tapering smoothly, well-covered with hair and carried gaily like a saber.

LEGS
Thick-boned, with straight forelegs, and strong, muscular hindquarters. The elbows should be held close to the body, rather than turned out.

COAT
Long and rough, never silky or woolly, with a dense undercoat. For showing purposes the coat is not trimmed. The color is white, with any combination of lemon, orange, tricolor, or grizzle markings.

SIZE
Average height: 15½-17in (39-43cm).

Grand Basset Griffon Vendéen
A breed that still earns its living through the chase of the boar, the Basset Griffon Vendéen is not only one of the more well-established European breeds, but also one that is slowly gaining recognition elsewhere.

Labrador Retriever

HEAD
Broad skull, with moderate stop, and medium-long muzzle.

T HE MOST POPULAR RETRIEVER OF ALL, the Labrador is renowned for its versatility. Used as guide dogs for the blind and as drug-sniffing dogs, Labradors are also excellent gundogs, in and out of water, and make reliable family pets.

History

This breed originated not in Labrador but on the coast of Newfoundland, where they were trained to bring in fishing nets through icy waters. In the nineteenth century, Newfoundland's fishermen came to the English West Country to sell fish, and some were persuaded to sell their dogs too. The breed was immediately successful as a gundog, and was recognized in Britain in 1903 and in the US in 1917. It was the Earl of Malmesbury who first called them Labradors in 1887.

COAT
Short, straight, dense coat, without any curl. It should be hard to the touch, and exceptionally waterproof. Colors are solid black, yellow, or chocolate.

Temperament

The Labrador is gentle, loyal, even-tempered, intelligent, and exceptionally reliable with children. It is always eager to please, but will guard against intruders. The breed is much better suited to country life, rather than that of the town.

Chesapeake Bay Retriever
This breed has a dense oily coat, webbed feet, and yellow or amber eyes. It was developed in the US in the early nineteenth century from two dogs, "Canton" and "Sailor", thought to be Newfoundlands, which had been shipwrecked off Maryland. These were crossed with Flat-coated and Curly-coated Retrievers, and possibly also with the Otterhound; though there is dispute about this.

SIZE
Dogs 22¹/2-24¹/2in (57-62cm) tall; bitches 21¹/2-23¹/2in (54-57cm).

FEET
Compact, round, with well-arched toes and generous pads. Nails to match coat.

EYES
Medium-sized, brown or hazel, with intelligent, friendly expression.

Nose should be large with well developed nostrils

Powerful jaws with upper teeth closely overlapping lower teeth

EARS
Not too long or heavy, hanging close to the head rather far back and set low.

FACIAL CHARACTERISTICS
Labrador Retriever

Labrador Retriever
Equipped with an excellent nose, Labradors were used in both World Wars to detect mines, and as police dogs their present-day duties include sniffing out drugs.

Curly-coated Retriever
Distinctive in its tightly curled black or brown coat, the Curly-coated Retriever was widely used in the nineteenth century to retrieve waterfowl and other game in all weathers. Its relations probably include the St John's Newfoundland (now defunct), the Water Spaniel, and the Poodle.

BODY
Well-built, with deep, broad chest, a short level back, and wide loins.

Famous owners of Labrador Retrievers have included Bing Crosby, and François Mitterrand.

LEGS
Forelegs straight from elbow, powerful hindquarters.

TAIL
Distinctive "otter tail", covered with thick, dense fur, medium length, thick at root, and tapering.

Setters

HEAD
Long and lean, with deep, square-ended muzzle.

SETTER-TYPE DOGS have long been used for hunting, and they are also among the most graceful and natural of field dogs. The Irish, English, and Gordon Setters are similar in shape and style, but have widely varying coat colors.

History

Derived from a variety of spaniels, setters, and pointers, the Irish Setter was initially a red and white dog, with shorter legs than today's breed. In the nineteenth century, following intensive selective breeding efforts, the lustrous, pure chestnut-red setter emerged, to win both prizes and hearts. Around the same time, the good-natured and handsome English Setter was being lovingly developed, principally by Sir Edward Laverack, and is consequently also known as the "Laverack Setter". The Gordon Setter was carefully bred by the Dukes of Gordon on their Scottish estate, and owes its black and tan coloration to a collie ancestor.

Temperament

Setters are generally affectionate, high-spirited, and full of vitality. Some are difficult to train, probably as a result of their independent spirit, but given firm handling and plenty of exercise, these dogs can be a joy to own.

Irish Setter

The Irish Setter finally had its name settled by the Ulster Irish Setter Club in 1876. Known long ago in its native Ireland as the "Red Spaniel", today the breed is also called the "Red Setter".

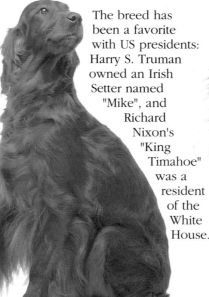

The breed has been a favorite with US presidents: Harry S. Truman owned an Irish Setter named "Mike", and Richard Nixon's "King Timahoe" was a resident of the White House.

Gordon Setter

The largest and strongest of the setters, this breed possesses excellent stamina, and the useful ability to work for long periods without drinking. Once known as the Black and Tan Setter of Scotland, it has a calmer temperament than the other setters, and hunts slowly and methodically.

Top of skull and top of muzzle are parallel and of equal length

EYES
Almond-shaped, set wide apart, hazel or dark brown in color.

Nose should be dark brown or black, with wide nostrils

EARS
Set low and well back, and hanging close to head, nearly long enough to reach the nose.

FACIAL CHARACTERISTICS
Irish Setter

BODY
Chest deep and rather narrow. Top line of body from withers to tail slopes slightly downward.

TAIL
About long enough to reach the hock. Carried level or just above the line of the back.

COAT
Medium-length, straight, silky hair, with feathering on ears, chest, belly, tail, and backs of legs. Color is deep chestnut. A little white on the chest and toes is permitted.

LEGS
Straight, sinewy forelegs; hind legs long and muscular.

English Setter
This dog is a dependable hunter over all terrain, but its long coat tends to attract seeds and burrs.

FEET
Rather small feet with arched toes. Feathered fur between toes.

SIZE
Dogs 24-26in (6l-66cm) tall; bitches slightly less.

61

Cocker Spaniel

HEAD
Rounded skull, with broad, deep muzzle, and square jaws.

Aotheough now primarily a show-dog and pet, the Cocker Spaniel has a sporting background, which is clearly reflected in its intelligent and energetic nature. The name "Cocker" is probably short for "Woodcocker", a reference to the dog's considerable skills as a flusher of woodcock.

History

English Cocker Spaniels were introduced into America in the 1880s, and it wasn't long before a distinctly new breed had been developed to suit the special needs of US sportsmen. By the 1930s the two types were significantly different, and by the 1940s they were officially recognized as two separate breeds. After World War II Cocker Spaniels became one of the most popular dogs in America, and were soon introduced back into Europe, where they are known as American Cockers.

Temperament

Bold and keen to work, the Cocker Spaniel is equally suited to life as a gundog, or as a household pet.

Brittany
With its ability to point as well as retrieve game, this dog remains a popular choice among sportsmen. Temperamentally, it is also suited to be an excellent house dog.

BODY
Short, compact body, with a deep chest, and gently sloping back.

FEET
Compact and round, with strong pads.

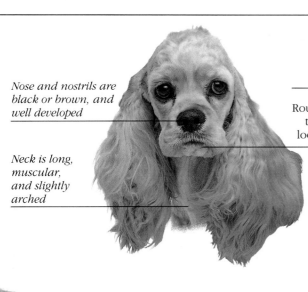

Nose and nostrils are black or brown, and well developed

EYES
Round and full, dark hazel to black in color, and looking directly forward.

Neck is long, muscular, and slightly arched

Scissor bite: upper teeth closely overlap lower teeth

EARS
Long, well haired, and set low.

FACIAL CHARACTERISTICS
Cocker Spaniel

Cocker Spaniel

This is a strong, athletic dog that needs lots of exercise, and also regular grooming.

TAIL
Customarily docked by three-fifths of its length. Carried in line with, or just above, the back.

English Springer Spaniel

Another all-rounder in the field, the English Springer is one of the largest of the spaniels. It derives its name from its original role, which was to flush, or "spring", game for falconers.

COAT
Dense, silky, flat or wavy coat, of good length. Prominent feathering. Many colors acceptable, including black, brown, red, cream, black and tan, brown and tan, particolors, and tricolors.

SIZE
Dogs 14-15in (36-39cm) tall; bitches 13-14in (34-36cm).

LEGS
Forelegs straight and muscular, hind legs strong and parallel.

English Cocker Spaniel

THIS EXCELLENT GUNDOG flushes out woodcock, pheasant, or partridge, and retrieves them from both land and water. But today the English Cocker Spaniel is perhaps better known as a show-dog. Extremely popular in Britain and also the US, it has won more championships at Cruft's than any other breed.

History

"Spaniel" is probably a corruption of the Old French for "Spanish dog", *espaignol.* The spaniel family can, as the name suggests, be traced back to fourteenth-century Spain. By the 1600s many types of spaniel were being used as gundogs in western Europe, and by the eighteenth century two members of the family had made their mark in Britain: the larger Springer Spaniel, and the Cocker Spaniel. The breed that we know today was firmly established in the late nineteenth century, and by the 1930s it had become the most popular dog in Britain.

Temperament

A very active, playful, and intelligent animal, the English Cocker Spaniel can be rather wilful at times. Its enthusiastic nature is demonstrated by its tail, which wags furiously most of the time, especially when the dog is on the move, or working in the field.

HEAD
Skull and muzzle of equal length, with definite stop between. Jaws are strong and nose is broad.

BODY
Broad, deep chest, well-sprung ribs, and wide, short loins.

FEET
Cat-like and compact, with thick pads and strong toes.

SIZE
Dogs 16-17in (41-43cm) tall; bitches 15-16in (38-41cm).

Irish Water Spaniel
Recognizable by its dark ringlets, this breed's speciality is hunting waterfowl.

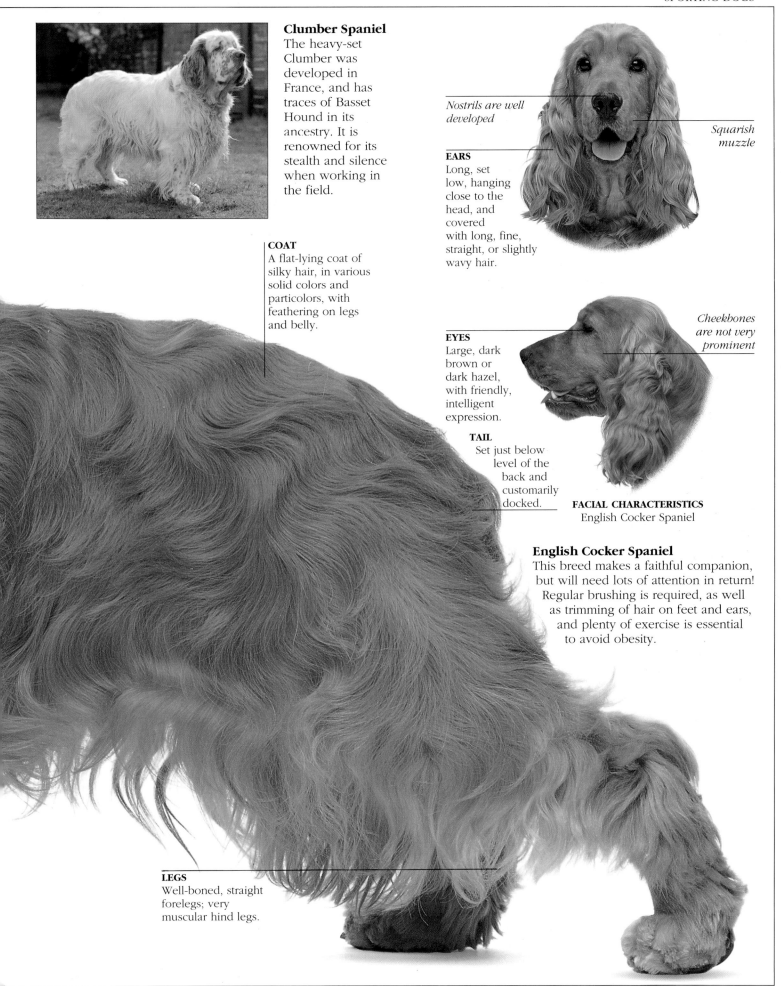

Clumber Spaniel
The heavy-set Clumber was developed in France, and has traces of Basset Hound in its ancestry. It is renowned for its stealth and silence when working in the field.

Nostrils are well developed

Squarish muzzle

EARS
Long, set low, hanging close to the head, and covered with long, fine, straight, or slightly wavy hair.

COAT
A flat-lying coat of silky hair, in various solid colors and particolors, with feathering on legs and belly.

EYES
Large, dark brown or dark hazel, with friendly, intelligent expression.

Cheekbones are not very prominent

TAIL
Set just below level of the back and customarily docked.

FACIAL CHARACTERISTICS
English Cocker Spaniel

English Cocker Spaniel
This breed makes a faithful companion, but will need lots of attention in return! Regular brushing is required, as well as trimming of hair on feet and ears, and plenty of exercise is essential to avoid obesity.

LEGS
Well-boned, straight forelegs; very muscular hind legs.

Vizsla

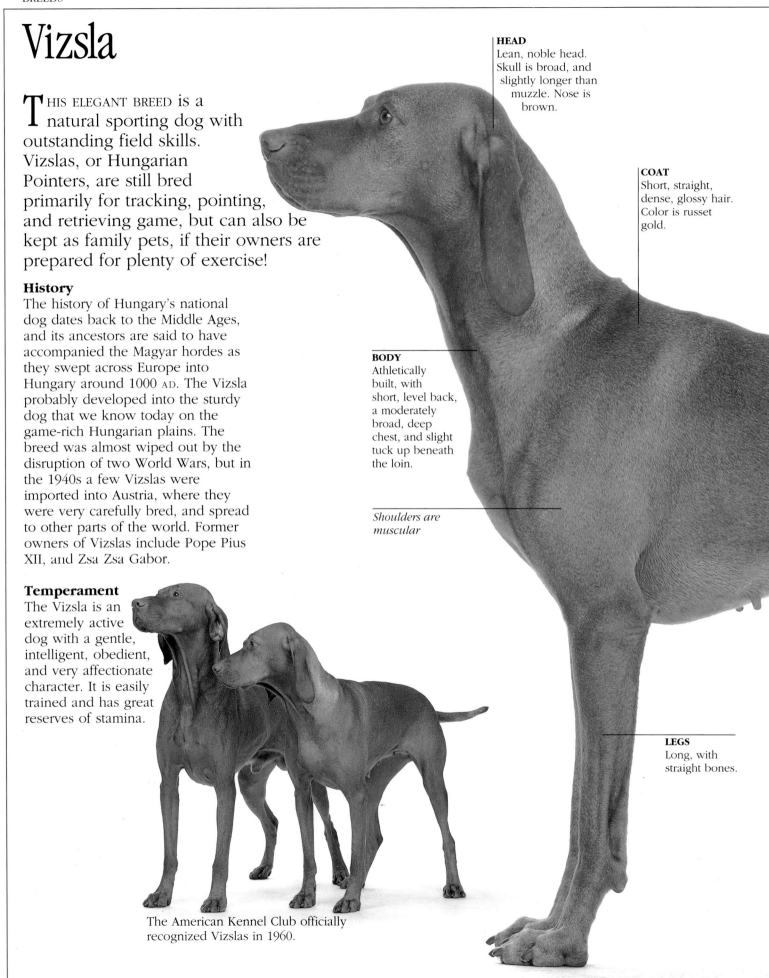

THIS ELEGANT BREED is a natural sporting dog with outstanding field skills. Vizslas, or Hungarian Pointers, are still bred primarily for tracking, pointing, and retrieving game, but can also be kept as family pets, if their owners are prepared for plenty of exercise!

History

The history of Hungary's national dog dates back to the Middle Ages, and its ancestors are said to have accompanied the Magyar hordes as they swept across Europe into Hungary around 1000 AD. The Vizsla probably developed into the sturdy dog that we know today on the game-rich Hungarian plains. The breed was almost wiped out by the disruption of two World Wars, but in the 1940s a few Vizslas were imported into Austria, where they were very carefully bred, and spread to other parts of the world. Former owners of Vizslas include Pope Pius XII, and Zsa Zsa Gabor.

Temperament

The Vizsla is an extremely active dog with a gentle, intelligent, obedient, and very affectionate character. It is easily trained and has great reserves of stamina.

The American Kennel Club officially recognized Vizslas in 1960.

HEAD
Lean, noble head. Skull is broad, and slightly longer than muzzle. Nose is brown.

COAT
Short, straight, dense, glossy hair. Color is russet gold.

BODY
Athletically built, with short, level back, a moderately broad, deep chest, and slight tuck up beneath the loin.

Shoulders are muscular

LEGS
Long, with straight bones.

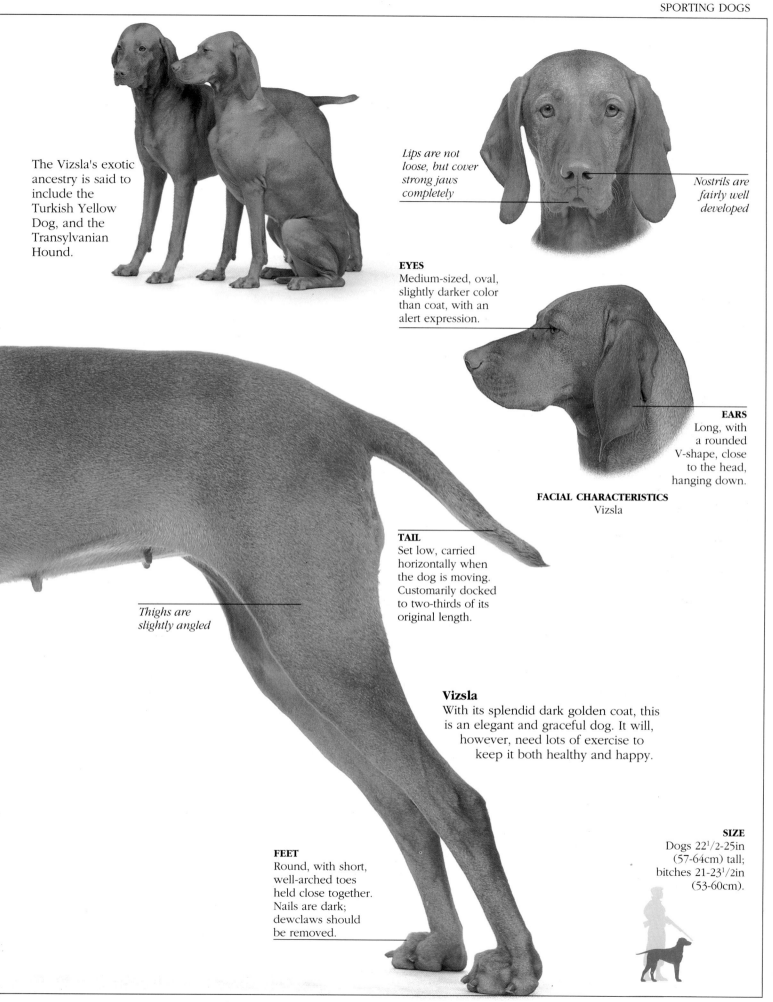

The Vizsla's exotic ancestry is said to include the Turkish Yellow Dog, and the Transylvanian Hound.

Lips are not loose, but cover strong jaws completely

Nostrils are fairly well developed

EYES
Medium-sized, oval, slightly darker color than coat, with an alert expression.

EARS
Long, with a rounded V-shape, close to the head, hanging down.

FACIAL CHARACTERISTICS
Vizsla

TAIL
Set low, carried horizontally when the dog is moving. Customarily docked to two-thirds of its original length.

Thighs are slightly angled

Vizsla
With its splendid dark golden coat, this is an elegant and graceful dog. It will, however, need lots of exercise to keep it both healthy and happy.

FEET
Round, with short, well-arched toes held close together. Nails are dark; dewclaws should be removed.

SIZE
Dogs 22$\frac{1}{2}$-25in (57-64cm) tall; bitches 21-23$\frac{1}{2}$in (53-60cm).

Weimaraner

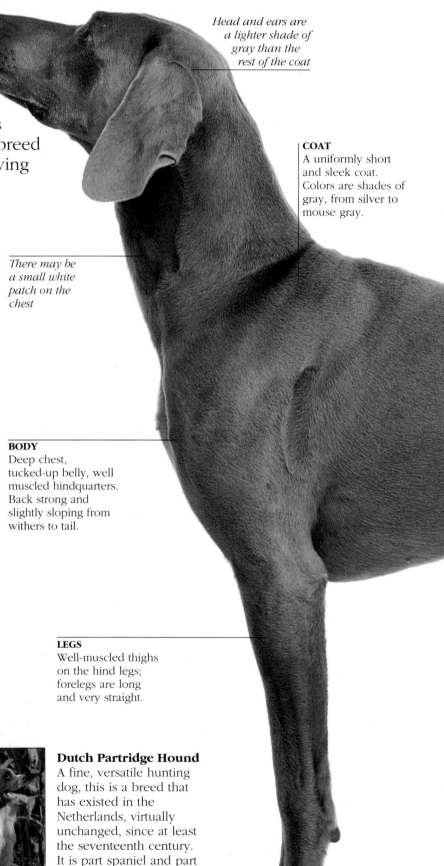

Head and ears are a lighter shade of gray than the rest of the coat

THIS LARGE GRAY DOG is renowned for its all-round hunting skills. It was first used to hunt big game such as wolves, bears, and boars, but later the breed was adapted for the tracking and retrieving of game birds.

COAT
A uniformly short and sleek coat. Colors are shades of gray, from silver to mouse gray.

There may be a small white patch on the chest

History
Large gray hunting dogs have been used in Germany since the seventeenth century, but the Weimaraner only emerged as a distinct breed early in the nineteenth century. It was developed by the nobility of the grand duchy of Weimar, probably by crossing Bloodhounds with a variety of hunting dogs. Its excellent nose is undoubtedly a result of these origins. As big game died out in Germany with the encroachment of civilization, the Weimaraner was adapted into a pointing dog for use with game birds. Although no longer the exclusive preserve of the gentry, the breeding of Weimaraners was still tightly controlled, and was not permitted at all outside Germany until the 1930s. The breed has since gained a significant following in both the US and Britain.

BODY
Deep chest, tucked-up belly, well muscled hindquarters. Back strong and slightly sloping from withers to tail.

Temperament
Originally bred as a gentleman's personal sporting dog and companion, the Weimaraner is active, strong-willed, intelligent, and fearless, and needs plenty of exercise and firm control.

LEGS
Well-muscled thighs on the hind legs; forelegs are long and very straight.

Dutch Partridge Hound
A fine, versatile hunting dog, this is a breed that has existed in the Netherlands, virtually unchanged, since at least the seventeenth century. It is part spaniel and part setter, and may have played an important role in the development of other major breeds of gundog. It makes an excellent pet.

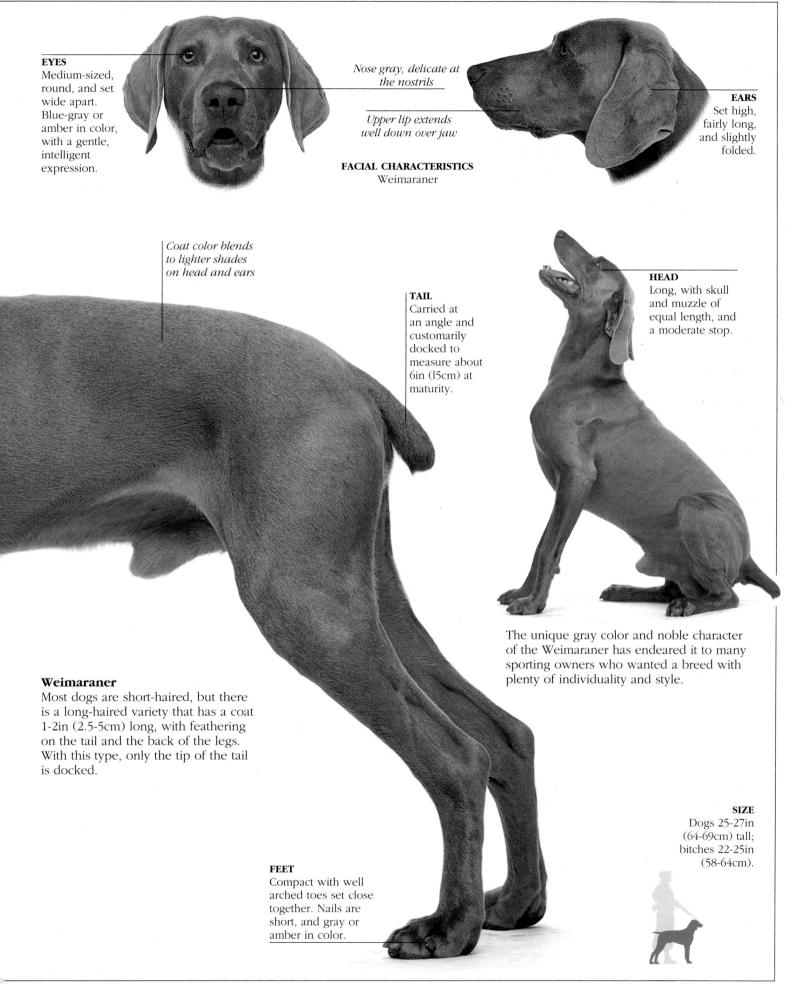

EYES
Medium-sized, round, and set wide apart. Blue-gray or amber in color, with a gentle, intelligent expression.

Nose gray, delicate at the nostrils

Upper lip extends well down over jaw

EARS
Set high, fairly long, and slightly folded.

FACIAL CHARACTERISTICS
Weimaraner

Coat color blends to lighter shades on head and ears

TAIL
Carried at an angle and customarily docked to measure about 6in (15cm) at maturity.

HEAD
Long, with skull and muzzle of equal length, and a moderate stop.

The unique gray color and noble character of the Weimaraner has endeared it to many sporting owners who wanted a breed with plenty of individuality and style.

Weimaraner
Most dogs are short-haired, but there is a long-haired variety that has a coat 1-2in (2.5-5cm) long, with feathering on the tail and the back of the legs. With this type, only the tip of the tail is docked.

FEET
Compact with well arched toes set close together. Nails are short, and gray or amber in color.

SIZE
Dogs 25-27in (64-69cm) tall; bitches 22-25in (58-64cm).

Terriers

If one group of dogs can claim to have been "Made in Britain", it is the terriers. These hunting dogs, designed for the tackling of such burrowing animals as badgers, foxes, rabbits, and rats, were largely developed in the British Isles. When the Romans first invaded they found these "workers in the earth" already being used, and called them *terrarii* from the Latin for earth, *terra*.

Bedlington Terrier

Terrier types

In some cases the terrier's job was to find and kill the animals underground, but, as an alternative, they were trained to force the quarry out of its den and up to the surface where it could be dealt with, in some way, by the hunter. Terriers are generally small, short-legged and stocky animals with alert and spirited temperaments. Tough working dogs, the terriers come in wide varieties that can be split into two basic coat types: the smooth or short-haired, such as the Smooth Fox Terrier; and the long or rough-haired, exemplified by the Scottish and Skye Terriers. The biggest terrier, the Airedale, has all the

Scottish Terrier

principal features of the terrier group, but its size, springing from its origins as a cross between the now extinct Black and Tan Terrier and the Otterhound, stopped it from pursuing game underground. It was developed as a dual-purpose breed to hunt both badger and otter. Terriers are linked to the big mastiff breeds via the Bull Terrier, a dog developed from crossing the Bulldog with another breed that no longer exists, the White English Terrier.

British breeds

England produced breeds such as the Fox Terrier, Airedale, Bull Terrier, Bedlington, and Manchester Terriers. Scotland gave us the Cairn, Skye, and West Highland, as well as the Scottish. Ireland was the birth place of the Irish and Kerry Blue, and Wales contributed the Welsh and Sealyham. Shakespeare may be referring to a terrier when he mentions "the dog Tray", which some people believe to be an abbreviation of the word "terrier". Almost every region of Britain produced their own variety of terrier; many of these are now extinct, have been absorbed into other breeds, or are narrowly localized. They include the Devon, Poltalloch, Clydesdale, Aberdeen, Roseneath, and Cheshire terriers.

Border Terriers

Soft-coated Wheaten Terrier

Welsh Terrier

Model heroes

It is possible that more terriers have been declared canine war heroes than any other breed. "Crib" was a Bull Terrier with the Buffs in the Peninsular War, who fought a battle with a Poodle from the French lines in No Man's Land and prevailed. "Billy", a brindled Bull Terrier, served with the Royal Ulster Rifles in the Transvaal at the turn of the century, was wounded, and learned how to feign a limp in order to be given a ride on a cavalry horse. "Bob" was a terrier attached to the Scots Guards during the Crimean War and chased Russian cannon balls when they landed behind the British lines. "Scout" was an Irish terrier of the Royal Dragoons who led the victorious troops into Bloemfontein, South Africa, and was awarded the Queen's medal with six bars, and the King's medal with two bars. "Drummer Jack", a Fox Terrier, served with the Coldstream Guards in World War I,

Jack Russell Terrier

winning the 1914 Star, Victoria Medal, and General Service Medal. There were many more such valiant terriers. In art and literature, terriers have played a major part. Painters such as Brueghel, Le Nain, and, above all, Landseer all featured terriers in their work. Landseer owned, and used as a model, "Brutus", a Rough White Terrier, who appears in a number of famous paintings, including "Rat Catchers" and "Attachment".

Rugged individualists

No other sort of dog has more gritty tenacity, cockiness, or sparkle than the terriers. These are rugged individuals that you read about being rescued alive after many days down a collapsed mine shaft or recovering from appalling injuries inflicted by fighting other dogs or badgers in illegal contests organized by barbaric and despicable owners. Most terriers kept in Britain nowadays are not used, fortunately, for any form of hunting, but make delightful, loyal, and lively pets and companions.

Kerry Blue Terrier

Manchester Terrier

Airedale Terrier

THIS GIANT AMONG TERRIERS is named after the Yorkshire valley in which it originated. Designed for hunting otter, as were the smaller Irish and Lakeland Terriers, the Airedale is a strong, energetic dog, and a good swimmer. It is never happier than when splashing about in water.

History
The breed was developed in the last century by crossing Otter Hounds with the now-extinct Black and Tan Terrier, and has been used to hunt bears, wolves, wild boar, and stags, as well as otters. Originally known as the Bingley, Waterside, or the Working Terrier, it was one of the first dogs to be recruited by the British Army in World War I, and was used as a guard and messenger in the trenches of Flanders. One Airedale, "Jack", actually won a posthumous Victoria Cross for gallantry in the field.

Temperament
Airedales are friendly and loyal, and make excellent pets, as well as ideal house guards. They can be a bit unruly, and owners must treat them with firmness as well as kindness.

Welsh Terrier
This breed looks like a small version of the Airedale. Their common ancestor, the Black and Tan Terrier, is probably responsible for this similarity in appearance. The Welsh Terrier has remained popular in the US since it was first shown there in 1888.

BODY
Chest is deep but not broad; back is short, strong, and level.

COAT
Stiff, wiry, wavy, and lying close to the body. Colors are dark grizzle, black, or black mixed with red on the body, with tan head, ears, underbody, and legs.

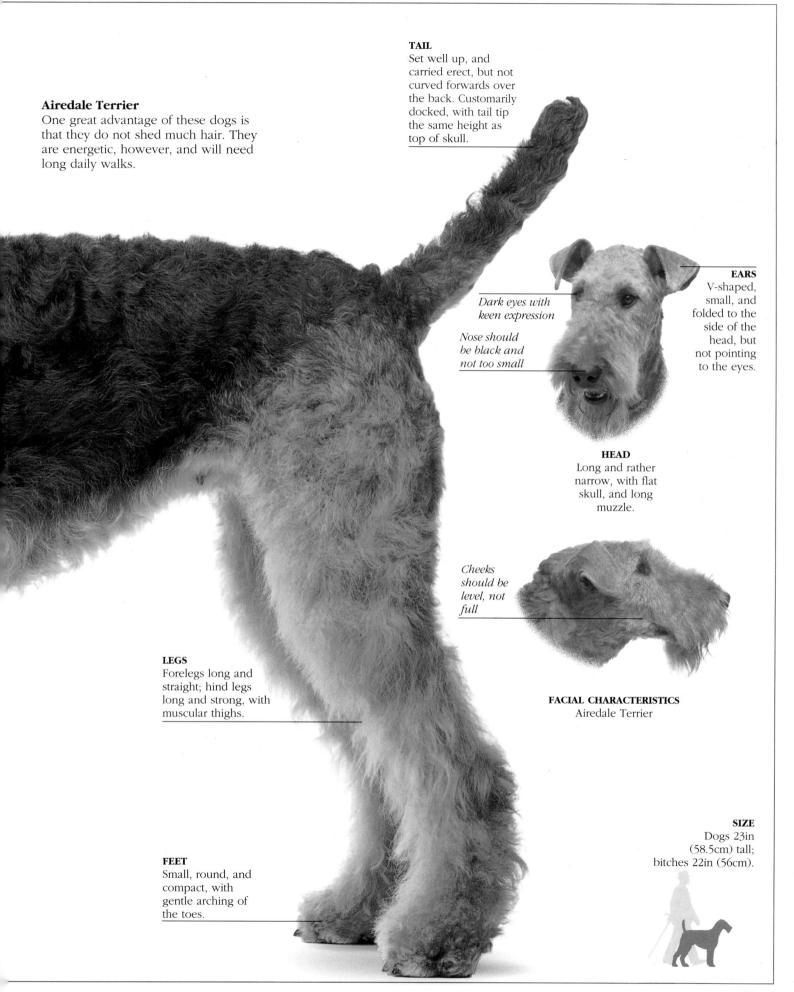

TAIL
Set well up, and carried erect, but not curved forwards over the back. Customarily docked, with tail tip the same height as top of skull.

Airedale Terrier
One great advantage of these dogs is that they do not shed much hair. They are energetic, however, and will need long daily walks.

Dark eyes with keen expression

Nose should be black and not too small

EARS
V-shaped, small, and folded to the side of the head, but not pointing to the eyes.

HEAD
Long and rather narrow, with flat skull, and long muzzle.

Cheeks should be level, not full

LEGS
Forelegs long and straight; hind legs long and strong, with muscular thighs.

FACIAL CHARACTERISTICS
Airedale Terrier

SIZE
Dogs 23in (58.5cm) tall; bitches 22in (56cm).

FEET
Small, round, and compact, with gentle arching of the toes.

Bedlington Terrier

I T MAY LOOK LIKE A LAMB, but this fascinating and rather curious dog is no softie! It is hardy, tough, and quick, and originated in the coalfields of Northumberland, England, where it was bred for hunting vermin, otters, and even foxes. Despite its unusual shape and curly coat, the Bedlington is a formidable fighter, with very strong jaws.

HEAD
Pear-shaped, with a narrow skull, and no stop.

History

At first known as the Rothbury Terrier, after its place of origin, the early Bedlington had a heavier body, and shorter legs. In the late eighteenth and early nineteenth centuries, it was crossed with Whippet, Dandie Dinmont, and possibly Poodle-type dogs, and a taller, finer, speedier breed emerged, but still retained its qualities of pluck and endurance. The "new" Bedlington was a poacher's dream, and became known as the Gypsy Dog. Gradually the breed was refined into an excellent companion dog, and the arts of clipping and trimming have put the finishing touches to its distinctive appearance.

EARS
Triangular with rounded tips, set low, and hanging flat against the cheeks.

Bedlington Terrier
Grooming the Bedlington Terrier can be a fairly intricate process, and first-time clipping should always be done by a specialist. For the house-proud, one great advantage of this breed is that it does not shed its coat.

Temperament

Echoing its ancestry, the Bedlington can have a tendency to pick fights with other dogs, but generally makes a charming and loyal pet.

The name "Bedlington" has been used since the early nineteenth century.

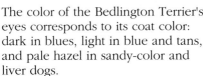

The color of the Bedlington Terrier's eyes corresponds to its coat color: dark in blues, light in blue and tans, and pale hazel in sandy-color and liver dogs.

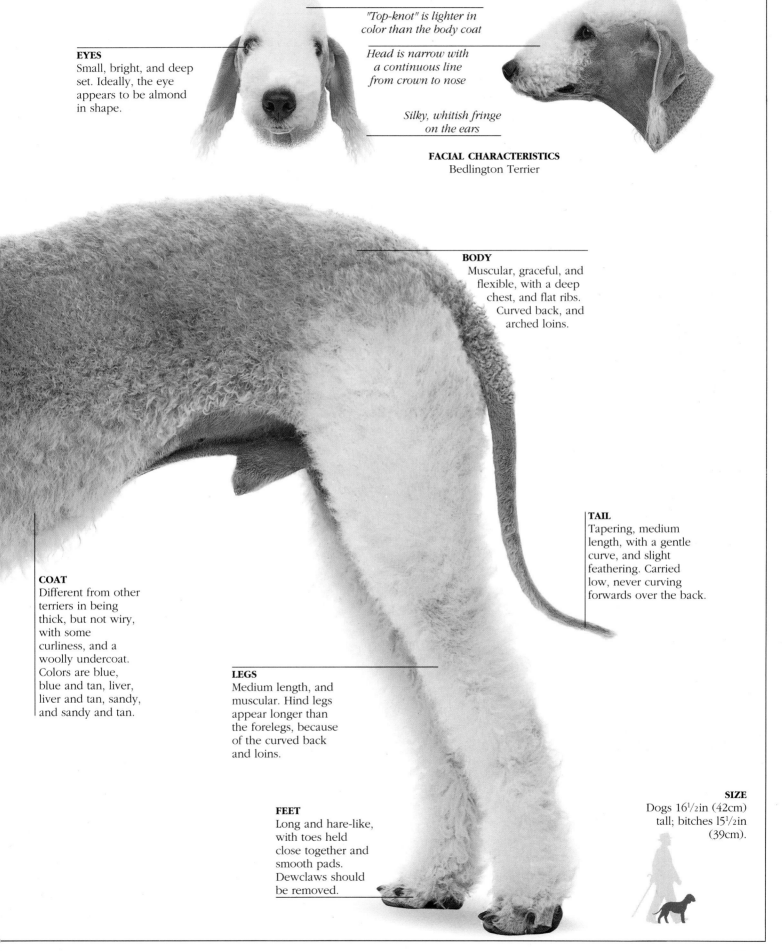

EYES
Small, bright, and deep set. Ideally, the eye appears to be almond in shape.

"Top-knot" is lighter in color than the body coat

Head is narrow with a continuous line from crown to nose

Silky, whitish fringe on the ears

FACIAL CHARACTERISTICS
Bedlington Terrier

BODY
Muscular, graceful, and flexible, with a deep chest, and flat ribs. Curved back, and arched loins.

TAIL
Tapering, medium length, with a gentle curve, and slight feathering. Carried low, never curving forwards over the back.

COAT
Different from other terriers in being thick, but not wiry, with some curliness, and a woolly undercoat. Colors are blue, blue and tan, liver, liver and tan, sandy, and sandy and tan.

LEGS
Medium length, and muscular. Hind legs appear longer than the forelegs, because of the curved back and loins.

FEET
Long and hare-like, with toes held close together and smooth pads. Dewclaws should be removed.

SIZE
Dogs 16½in (42cm) tall; bitches 15½in (39cm).

Border Terrier

THE RUGGED AND REMOTE FRONTIER COUNTRY between Scotland and England produced a doughty, no-nonsense breed in the form of the Border Terrier. Its rough, dense coat was ideal for long, wet days following huntsmen in pursuit of the fox, and it was tough and small enough to engage its foe underground at the end of the chase.

History

The first Border Terrier types came on the scene in the late seventeenth century, and it shares a common ancestry with other terriers of the region including the Lakeland, Dandie Dinmont, Bedlington, and the now-extinct, all-white Redesdale. Before 1880, when its modern name was finally established, it was often called the Reedwater or Coquetdale Terrier. The Border Terrier Club was formed in the UK in 1920.

Temperament

As a companion dog, the Border is lively, affectionate, and loyal. It is happy in houses and apartments in town, but it needs frequent exercise to burn off its abundant energy.

HEAD
Otter-like, with broad skull, and short muzzle.

COAT
A tough and wiry outer coat with a short, dense undercoat. Colors are bluish-gray and tan, blue and tan, red, or fawn. A little white on the chest is permitted.

BODY
Long, narrow, and deep, with strong loins.

TAIL
Quite short, thick, and tapering. Set high and carried aloft when active.

Although traditionally tenacious and hostile when in pursuit of the fox, the Border Terrier is generally an amiable creature.

Border Terrier
This appealing breed is renowned for its vitality, and is said to be capable of keeping pace with a horse.

EARS
V-shaped, small, and falling forward to lie close to the cheeks.

Neck is fairly long

EYES
Dark in color, with an alert expression.

Nose is preferably black

FACIAL CHARACTERISTICS
Border Terrier

LEGS
Not too heavy; forelegs are straight, hind legs have rounded thighs.

FEET
Small, with thick pads and arched toes.

SIZE
Weight: dogs 13-15¹/2lb (5.9-7kg); bitches 11¹/2-14lb (5.2-6.4kg).

Bull Terrier

D ESPITE ITS FIERCE and intimidating appearance, the Bull Terrier is good with people and gentle with children. It does, however, need a firm hand, as it is extremely powerful and can be a danger to other dogs.

History
In the eighteenth century Bulldogs were crossed with terrier-types to create "Bull and Terrier" fighting dogs. Into these the blood of English Toy Terriers and Whippets was introduced, adding speed and agility to ferocity and strength. About 1860, a Birmingham dog dealer named James Hinks refined the breed by incorporating strains of the English White Terrier and possibly Dalmatians and Spanish Pointers. This produced a white, well-muscled dog with a smooth head and shorter legs than its forebears. In the 1920s, to avoid the genetic tendency to deafness associated with the all-white type, some color was introduced into the dog's coat. The colored version of the breed is recognized separately in the US.

Temperament
Although wary of strangers and often fiercely aggressive towards other dogs, this breed will make a devoted pet if given sufficient attention and exercise.

HEAD
Long, strong, and egg-shaped, with smoothly curving, convex profile.

Bull Terrier
In the second half of the nineteenth century, White Bull Terriers became particularly fashionable among the gambling classes.

BODY
Short and well muscled, with deep, broad chest.

SIZE
Ideal height: 2l-22in (53-56cm).

In March 1865 a brindle Bull Terrier named "Pincher" set an astonishing ratting record: 500 rats killed in 36 minutes 26.5 seconds!

FEET
Round and compact, with arched toes.

Staffordshire Bull Terrier

The Staffordshire Bull Terrier was initially bred for the bloody sports of bull- and bear-baiting, and although it is now recognized as a faithful, reliable, and affectionate pet, it still enjoys a good fight!

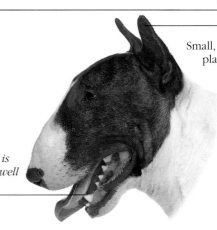

EARS
Small, thin, and placed close together. Carried erect.

Underjaw is deep and well defined

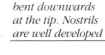

Black nose pad, bent downwards at the tip. Nostrils are well developed

EYES
Triangular, slanting, and deep set with a piercing expression. Black or dark brown in color.

FACIAL CHARACTERISTICS
Bull Terrier

TAIL
Short, tapering, set low, and carried horizontally.

LEGS
Straight and parallel, with heavy bones, and powerful thighs.

COAT
Short, hard, and flat, with a slight gloss. The colored variety can be any color, or any color with white markings.

American Staffordshire Terrier

The Staffordshire Bull Terrier crossed the Atlantic in the nineteenth century and gave rise to a heavier, bigger-boned version that is now recognized as a distinct breed, known as the American Staffordshire Terrier. In the US, some of these dogs have cropped ears.

Cairn Terrier

ONE OF THE SMALLEST of the working terriers, the Cairn gets its name from the Gaelic word *cairn,* meaning a heap of stones. The landscape of the Scottish Highlands is dotted with cairns, which reputedly mark the graves of ancient Romans. The Cairn Terrier's speciality was to hunt the sort of quarry that would take refuge in such rocky piles — rodents, weasels, foxes, and occasionally the fierce Scottish wild cat.

History

The history of this engaging and ever active little terrier goes back at least five hundred years. It was developed on the Isle of Skye, and has common ancestors with those other Highlanders, the Scottish Terrier and the West Highland White. When not hunting predators, the Cairn was used to chase rabbits, dig up moles, and take to the water in pursuit of otters. Cairn Terriers were officially recognized by the British Kennel Club in 1912, but some breeders were crossing them with West Highland White Terriers, and registering the lighter pups as West Highland Whites, and the darker ones as Cairns. In 1924, in an attempt to keep the breeds distinct, the British Kennel Club refused to register the offspring of crosses. The breed was first recognized by the American Kennel Club in 1913.

Temperament

As a companion pet, the Cairn is second to none, being intelligent, loyal, friendly, and perky.

HEAD
Broad, well-proportioned skull, with a well-defined stop, leading to a powerful muzzle. Eyebrows are shaggy.

BODY
Strong and compact, with a deep chest, and level back.

Australian Terrier
One of the few terriers to have been developed outside Britain, the Australian Terrier's rugged appearance is well suited to the harsh terrain of its homeland.

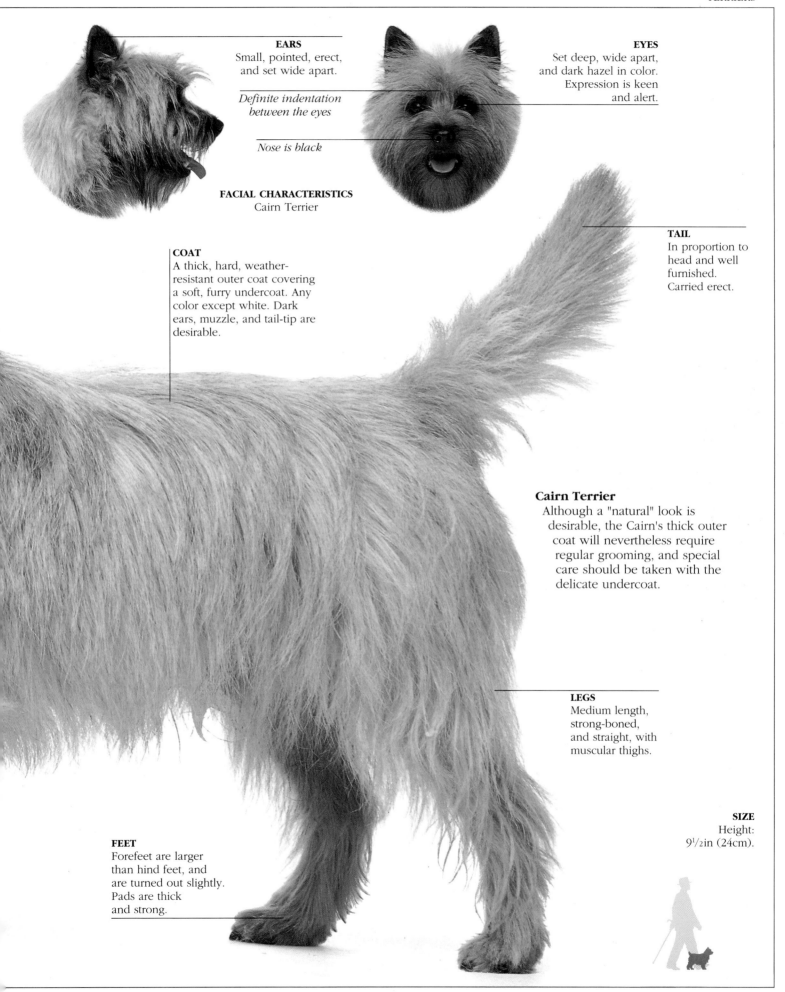

EARS
Small, pointed, erect,
and set wide apart.

EYES
Set deep, wide apart,
and dark hazel in color.
Expression is keen
and alert.

*Definite indentation
between the eyes*

Nose is black

FACIAL CHARACTERISTICS
Cairn Terrier

TAIL
In proportion to
head and well
furnished.
Carried erect.

COAT
A thick, hard, weather-
resistant outer coat covering
a soft, furry undercoat. Any
color except white. Dark
ears, muzzle, and tail-tip are
desirable.

Cairn Terrier
Although a "natural" look is
desirable, the Cairn's thick outer
coat will nevertheless require
regular grooming, and special
care should be taken with the
delicate undercoat.

LEGS
Medium length,
strong-boned,
and straight, with
muscular thighs.

SIZE
Height:
9½in (24cm).

FEET
Forefeet are larger
than hind feet, and
are turned out slightly.
Pads are thick
and strong.

Dandie Dinmont Terrier

T HIS GAME LITTLE TERRIER takes its name from a fictional character, a dog-owning farmer in the novel *Guy Mannering* by Sir Walter Scott. Originally an accomplished hunter of vermin, rabbits, otters, and badgers, the Dandie Dinmont is now chiefly valued for its distinctive appearance, and companionable nature.

History

Originating in the border country between England and Scotland, the Dandie Dinmont can be traced back as a distinct breed to the seventeenth century. It features in a painting of the Duke of Buccleuch by Gainsborough, and was a favorite pet of Louis Philippe of France. Its long, arched back and scimitar-like tail set it apart from other terriers, and its ancestry may include strains of Otter Hound and Basset Hound, as well as Skye, Border, Cairn, Scottish, and Bedlington Terriers.

Temperament

The Dandie Dinmont is friendly, playful, and intensely loyal. It makes an alert house guard, and gives a surprisingly loud bark.

COAT
A mixture of hard and soft hairs, preferably 2in (6cm) long. Colors are black to pale gray ("pepper"), or reddish-brown to fawn ("mustard"). A little white on the chest is permitted.

Skye Terrier
One school of thought has it that this breed owes its origins to the shipwreck of a seventeenth-century Spanish galleon off the coast of Skye in the Scottish Hebrides. On board were Maltese dogs that are said to have mated with the canine inhabitants of the island to produce today's charming, perky, little terrier.

FEET
Hind feet are smaller than forefeet. Dark nails, but varying in color to correspond to coat color.

Profuse "pepper" or "mustard" "top-knot"

EYES
Large and round, set wide and low. Dark hazel in color.

EARS
Long, hanging close to cheeks, set wide apart, and well back.

Distinctly soulful expression

FACIAL CHARACTERISTICS
Dandie Dinmont Terrier

HEAD
Large, with a broad skull, well-domed forehead, and strongly developed jaws. Nose and inside of the mouth are black.

Dandie Dinmont Terrier
Regular, careful grooming is necessary for show-dogs, with the fluffy "top-knot" demanding particular attention.

To keep it in tip-top condition, the Dandie Dinmont needs daily walks, and a fairly lean diet.

BODY
Deep chest, well-sprung ribs, and long, strong back; rather low at the shoulder and slightly arched over the loins.

TAIL
Thick at base, and tapering to a point. Underside neatly feathered. Curved, and carried above body level, but perpendicular when excited.

SIZE
Weight: 18-24lb (8-11kg).

LEGS
Well-boned and muscular; hind legs are a little longer than forelegs. No feathering or dewclaws.

Fox Terriers

HEAD
Flat, rather narrow skull with lean cheeks. Nose black.

COAT
Dense and wiry outer coat, with a soft undercoat. Color is mainly white. Markings can be black, black and tan, or tan, but not slate gray, red, or liver.

BODY
Short, level back, deep chest, slightly arched and muscular loins.

T HESE ARE THE CLASSIC English terriers — full of energy, irrepressible, and pugnacious. Experts differ as to whether the Wire or the Smooth Fox Terrier is the older type, but both share identical characteristics, except for the texture of the coat.

History
The Wire Fox Terrier was originally developed for fox-hunting in the early nineteenth century. It carries the blood of several terriers, including the rough-coated Black and Tan, while the Smooth variety descends from the smooth-coated Black and Tan with a mixture of Beagle, Bulldog and Greyhound. The breed has an enviable record in the services: one Wire Fox Terrier, "Drummer Jack", was attached to the Coldstream Guards during World War I and was awarded the General Service medal. Another, "Igloo", went to the Antarctic between 1928 and 1930 with Admiral Byrd (fully equipped with four fur-lined boots and a camel-hair coat). Both Smooth and Wire Fox Terriers have been exported from England all over the world, and their relative popularity has fluctuated over the years. Originally less favored, the Wire Fox Terrier overtook its rival and reached its zenith of popularity in the 1920s.

Temperament
As a companion dog, the Fox Terrier is affectionate and protective. It does, however, need firm handling to curb its hunting instinct.

Wire Fox Terrier
This dog first appeared in the show ring in 1872. It is now more popular than the Smooth variety.

Smooth Fox Terrier
The Smooth Fox Terrier has a straight, thick, flat-lying coat. Originally a fine "ratting" dog, it was officially recognized as a breed in the 1860s. This was the dog pictured on the early "His Master's Voice" gramophone record labels.

SIZE
Dogs up to 15in (39cm) tall; bitches up to 12in (30cm).

This breed has excellent balance, and is perfectly poised for action.

The Wire Fox Terrier's coat is sometimes likened to coconut matting.

This jaunty character is a firm favorite as a family pet.

TAIL
Customarily docked. Gaily carried high, not curled over the back.

EARS
V-shaped, small, and folded forward to lie close to the cheeks.

EYES
Small, round, and dark in color. The expression is alert and fiery.

Scissor bite: upper teeth closely overlapping lower teeth

Neck fairly long and muscular, broadening to shoulder

LEGS
Strong-boned, straight and parallel. The thighs are powerful.

FEET
Round, neat and compact, with moderate arching of the toes. The pads should be tough and thick.

FACIAL CHARACTERISTICS
Wire Fox Terrier

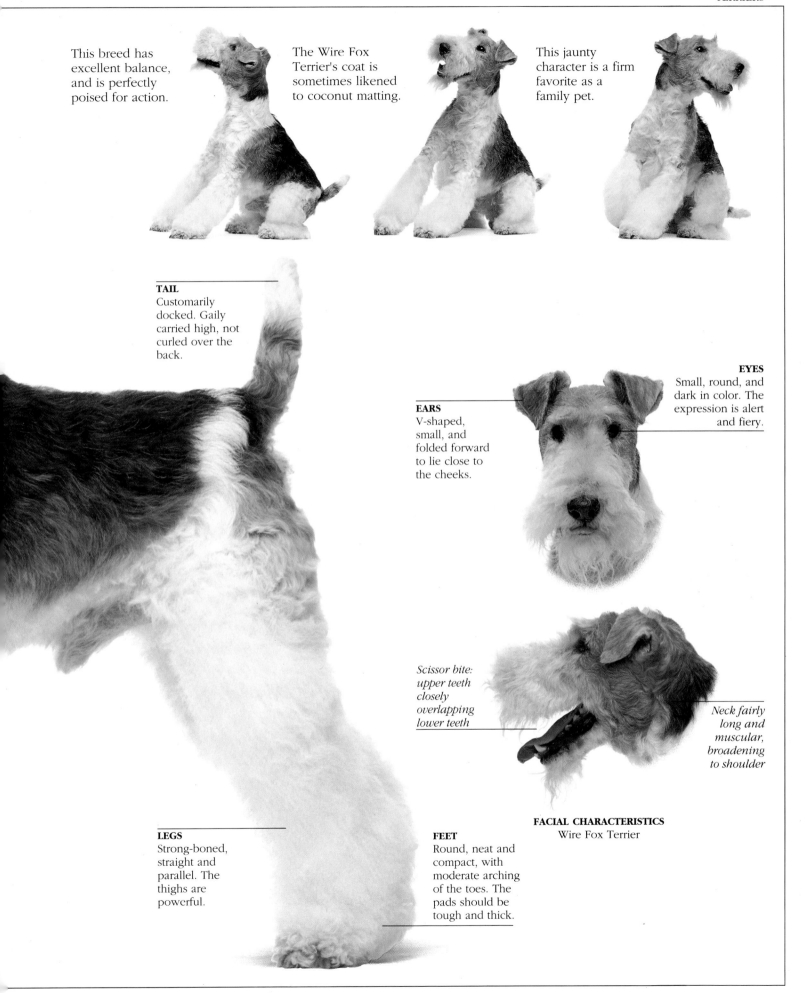

Jack Russell Terrier

THE ESSENTIAL APPEAL of this exuberant animal is its character — full of intelligence, enthusiasm, and tenacity. Most of the world's major canine clubs refuse to accept the Jack Russell as an official breed, but some aficionados positively welcome the fact that its excellent practical qualities have not been sacrificed for the show-ring.

History
One of the Church of England's "hunting parsons", the Reverend Jack Russell of Devon established the breed in the early nineteenth century, and also gave it his name. The Reverend was a keen foxhunter, and needed a nippy dog with plenty of fighting spirit that could keep up with the hounds, and have the courage to face up to its quarry underground. When not pursuing foxes, the Jack Russell was quite happy to perform as a specialist exterminator of vermin. Character has always been the most important ingredient of the breed, so its physical appearance has tended to vary quite widely.

Temperament
The Jack Russell Terrier is excitable, cheerful, and loyal, and makes an excellent guard dog.

COAT
There are two main varieties of coat: one is short and smooth, the other is longer, and rougher. Color is predominantly white, with black, tan, or black and tan markings, or all-tan.

BODY
Strong, with a straight back, slightly arched loins, and a fairly narrow chest.

TAIL
Short, and carried high.

These highly appealing creatures have yet to be officially recognized by the British or American Kennel Clubs.

EARS
V-shaped, small, and falling forwards.

Lips are black

HEAD
Flat, rather wide skull, with slightly tapering muzzle, and black nose.

EYES
Dark brown in color, almond-shaped, and deep-set with lively expression.

Slight stop

FACIAL CHARACTERISTICS
Jack Russell Terrier

Jack Russell Terrier

This breed is endowed with abundant energy resources, but is likely to lose its fine shape if it isn't given plenty of vigorous exercise.

LEGS
Short, with muscular thighs.

FEET
Compact, with well arched toes.

SIZE
Up to 12in (30.5cm) tall.

Kerry Blue Terrier

HEAD
Long and well
proportioned in
relation to the
body. Nose is black,
with large, wide
nostrils. Jaws are
deep and
powerful.

SOMETIMES CALLED the Irish
Blue, the Kerry Blue Terrier
is the national dog of the
Republic of Ireland. Its past is
steeped in mystery — it could
be a descendant of the Spanish
dogs that reached the Irish coast
from the shipwrecked Armada in
1588, or it is sometimes reputed to
be related to the considerably larger
Irish Wolfhound.

History

Some believe the Kerry Blue to be
simply a true native of Ireland, and
in the eighteenth century, it was
certainly used in the Emerald Isle as
a fighting, hunting, herding, and
house-guarding dog. Since then, it
has probably received some
injections of Dandie Dinmont and
Bedlington Terrier blood. Kerry
Blues made their show debut in
England in 1922, and the American
Kennel Club officially recognized
them two years later.

Temperament

The Kerry Blue is a good-natured,
vivacious, and loyal animal, though
with a tendency to stubbornness. It
makes a good house dog, but
requires firm handling.

For showing, the Kerry Blue demands
elaborate trimming and grooming.

The Kerry Blue is a
very clean character,
and does not shed
its curly hair.

EYES
Small and dark in color. Expression should be keen and fiery.

Beard is bushy

COAT
Very thick, soft, silky, and curly. Color is blue-gray, sometimes with areas of darker hair.

TAIL
Customarily docked. Medium-length, set high, and carried erect.

EARS
V-shaped, small, and falling forward to lie close to the cheeks.

Moustache is profuse

FACIAL CHARACTERISTICS
Kerry Blue Terrier

Kerry Blue Terrier
Kerry Blues are born black; their coat usually turns to the distinctive blue-gray within eighteen months.

BODY
Short, with deep, well-sprung chest, and level back.

LEGS
Medium-length and strong. Forelegs are straight; hind legs are powerful.

FEET
Moderately small, round, and compact, with black nails.

SIZE
Height: dogs 18-19in (46-48cm); bitches slightly less.

Manchester Terrier

ORIGINALLY BRED for the dual purposes of rabbit-coursing and rat-killing, the Manchester Terrier was a quick-tempered, game, and rather snappy dog. Gradually the rougher aspects of its character were bred out, but luckily it retained the lively spirit and alertness so typical of the breed.

History

This is yet another dog that has the now-extinct Black and Tan Terrier as its ancestor. A nimble but powerful "ratter", the Black and Tan was crossed with a Whippet by an eighteenth-century Manchester breeder, John Hulme, and the first Manchester Terrier was born; West Highland Terrier blood may have been introduced later. The Toy variety of the breed is the same except that it weighs less and has ears that are larger in proportion to its head.

Temperament

Although not widely popular, the Manchester Terrier has a devoted following of enthusiasts, and is undoubtedly a handsome, active, and affectionate companion.

Manchester Terrier
This unusually sleek terrier reached the US, Canada, and Germany in the nineteenth century. Considering the similarities in both coat texture and color, it is highly likely that the Manchester was involved in the Doberman Pinscher's genetic make-up.

TAIL
Fairly short and tapering, carried below the level of the back.

Hind legs have good driving power

LEGS
Straight; forelegs are set well under the body, hind legs are strong.

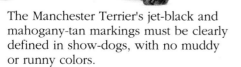

The Manchester Terrier's jet-black and mahogany-tan markings must be clearly defined in show-dogs, with no muddy or runny colors.

HEAD
Long, flat, and narrow, tapering to the nose.

BODY
Short, with slightly arched loins, and well-sprung ribs.

EARS
If button in type, should be carried above the top line of the head, hanging down above the eyes. If cropped, should come to a point and be carried erect.

EYES
Small, not prominent, and almond-shaped. Dark in color, and sparkling.

Perfect scissor bite, with upper teeth closely overlapping lower teeth

COAT
Short, smooth, dense, and glossy. Colors are black and tan, in clearly defined zones. Tan spots should be over each eye, on the throat (in a V-shape), cheeks, chest, partly inside the ears, under the tail, and on forelegs up to the knee. There should be pencil stripes on each toe.

Mouth is tight-lipped

Neck tapers from the shoulders to the head

FACIAL CHARACTERISTICS
Manchester Terrier

Forelegs are far-reaching

FEET
Small and compact, with well-arched toes, and black nails. Hind feet are cat-like.

SIZE
Dogs 16in (41cm) tall; bitches 15in (38cm).

Norwich Terrier

E AST ANGLIA'S CONTRIBUTION to the range of British terriers is the Norwich and Norfolk breeds. Very similar apart from the ears, they have only recently been recognized as separate breeds by the American and British Kennel Clubs.

History

The ancestry of the Norwich Terrier is unclear, but it seems likely that it contains Border, Cairn, and Irish Terrier blood. Bred for hunting vermin, it became popular with undergraduates at Cambridge University in Victorian times, and consequently was often called the Cantab Terrier. After World War I, the breed crossed the Atlantic, and was known as the Jones Terrier, after Frank Jones, one of the early serious breeders. The Norwich Terrier was first recognized in 1932 in the UK, with both prick-eared and drop-eared varieties being accepted, but in 1965 the drop-eared version was renamed the Norfolk Terrier. In the US, the two separate breeds were recognized in 1979.

Temperament

Both East Anglian terriers are tough, lively, loyal, and untroublesome dogs, that make ideal pets and watchful house guards.

COAT
Hard, wiry, and lying close. Long and rough on the neck and shoulders, short and smooth on the skull. Colors are black and tan, wheaten, grizzle, or shades of red, preferably without any white marks.

SIZE
10in (25.5cm) tall.

Norfolk Terrier
Unlike the Norwich, the Norfolk Terrier's ears are medium-sized, V-shaped, and slightly rounded at the tip.

American and British breed standards allow this fearless dog to have "honourable scars from fair wear and tear".

TAIL
Docked to half the original length, and carried erect.

BODY
Short and compact, with a level back, and well-sprung ribs.

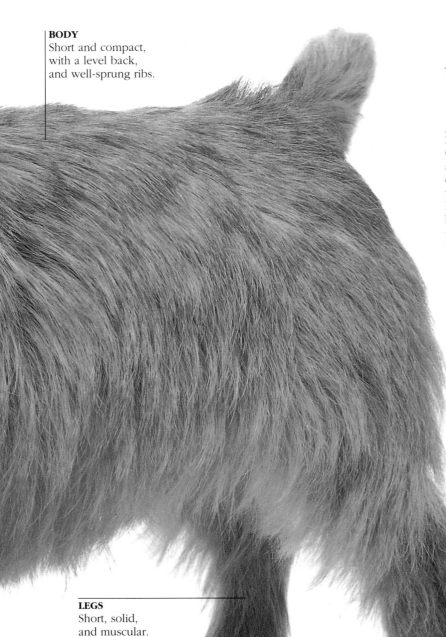

EARS
Set fairly well apart, erect, with pointed tips.

EYES
Oval-shaped, small, and dark in color, with black rims. Expression is bright and alert.

Neck is of medium length and strong

HEAD
Wide skull, with definite stop, and wedge-shaped muzzle. Nose and lips are black.

Pronounced whiskers and eyebrows

FACIAL CHARACTERISTICS
Norwich Terrier

LEGS
Short, solid, and muscular.

FEET
Round, with thick pads. Nails are black.

Norwich Terrier
This is an ideal house dog, because its hard, close coat does not collect dirt or need trimming, and only minimal grooming is required.

Schnauzers

CURRENTLY, there are three types of Schnauzer — Giant, Standard, and Miniature. Their name is derived from the German word *Schnauze*, meaning muzzle. The Schnauzer muzzle is remarkable in that it is adorned with a distinctive, prominent moustache.

History

The Schnauzers originally came from the cattle- and sheep-farming area of Württemberg and Bavaria in southern Germany, where a standard-sized, Schnauzer-like dog had been recorded in the sixteenth century. Its forebears probably included Poodle-type dogs, as well as the Wire-haired German Pinscher. The early Schnauzers were general-purpose dogs, being very good ratters and guards, and they were also popular as coach dogs because of their great stamina. Today, the Standard and Giant Schnauzers are classified as Working Dogs in the US, and as Utility Dogs in the UK and Australia.

Temperament

Generally, all three Schnauzers are alert and energetic, and make good companions and family pets.

HEAD
Broad and long, gradually tapering to blunt muzzle. Prominent eyebrows, thick moustache and whiskers.

BODY
Stocky; deep chest of moderate width, and straight, sloping back.

Giant Schnauzer
The strongest of the Schnauzers stands 25^1/2-27^1/2in (65-70cm) tall at the shoulder, and was originally used as a cattle dog in Bavaria.

LEGS
Forelegs are straight and strong; thighs on the hind legs are well-muscled.

The Miniature Schnauzer is a brisk, bright little dog, and is the most popular of the Schnauzers.

TAIL
Set high and carried erect. Customarily docked.

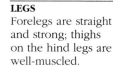

Slight stop from skull to muzzle accentuating prominent eyebrows

EARS
V-shaped, set high, and falling forward.

The Miniature Schnauzer is classified as a Terrier in the US, and as a Utility Dog in the UK and Australia. The dog illustrated here has cropped ears, which would be illegal in the UK, but is optional in the US and other countries.

EYES
Medium-sized, oval, and dark, with a keen, lively expression.

Nose should be black, with wide nostrils

FACIAL CHARACTERISTICS
Miniature Schnauzer

Miniature Schnauzer

As its size suggests, this dog is not only smaller and more manageable than the Giant and Standard Schnauzers, but also tends to be less aggressive in temperament.

COAT
Coarse, wiry outer coat, and dense undercoat. It should never feel soft. Long on legs and head, short elsewhere. Colors are "pepper" and "salt" (a mixture of dark and light gray hair, with tan shading permitted), pure black, or black and silver.

FEET
Cat-like, round and short, with well arched toes and thick, black pads.

SIZE
Miniature: 12-14in (30.5-35.5cm) tall. Standard: 18-20in (46-51cm).

Sealyham Terrier

THIS MAGNIFICENTLY BEARDED animal was bred to accompany hounds in pursuit of the otter, badger, and fox. It therefore had to have stamina, a good turn of speed, gameness to follow its quarry underground, and the bulk, determination, and toughness to battle to the very end.

History

The Sealyham is a one-man dog in a very special sense; it was created between 1850 and 1891 by the careful selective breeding program of only one man, Captain John Edwardes, of Sealyham, an estate near Haverfordwest in Wales. No one knows exactly how he did it, as the Captain kept no records of his work. It is likely, however, that he used the Bull Terrier, West Highland White, Dandie Dinmont, and perhaps the Pembroke Corgi. The show debut of the breed took place in 1903, in its home town of Haverfordwest. It was recognized by the American and British Kennel Clubs in 1911, and the American Sealyham Terrier Club was founded in 1913, five years after its British counterpart.

Temperament

A typical terrier, with plenty of pluck, the Sealyham makes an affectionate companion.

COAT
Long, hard, wiry outer coat covering a weather-resistant, soft, dense, undercoat. Colors are white, or white with lemon, with tan or badger markings on the head and ears.

BODY
Medium-length and strong, with level back, and deep, broad chest.

LEGS
Short and strong. Forelegs are straight; hind legs are longer and lighter-boned.

SIZE
Height:
10½in (27cm).

This bearded breed is fearless, frank, and friendly.

Considering the Sealyham's size, its hind legs are surprisingly powerful.

Bouncy, well-balanced, and particularly poised, the Sealyham Terrier has all the attributes of a natural performer.

Sealyham Terrier
Careful grooming is a daily requirement for show-dogs, in addition to regular attention from a professional groomer.

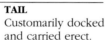

TAIL
Customarily docked and carried erect.

EARS
Medium-sized, with rounded tips. Folded level with the top of the head, with the forward edge lying close to the cheek.

EYES
Round and very dark, with a keen, piercing expression. Set deep and fairly wide apart.

HEAD
Long, broad, and powerful. Nose is black with large nostrils.

Neck is thick and muscular

Jaw is square

FACIAL CHARACTERISTICS
Sealyham Terrier

FEET
Large, compact, and round, with thick pads and well-arched toes pointing forwards.

Soft-Coated Wheaten Terrier

ALTHOUGH THE OLDEST of the terriers native to Ireland, the Soft-Coated Wheaten now has its stronghold in the US. It derives its name from its coat, which is the color of ripening wheat.

Very appropriately for an Irish breed, the Soft-Coated Wheaten made its show debut on St. Patrick's Day, in Dublin, in 1937.

History

Its relations are thought to include the Black and Tan, Irish, and Kerry Blue Terriers. Originally it was a working terrier on the farm, earning its keep by acting as cattle-drover, guard dog, and foe of badgers, rats, rabbits, and even otters! In the 1930s, its numbers diminished alarmingly, but careful breeding ensured its safety. The Soft-Coated Wheaten was recognized by the British Kennel Club in 1943, and although it crossed the Atlantic in 1946, it was not officially recognized by the American Kennel Club until 1973. Soft-Coated Wheatens are now steadily increasing in popularity, particularly in the US.

Temperament

An intelligent, cheerful character, the Soft-Coated Wheaten makes an excellent companion dog, and loves outdoor exercise.

HEAD
Medium-length, with flat-topped skull, definite stop, and square muzzle, equal to skull in length.

FEET
Round and compact, with black pads and nails. Dewclaws should be removed.

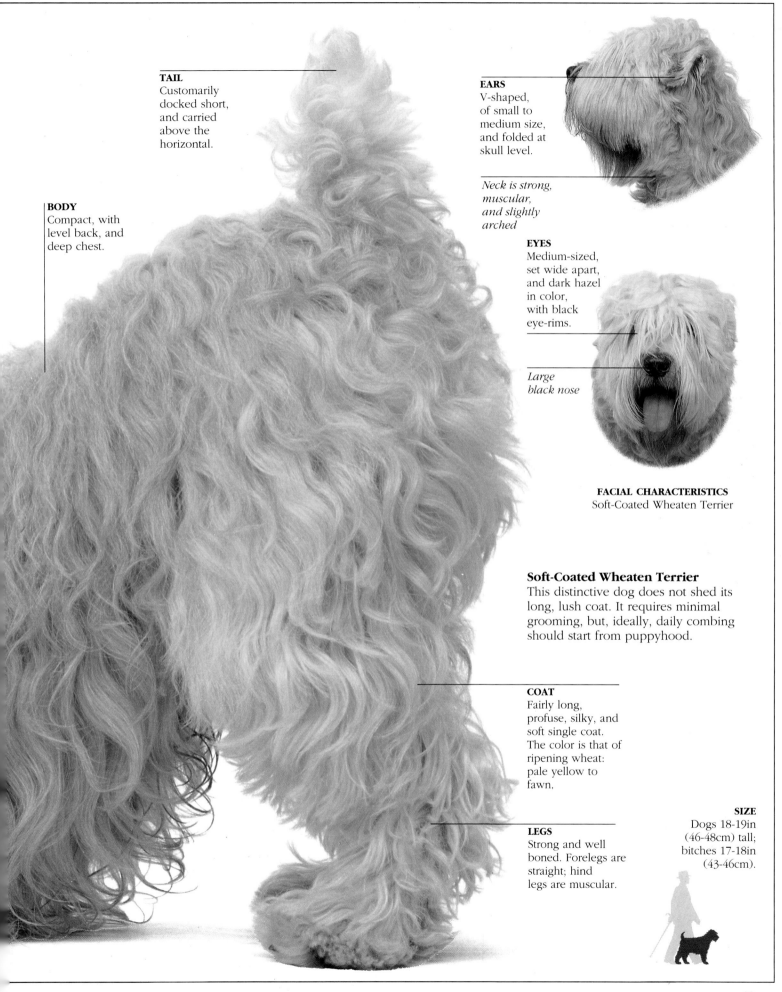

TAIL
Customarily docked short, and carried above the horizontal.

EARS
V-shaped, of small to medium size, and folded at skull level.

Neck is strong, muscular, and slightly arched

BODY
Compact, with level back, and deep chest.

EYES
Medium-sized, set wide apart, and dark hazel in color, with black eye-rims.

Large black nose

FACIAL CHARACTERISTICS
Soft-Coated Wheaten Terrier

Soft-Coated Wheaten Terrier

This distinctive dog does not shed its long, lush coat. It requires minimal grooming, but, ideally, daily combing should start from puppyhood.

COAT
Fairly long, profuse, silky, and soft single coat. The color is that of ripening wheat: pale yellow to fawn.

LEGS
Strong and well boned. Forelegs are straight; hind legs are muscular.

SIZE
Dogs 18-19in (46-48cm) tall; bitches 17-18in (43-46cm).

West Highland White Terrier

C ONSIDERED BY ITS DEVOTEES to be one of the most attractive of the Scottish terriers, the West Highland White is also a hardy and tenacious dog. It requires firm handling and plenty of attention from its owner.

History

Bred to hunt otter, fox, and vermin, the West Highland White shares its ancestry with the Scottie, Cairn, and Dandie Dinmont. Selective breeding of all-white dogs around Poltalloch in Argyll in the nineteenth century established the characteristic features we know today. The "Westie" was once called the Poltalloch Terrier, and also the Roseneath Terrier, after the Dumbartonshire estate of the Duke of Argyll, a famous fancier of the breed.

Temperament

The West Highland White is an affectionate, self-confident, and cheeky character. Despite its small size, it makes a good guard dog, being alert and courageous.

Head is thickly coated, and frames the face

COAT
A harsh, straight outer coat about 2in (5cm) long covering a short, soft undercoat. Color is pure white.

SIZE
About 11in (28cm) tall.

Scottish Terrier

The "Scottie" has been known by several names, including the West Highland and the Aberdeen, a reflection of its old and mixed Celtic background. The dog that we know today was developed towards the end of the nineteenth century.

West Highland White Terrier

"Westies" require regular grooming as the white coat tends to shed hair more or less continuously. On the plus side, they have a dry skin with no "doggy" odor.

One reason for the selective breeding of the "Westie" is that a pure white coat that shows up against dark foliage confers an obvious advantage in a dog that is used to hunt prey.

TAIL
Set on high, but not long enough to extend above the top of the skull. Straight, unfeathered, and carried jauntily, but not curled over the back.

BODY
Compact and strong with a deep chest and level back.

EARS
Small, erect, sharply pointed, and covered in smooth hair.

Nose black and quite large

HEAD
Slightly domed skull with a moderate stop down to muzzle, and heavy eyebrows.

EYES
Medium-sized, sharp, and as dark as possible. Set wide apart.

FEET
Round, with the forefeet larger than the hind feet. Covered with short, harsh hair and thickly padded. The nails are preferably black.

LEGS
Short and muscular.

FACIAL CHARACTERISTICS
West Highland White Terrier

Non-Sporting Dogs

The Non-Sporting group of dogs, known as Utility Dogs in the UK, are a miscellaneous collection left over when the other breeds have been neatly pigeon-holed into the other groups. But they are none the worse for that! The name "Utility", meaning fitness for a purpose, barely touches on the individuality and specialization of these dogs, and certainly doesn't give them any common characteristic. A better appellation might be "Special Dogs", for they include, in many ways, the most interesting, the most out-of-the-ordinary dogs.

Shar Pei

As you might expect, they are as widely varied as there are breeds in the group, and all have been selectively bred either for esthetic effect, or to perform some precise and often unusual function, a kind of work not included in the Sporting and Working categories. In some cases their history goes back for many centuries, making them some of the oldest documented breeds of dog.

Unusual occupations

A good example of unusual function is that of the Lhasa Apso, which comes from the Lamaist temples and monasteries of Tibet. There they were used both as watchdogs and as "bearers of good fortune". Of more practical, but still singular, use, were such breeds in the group as the Dalmatian, descended from some form of pointer-cross and employed in days gone by to run alongside carriages as a deterrent to highwaymen, and the Chow Chow, first bred in Mongolia three thousand years ago for use in war, and later raised in China and surrounding Eastern countries as a valuable source of meat and fur. Sadly, "Red Dogs" of the Chow Chow type are still regarded as table delicacies in the Far East.

Distinctive breeds

Perhaps the most glamorous and eye-catching of the Non-Sporting breeds is the Bichon Frise, easily mistaken

Boston Terrier

Chow Chow

for a puff-ball! Another highly decorative companion, the Poodle, is descended from a German gundog, the Pudel, that retrieved game from water. Most famous perhaps, and certainly most British of all this group, is the Bulldog. This attractive and surprisingly good-natured fellow has a long record of exploitation

Poodle

by man in the barbaric "sport" of bull-baiting, which goes back to at least the fourteenth century. A more recently developed Non-Sporting Dog is the Boston Terrier, one of the few breeds to originate in the US, and which had its beginnings in the middle of the nineteenth century.

decorated with the Bronze Star and five other ribbons, and another was promoted to Corporal. The football teams of the Universities of Yale and Georgia have had Bulldog mascots, and modish nineteenth-century German students had a fad for French Poodles. Illustrious owners of Non-Sporting Dogs include Sigmund Freud, who owned a Chow, "Jo-Fi"; John Steinbeck, who had a Standard

Winning dogs

Non-Sporting Dogs are no reserved team of "also rans" among dog breeds. They have, in the shape of the Toy and Standard Poodles, been awarded the Best of Show accolade at Cruft's in Britain twice in the past seven years. The Boston Terrier, the Bulldog, the Poodle, and the Keeshond, all Non-Sporting breeds, are national dogs of the US, Britain, Holland, and France respectively.

Keeshond

Famous pets

King William of Orange had his life saved by two Schipperkes in 1572, and Prince Rupert's favorite, a white Poodle called "Boy", was thought by some of Cromwell's Roundheads to possess supernatural gifts. He was killed at the Battle of Marston Moor in 1644. The American President Warren Harding had a pet white English Bulldog, "Oh Boy". An English Bulldog working for the American forces during World War I was

Dalmatian

Poodle, called "Charley"; and Eugene O'Neill whose Dalmatian was named "Blemie". Gertrude Stein was devoted to her white poodle, "Basket", as was Maeterlinck to his French Bulldog, "Pelleas". The off-beat, the unusual, and the eccentric; the Non-Sporting group has them all.

Bichon Frise

COMPANION OF SAILORS, a favorite at the sixteenth-century French court, successful circus performer, a rising star at today's shows — the Bichon Frise has had a career as glamorous as its extraordinary looks would suggest.

History

Although it is thought of as a French breed, the Bichon Frise may have originated on the Canary Islands, from where it was brought to the European mainland by Italian travelers during the fourteenth century. A descendant of the now-extinct Water Spaniel, it proved popular with the French and Spanish nobility, and made frequent appearances in the paintings of Goya. At that time, there were four varieties, the Maltais, Bolognais, Havanais, and Tenerife, but the French Revolution was to see the decline not only of the aristocracy, but also of the little dog that it had favored. The Bichon Frise traded the golden life of palaces and chateaux for the gilt and spangles of the circus ring, where, like the Poodle, it was employed as an easily trained, cheerful, trooper. Its numbers still fell, however, especially during World War I, and it was not until the 1930s that the dog enjoyed a resurgence in France. A standard was drawn up in 1933 when the dog became known by its present name, which translated means "curly lap-dog".

Temperament

A dog that loves human company, the Bichon Frise nevertheless has a strong, independent spirit.

SIZE
Up to 12in (30cm) tall; ideally smaller.

TAIL
Set quite low. Carried curved, but not curled, over the back.

Bichon Frise
A charming puff-ball of a dog, with a coat that makes it literally stand out from the crowd, the Bichon Frise has a robustness and tenacity that belies its "child's-toy" appearance.

LEGS
The forelegs are straight and perpendicular when seen from the front and should not be too finely boned. The thighs are broad and well rounded.

To maintain the "powder-puff" appearance of the Bichon Frise takes extensive trimming, brushing, and bathing. For pets that aren't destined for showing, normal grooming keeps the coat in a pleasant, curly condition.

COAT
Fine and silky, with soft, corkscrew curls when not brushed out. Color should be white; shadings of buff, cream, or apricot are allowed, but must not exceed ten per cent of the coat. Under the coat, a dark pigment is desirable.

HEAD
Lines drawn between the outer corners of the eyes and the tip of the nose should create an equilateral triangle.

EYES
Fairly large and round; dark in color. The white of the eye should not be visible when the dog looks forwards.

BODY
The chest is well developed and deep, with the loins slightly arched, muscular, and well tucked up. The pelvis is broad.

Nose is large, round, and black

EARS
Narrow, delicate, hanging close to the head, and covered with long, fine hair.

Muzzle should not be too thick nor too snipey

FEET
Tight, rounded, and well knuckled up. Pads are black, with black nails a desirable feature.

FACIAL CHARACTERISTICS
Bichon Frise

Boston Terrier

THIS LIVELY, INTELLIGENT, plucky little dog, one of the few breeds to have been developed in the United States, has few special requirements, and makes an excellent house-dog and companion.

History

Originally the Boston Terrier was bred for the purpose of dog fighting, a "sport" which was centered around Boston in the nineteenth century. The early Boston Terriers were produced by crossing Bulldogs with white Bull Terriers, although later the breed was substantially modified by selective inbreeding and by crossing with the French Bulldog. In 1891 the American Bull Terrier Club of Boston applied for breed recognition, which was refused until the offending words "Bull Terrier" were removed. The Boston Terrier Club of America was eventually recognized in 1893. Since then, the breed has become one of the most popular in the US, both as a show-dog and a pet. It has also enjoyed popularity in Britain, Canada, and Australia, but to a lesser extent.

Temperament

The Boston Terrier is an intelligent, boisterous, and affectionate dog, with none of the aggressive tendencies of its ancestors.

Boston Terrier
Because of the structure of the puppy's head, most Boston Terriers have to be delivered by Caesarean section. This surgery is expensive, and breeding tends to be limited to those of very fit stock.

COAT
Short, fine hair, giving a smooth, shiny coat. Color is preferably brindle with white markings.

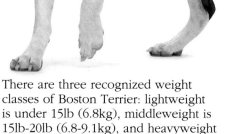

There are three recognized weight classes of Boston Terrier: lightweight is under 15lb (6.8kg), middleweight is 15lb-20lb (6.8-9.1kg), and heavyweight is 20-25lb (9.1-11.4kg).

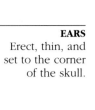

EYES
Large, dark in color, wide apart, and round. Alert, intelligent expression.

HEAD
Square and flat-topped, with a short muzzle and deep jowls.

EARS
Erect, thin, and set to the corner of the skull.

Stop is well defined

Flews completely cover teeth when mouth is closed

Nose is black and wide

Head should be in proportion to the size of the dog

FACIAL CHARACTERISTICS
Boston Terrier

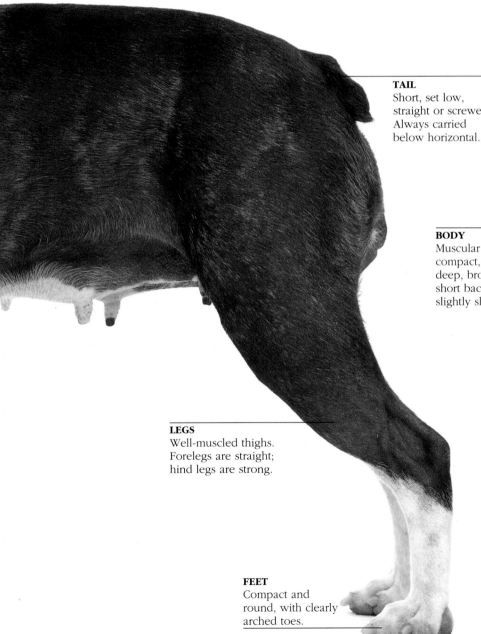

TAIL
Short, set low, straight or screwed. Always carried below horizontal.

BODY
Muscular and compact, with a deep, broad chest, short back, and slightly sloping rump.

LEGS
Well-muscled thighs. Forelegs are straight; hind legs are strong.

The ancestor of this perky breed was called "Hooper's Judge". Owned by Mr Hooper of Boston, this early Boston Terrier was a cross between a Bulldog and an English Terrier.

FEET
Compact and round, with clearly arched toes.

SIZE
Height is 15-17in (38-43cm).

Bulldog

DESPITE ITS FORMIDABLE appearance, the Bulldog is a gentle, affectionate, and loyal creature. These qualities, plus its reputation for courage and dogged endurance, prompted the British to adopt it as their national dog, and to preserve the breed after the abolition of bull-baiting.

History

The practice of setting dogs to attack bulls for the purposes of public entertainment had been established in Britain for over 600 years before it was finally made illegal in 1835. By the seventeenth century the dogs used for this "sport" had become known as Bulldogs, but they probably had longer legs and were certainly more aggressive than the breed we know today. This may reflect their ancestry, as they were probably derived from a Mastiff-type of dog introduced into Britain by the Phoenicians in the 6th century BC.

Temperament

Today's Bulldog has a very different temperament from that of its forebears. It is an affectionate and dependable animal, gentle with children, but known for its courage and its excellent guarding abilities.

BODY
Heavily built, but narrower at the loins. Shoulders are broad; back is short and slightly arched; chest is deep.

HEAD
Large, broad, and square. Well-defined stop. Cheeks are well rounded and heavily wrinkled.

LEGS
Straight and muscular; hind legs are longer than forelegs.

The Bulldog is classified as a Utility Dog in the UK, and as a Non-Sporting Dog in the US and Australia.

COAT
Fine, short, and smooth.
Colors include brindle,
reds, and fawn.

*Nose and
nostrils
are broad
and black*

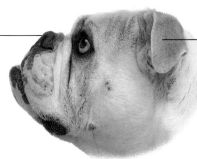

EARS
Small, thin,
set high and
wide apart.

TAIL
Short, set low, and
carried downwards.
May be straight or
screwed.

*Upper lips
hang over
lower jaws
at the sides
but join lower
lip at the
front and
completely
cover teeth*

*"Rose ear"
exposes the
pink inside*

EYES
Very dark,
round, set wide
apart and low
down in the
skull.

FACIAL CHARACTERISTICS
Bulldog

French Bulldog
Probably derived in part from smaller
examples of the English Bulldog, the
French Bulldog is a muscular, energetic,
little dog weighing 19-22lb (9-10kg). It
has an affectionate, dependable nature,
and characteristic bat-shaped ears.

Bulldog
This prizefighter of a dog
won a place in Englishmen's
hearts for its tremendous
courage: scorning a less direct
approach, it would always attack
from the front.

FEET
Compact and round,
with forefeet turning
slightly outwards.
Toes are well spaced.

SIZE
Weight:
dogs 50lb (23kg);
bitches 40lb (18kg).

Chow Chow

T HIS EXOTIC ANIMAL has two unique anatomical features — its mouth and tongue are blue-black in color, and it walks with a stilted gait, due to its virtually straight hind legs.

In China, the Chow Chow's appearance has given it the name *hsiung kon*, meaning bear dog.

History

In ancient times, the Chow Chow was the adversary of evil spirits, guarding temples against their malign influence. Also known as the Tartar Dog, Dog of Barbarians, or the Chinese Spitz, the breed probably originated in Mongolia or northern Siberia. It was then introduced into China, where it performed the roles of guard dog (against intruders rather than spirits) and hunting dog of emperors and aristocrats. Later, the breed unfortunately became a source of both food — its flesh is still considered a delicacy in many parts of Asia — and fur. The Chow's coat can be rough or smooth: the rough is more common, and has the distinctive ruff on the neck and culottes on the legs, but the smooth coat is still quite thick and dense, and stands up from the body.

Temperament

The Chow's rather independent and quiet nature contrasts sharply with the loyalty and affection it characteristically shows towards its owner.

TAIL
Set high, and arching forwards over the back.

COAT
Soft, dense undercoat, and coarse, abundant outer coat which stands out from the body. Colors are solid black, blue, cream, red, or fawn.

SIZE
Average height:
18-20in (46-51cm).

Chow Chow
With its leonine ruff, massive bear-like face, and scowling expression, the Chow Chow can look a daunting creature, but is unlikely to fight unless provoked.

BODY
Muscular and well-balanced, with a broad, deep chest, and a short, straight back.

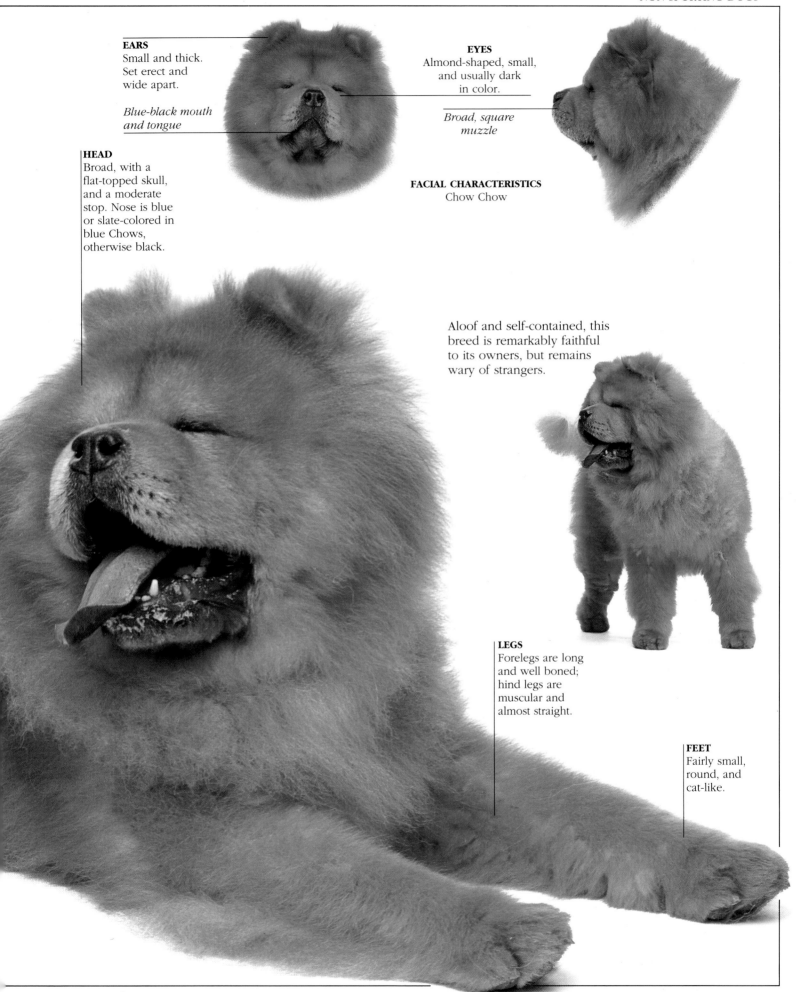

EARS
Small and thick.
Set erect and
wide apart.

*Blue-black mouth
and tongue*

EYES
Almond-shaped, small,
and usually dark
in color.

*Broad, square
muzzle*

FACIAL CHARACTERISTICS
Chow Chow

HEAD
Broad, with a
flat-topped skull,
and a moderate
stop. Nose is blue
or slate-colored in
blue Chows,
otherwise black.

Aloof and self-contained, this
breed is remarkably faithful
to its owners, but remains
wary of strangers.

LEGS
Forelegs are long
and well boned;
hind legs are
muscular and
almost straight.

FEET
Fairly small,
round, and
cat-like.

Dalmatian

WITH ITS WHITE COAT and distinctive dark spots, the Dalmatian is one of the most elegant and eye-catching of breeds. In nineteenth-century Europe, and particularly in Britain, it trotted alongside horse-drawn carriages — reputedly to protect passengers from the unwanted attentions of highwaymen, but probably also used for its marvellous decorative effect.

History

Although the Dalmatian is often considered a British dog because of its association with the aristocracy's stately processions, its history remains the subject of some debate. Some say its origins can be traced to northern India, and that it reached Europe by traveling with gypsy caravans in the Middle Ages via Dalmatia, Yugoslavia, whence it derived its name. Others, however, claim it may have had its roots in Egypt or Greece. Apart from its spots, the Dalmatian resembles the Pointer in appearance, and it is likely that the dogs are related.

Temperament

A lively, extroverted, and intelligent dog, the Dalmatian is naturally friendly, and a favorite with children. It likes regular exercise, and has great stamina.

HEAD
Long, flat-topped skull, and a moderate stop. Nose is black or brown.

BODY
Deep-chested, but not too wide. Loins are slightly arched.

COAT
Sleek and glossy, with short, fine hairs. Color is white, with either brown or black spots.

In modern times, "101 Dalmatians", Walt Disney's 1959 animated cartoon, has ensured the breed's continuing popularity.

An important requirement of the breed
is a well-balanced physique.

TAIL
Slightly curved and
long. Ideally it
should be spotted.

Dalmatian

Unlike leopards, they do change their
spots! Dalmatians are born white, then,
as puppies, develop faint smudges
which change to bold, distinctive marks
as they get older.

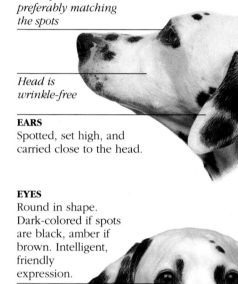

*Dark eye-rims,
preferably matching
the spots*

*Head is
wrinkle-free*

EARS
Spotted, set high, and
carried close to the head.

EYES
Round in shape.
Dark-colored if spots
are black, amber if
brown. Intelligent,
friendly
expression.

*Muzzle is long
and powerful*

FACIAL CHARACTERISTICS
Dalmatian

LEGS
Well-developed
thighs. Forelegs
are straight;
hindquarters
are rounded.

SIZE
Dogs 22-24in (56-
61cm) tall; bitches
20-22in (51-56cm).

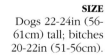

FEET
Round and compact,
with well-arched
toes. Nails are white,
or match the color
of the spots.

Keeshond

THIS TYPICAL SPITZ-TYPE breed could have
derived its name from "Jan Kees" — a
very common Dutch name, or from the two
patriots Kees de Witt and Kees de Gyselaer.
Used extensively as a guard dog on canal
boats, it became known as the Dutch Barge
Dog, although in Victorian England it was
perhaps rather unkindly named the
Overweight Pomeranian!

History

In the eighteenth century the
Keeshond was known as "a dog of
the people". It symbolized resistance
against the rule of William of
Orange, and one of the Dutch
patriot leaders, Kees de Gyselaer,
actually owned one of these dogs.
The Keeshond's ancestors remain
rather obscure, but it was probably
derived from earlier types of Spitz
dogs, such as the Wolf Spitz.
Keeshonden were first introduced
into the UK by Mrs Wingfield-Digby,
and by the late 1920s the breed had
arrived in the US.

Temperament

A bright, friendly character, quick to
learn and very alert. It makes a good
guard dog.

HEAD
Wedge-shaped
from above, with
a medium-length
muzzle.

BODY
Short, compact,
and powerful.
Chest is deep and
well rounded.

COAT
Gray and black
mixed with pale
gray, dense, soft
undercoat. Long,
hard gray outer
coat with black
tips, standing out
from body. Needs
thorough daily
grooming.

Keeshonden tend to be
one-person dogs, and
usually enjoy a very
long life.

Keeshond

The Keeshond does not take up much room in the home, and like its ancestors on the barges in Holland, can comfortably curl up to keep out of the way.

Grand Spitz

The doyen of the Spitz group of Northern dogs, this breed differs from the Keeshond and Wolf Spitz in being somewhat smaller and carrying a black, brown, or white coat.

TAIL
Moderate length, set high, with black tip. It is carried tightly curved over back.

Fox-like head, with large ruff

EYES
Oblique, dark eyes. Distinctive "spectacle markings".

EARS
Small, set high, velvety, and erect.

Dark muzzle with black nose

LEGS
Straight forelegs with good bones. Hind legs are slightly bent at hocks.

FACIAL CHARACTERISTICS
Keeshond

FEET
Cream-colored and compact, with black nails. Short, smooth hair on feet and lower legs.

SIZE
Height: 17-18in (43-46cm).

Lhasa Apso

PRIOR TO THE TWENTIETH CENTURY, this Tibetan breed was rarely seen outside its native land. The exact origins of its name remain obscure — "Lhasa" is probably taken from Tibet's capital city, but "Apso" could have been derived from the Tibetan *abso seng kye*, meaning barking sentinel dog, or from a version of *rapso*, Tibetan for goat, perhaps referring to the breed's long, wiry coat.

History
For at least two thousand years, the Lhasa Apso was bred only in Tibet by holy men and nobles. It was used as a watchdog in temples and monasteries, and was considered sacred, for when its master died, his soul was thought to enter the Lhasa Apso's body. Although they were thought to bring good luck to their owners, Lhasa Apsos were virtually impossible to buy. Happily, these very precious dogs and the equally prized Tibetan Terrier spread to other parts of the world, mainly because the Dalai Lama, Tibet's ruler, would present them to visiting foreign diplomats. The breed was first seen in Britain in the 1920s, and was introduced to the US in the 1930s.

Temperament
This is a hardy dog with a friendly, assertive manner. Intelligent and lively, it makes a good pet, but is naturally suspicious of strangers.

SIZE
Height:
9-11in (23-28cm).

COAT
Long, coarse, and straight outer coat, with thick undercoat. There is a definite parting along the spine. Many colors including white brown, honey, and slate.

Lhasa Apso
Because of the golden-honey colors in its coat, the Lhasa Apso is sometimes referred to as the Lion Dog of Tibet. This long, beautiful coat can easily become matted, and requires regular and thorough grooming from an energetic owner.

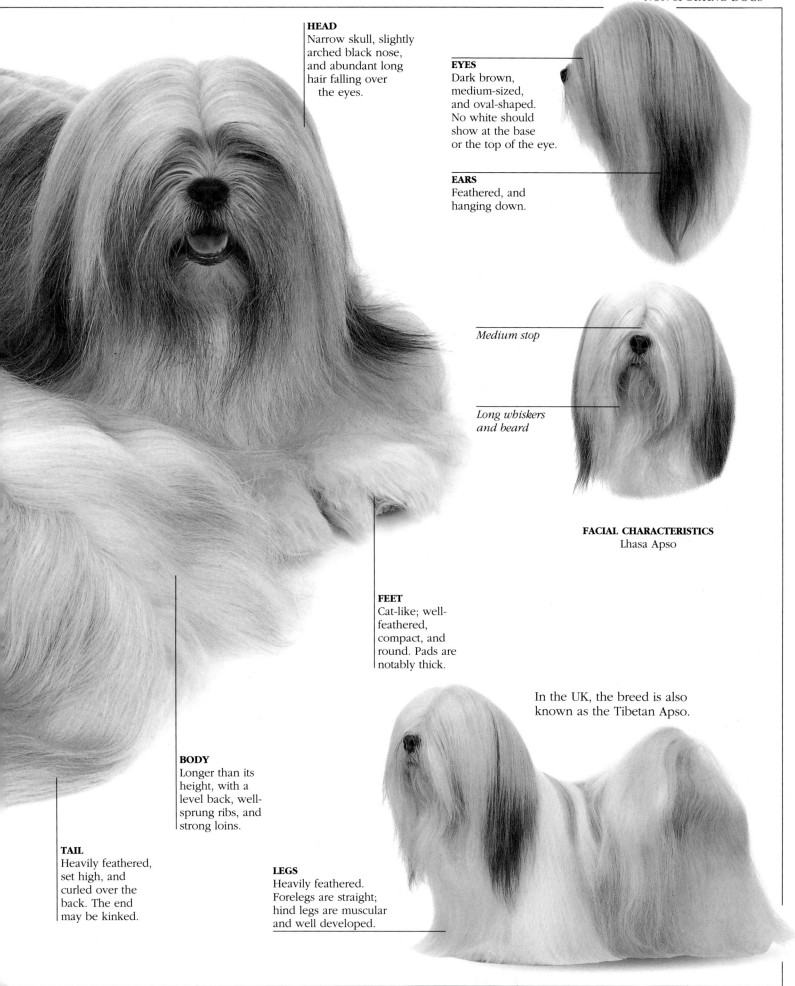

HEAD
Narrow skull, slightly arched black nose, and abundant long hair falling over the eyes.

EYES
Dark brown, medium-sized, and oval-shaped. No white should show at the base or the top of the eye.

EARS
Feathered, and hanging down.

Medium stop

Long whiskers and beard

FACIAL CHARACTERISTICS
Lhasa Apso

FEET
Cat-like; well-feathered, compact, and round. Pads are notably thick.

In the UK, the breed is also known as the Tibetan Apso.

BODY
Longer than its height, with a level back, well-sprung ribs, and strong loins.

TAIL
Heavily feathered, set high, and curled over the back. The end may be kinked.

LEGS
Heavily feathered. Forelegs are straight; hind legs are muscular and well developed.

Poodles

I T IS PERHAPS UNFORTUNATE that this animal has received more attention for the unique way it is clipped for showing, than for its exceptional intelligence and sporting past. Nevertheless, it has become one of the world's most well-loved breeds.

Standard Poodle
It is generally accepted that the Standard is the most healthy of the three varieties of Poodle.

History
Although the Poodle has been known throughout western Europe for at least 400 years, its exact origins are uncertain. Very versatile, it can happily perform in various environments. On the battlefield, "Boy", the constant companion of Prince Rupert of the Rhine was killed at the Battle of Marston Moor in 1644; in the field, French Poodles were used to retrieve game birds from water; and even at the circus, the combination of distinctive looks and a "show-off" nature meant that Poodles always pulled in the crowds. There are three varieties of Poodle: Standard, Miniature, and Toy; they differ only in size.

Temperament
Lively and good-natured dogs, all Poodles are intelligent, friendly, and can be extremely loyal.

Miniature Poodle
The Miniature is larger than the Toy, but smaller than the Standard, and was particularly popular in the 1950s.

LEGS
Forelegs and hind legs are straight and muscular.

SIZE
Toy up to 10in (25.5cm) tall; Miniature 10-15in (25.5-38cm) tall; Standard over 15in (38cm) tall.

FEET
Small and compact, with well-arched toes, ample pads, and dark nails.

Nose, lips, eyes, and eye-rims are usually black, but vary according to the coat color

EARS
Wide and long, set low, and hanging down close to the face. Abundant feathering.

EYES
Almond-shaped, dark, and set fairly wide apart. Expression is intelligent and playful.

Flat cheeks and tight-fitting lips

FACIAL CHARACTERISTICS
Poodles

COAT
Profuse, with firm texture, and characteristically curly. All solid colors.

HEAD
Lean, well chiselled, and carried high.

Clips	
English Saddle clip	
European Continental clip	
Sporting clip	
Puppy clip	

Toy Poodle
All Poodles have the advantage that they do not shed their curly hair, but it does grow continuously, and will need regular clipping.

BODY
Deep chest, short back, and muscular loins.

TAIL
Set high and carried up, in balance with the body. It is customarily docked.

Schipperke

THIS RATHER FIERCE-LOOKING creature probably derives its name from its work on the waters of lowland Belgium, being used as a guard dog and rat catcher on the canal boats. *Schipperke* means little captain or boatman in Flemish, but its name could also refer to its spruce, dark coat and proud military bearing.

History

The Schipperke has its roots in Flanders, where it has existed as a distinct breed for centuries. Some believe that it is descended from a now-extinct Belgian sheepdog breed, or from the Northern Spitz family, or even to be a terrier and Pomeranian cross. Whatever its origins, this lively, intelligent animal was, and is, much-loved, and became one of Belgium's national breeds. It reached the UK and the US in the late nineteenth century, and the Schipperke Club of America was established in 1929.

Temperament

The "Schip" is a loyal, energetic, inquisitive little dog. These characteristics, together with a robust constitution, make it ideally suited to life as a house dog.

BODY
Compact and muscular, with broad chest, and powerful loins.

Back is straight and strong

LEGS
Straight forelegs, and strong, muscular hind legs. Thighs are powerful, with longish hair on the backs.

When the Schipperke becomes excited, its mane of thick rough hair appears to rise.

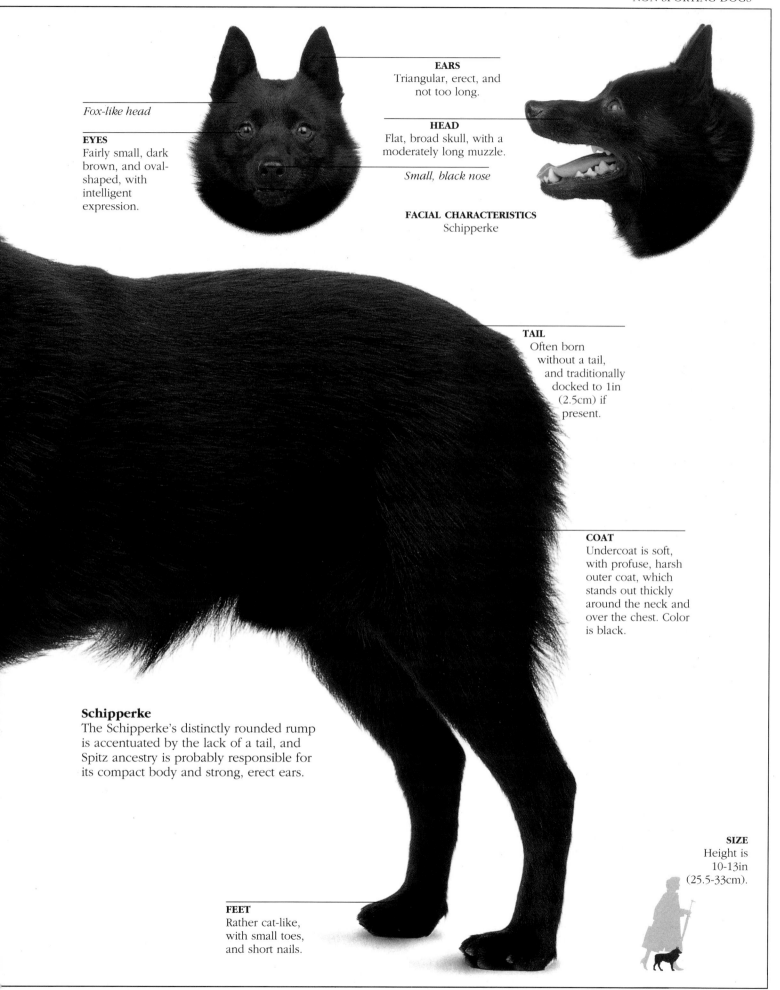

EARS
Triangular, erect, and
not too long.

Fox-like head

EYES
Fairly small, dark
brown, and oval-
shaped, with
intelligent
expression.

HEAD
Flat, broad skull, with a
moderately long muzzle.

Small, black nose

FACIAL CHARACTERISTICS
Schipperke

TAIL
Often born
without a tail,
and traditionally
docked to 1in
(2.5cm) if
present.

COAT
Undercoat is soft,
with profuse, harsh
outer coat, which
stands out thickly
around the neck and
over the chest. Color
is black.

Schipperke
The Schipperke's distinctly rounded rump
is accentuated by the lack of a tail, and
Spitz ancestry is probably responsible for
its compact body and strong, erect ears.

SIZE
Height is
10-13in
(25.5-33cm).

FEET
Rather cat-like,
with small toes,
and short nails.

Shar Pei

HEAD
Large, with a flat skull, and a broad stop. Nose is preferably black, or should conform to the coat color. A solid blue-black tongue is preferred.

ONE OF THE WORLD'S rarest dogs, this baggily wrinkled creature is likely to cause a stir wherever it goes! It derives its name from its bristly coat — *Shar Pei* means sharkskin or sandpaper in Chinese. It is a pleasant, amiable breed, and at first may seem undeserving of its other name, the Chinese Fighting Dog. In the past, however, it has achieved considerable success in canine combat, for its seemingly oversized skin makes it a difficult dog to get to grips with!

History

The Shar Pei's Oriental ancestors can possibly be traced back to 206 BC to AD 220, for works of art from the Chinese Han Dynasty feature a dog resembling it. Some believe the breed to be descended from a much larger dog, now extinct, found in Tibet and China's Northern Province around 2,000 years ago, while others consider it to be related to the Service Dogs of China's Southern Province. Its future has sometimes looked very bleak indeed — in 1947 the dog tax in China rose so steeply that many Shar Pei owners could no longer afford to keep them, and their numbers diminished alarmingly. In the 1970s, the Shar Pei's plight was taken up by breeders in the US, and in 1981, the first Shar Pei arrived in Britain.

Temperament

The Shar Pei is a joy to be with — it is independent, well-behaved, and loves people.

LEGS
Muscular and strong. Forelegs are straight; hind legs are fairly angulated.

SIZE
Height: 18-20in (46-51cm).

Shar Peis are generally healthy dogs, but are prone to entropion (inward rolling of the eyelids), an eye disease that can result in blindness unless surgically corrected. This procedure makes them ineligible for competition at shows.

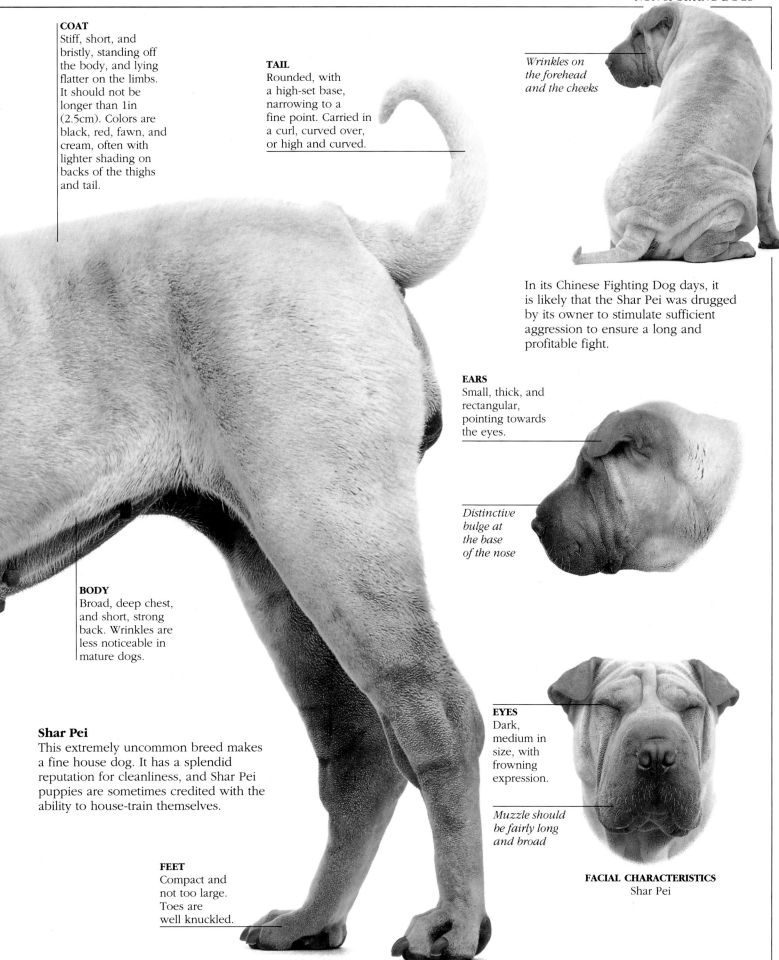

COAT
Stiff, short, and bristly, standing off the body, and lying flatter on the limbs. It should not be longer than 1in (2.5cm). Colors are black, red, fawn, and cream, often with lighter shading on backs of the thighs and tail.

TAIL
Rounded, with a high-set base, narrowing to a fine point. Carried in a curl, curved over, or high and curved.

Wrinkles on the forehead and the cheeks

In its Chinese Fighting Dog days, it is likely that the Shar Pei was drugged by its owner to stimulate sufficient aggression to ensure a long and profitable fight.

EARS
Small, thick, and rectangular, pointing towards the eyes.

Distinctive bulge at the base of the nose

BODY
Broad, deep chest, and short, strong back. Wrinkles are less noticeable in mature dogs.

Shar Pei
This extremely uncommon breed makes a fine house dog. It has a splendid reputation for cleanliness, and Shar Pei puppies are sometimes credited with the ability to house-train themselves.

EYES
Dark, medium in size, with frowning expression.

Muzzle should be fairly long and broad

FEET
Compact and not too large. Toes are well knuckled.

FACIAL CHARACTERISTICS
Shar Pei

123

Working and Herding Dogs

Man first domesticated the dog as far back as ten thousand and perhaps even thirty-five thousand years ago. It is likely that to begin with, he used them for food and fur, killing the adults and taking away the pups for fattening up. But it wasn't long before he realized that this, his earliest animal companion, could be useful to him in other ways, as a watchdog and later as a helper in the pursuit of game.

Innate abilities

As time passed, various breeds of dog emerged, and the first were hunting dogs of the hound kind. From then on, the potential

Great Pyrenees

of the dog, which as a wild species was, and still is, a versatile, multipurpose creature, was gradually cultivated. Breeds specializing in a wide range of tasks, not just hunting, evolved. The dog became far more than merely "man's best friend". The variety of skills that the different dog breeds could master derived from the biological make-up of the dog family, *Canis*, one of the most successful types of mammal on earth. Intelligence, strength, stamina, speed, nimbleness, excellent sight, and an even more remarkable sense of smell, the sociability of the pack animal, and the natural hunting skills of a predatory carnivore were all there; man had simply to select, concentrate, and

exaggerate some of these features by controlled breeding.

Developing skills

Over the centuries dogs became guards, sentries, and weapons of war. They pulled and carried loads, herded cattle, sheep, and other beasts, tracked criminals, and located people in trouble. In modern times, their role has been expanded, with some dogs acting as police auxiliaries,

Australian Cattle Dog

seeing-eyes, and sniffers-out of gourmet truffles, drugs, gas leaks, and explosives. Now there are even "hearing-ear" dogs that aid deaf people. In the "police" group are the Boxer, Doberman Pinscher, Rottweiler, German Shepherd, Great Dane, and Giant Schnauzer, all of which have been trained as sentry aids and guard dogs.

Farmers' aids

Other breeds in the Working group were developed as farmers' aids. This division includes the Collie, Puli, Old English Sheepdog, Shetland Sheepdog, German Shepherd, and Corgi, all of which are herders. Almost every nation has its breed of dog

Bearded Collie

used for herding purposes. Thus we have the Collie from Scotland, the Puli from Hungary, and the Corgi from Wales. The dog most commonly used on American farms for herding work is an unofficial breed called the American Shepherd, English Shepherd, or Border Collie. It is a Collie-type, but has a shorter muzzle, and smaller body, and is usually black and white in color.

Doberman Pinscher

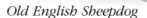

Old English Sheepdog

Draft breeds

In the last century, dogs were used in teams to draw the Sussex Mail between the towns of Steyning and Storrington in Britain, and to take fish from Southampton to London. Dog teams were also used in the early 1800s to pull the carts of butchers, bakers, hawkers, and knife grinders, as well as the traveling side shows that visited country fairs. Other draft breeds include the "snow dogs", such as the Alaskan Malamute, Siberian Husky, and the Samoyed, which still perform great feats of strength and endurance, not only for sport, but also for more serious purposes in the Far North. Such animals have been known to run 100 miles (160 kilometers) in just under eighteen hours, and a four-dog team can pull a load of 400 pounds (180 kilograms) for over thirty miles a day.

Specialization

The Working and Herding group also contains some rather less well known "specialists", like the Portuguese Water Dog that would dive to retrieve lost nets and other fishing gear and also bring back fish that had escaped the trawl; the Bernese Mountain Dog that worked for Swiss farmers, pulling loads of milk and cheese to market; and the Australian Cattle Dog with dingo blood running in its veins, the expert herder and the protector of livestock in the outback. The most legendary working dog of all, perhaps, is the St Bernard, the finder and bringer of brandy to travelers lost or trapped in snow drifts. ("A traveller, by the faithful hound, Half-buried in the snow was found." Longfellow, *Excelsior*) And finally, if there is one rare breed with the strangest occupation it has to be the Norwegian Lundehund, otherwise known as the Puffin Hound, which is trained to work in caves and cliffs as a raider of puffin nests.

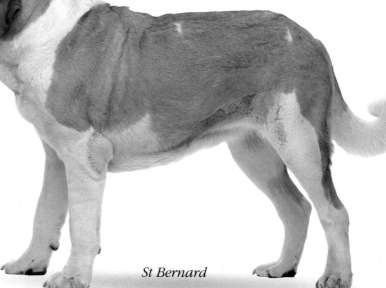

St Bernard

Akita

A MEMBER OF THE SPITZ FAMILY, the Akita is a strong, athletic breed that derives its name from the Japanese province of Akita, on Honshu Island. In its native land it is primarily used as a police and guard dog, but it has also become a popular family pet around the world.

History

The Akita is the largest of Japan's three Spitz-type dogs, and the breed has remained largely unchanged over the last three centuries. Known in its past as a hunter of wild boar, deer and even bear, for hundreds of years it was also famous for its dog fighting exploits, a "sport" that is now illegal in Japan. The breed's devotion is legendary — in Shibuya railway station, Tokyo, there is a statue to "Hachiko", who for nine years kept daily vigils on the spot, awaiting his dead master's return. The first Akita was introduced to the US in 1937, but the breed became more numerous after World War II, when servicemen brought them back from Japan.

Temperament

Renowned for its strength and courage, the Akita is affectionate and loyal, but needs a dominant personality to train it properly.

Body is greater in length than height

COAT
Coarse, stiff outer coat, with a soft, dense undercoat. All colors, with clear markings.

Shoulders are powerful

Forelegs are straight when viewed from the front

Akitas have very good hunting and retrieving skills, particularly in deep snow and water.

EARS
Very erect, triangular, and small, with slightly rounded tips.

Nose and lips are black

Muzzle is blunt

TAIL
Thick, set high, and carried arched over the back.

BODY
Well-muscled, with broad, deep chest, and level back.

HEAD
Large and broad, with well-defined stop.

EYES
Very deep set, triangular, and small in size. Color is brown with black rims.

FACIAL CHARACTERISTICS
Akita

Skin is fairly taut

LEGS
Forelegs are well boned; hind legs have muscular thighs.

Akita
This breed is highly thought of in its native land — since 1931, the Japanese government has officially appointed champion Akitas as national treasures.

FEET
Thick, compact, cat-like paws, with hard pads. Dewclaws of hind feet are usually removed.

SIZE
Dogs 26-28in (66-71cm) tall; bitches 24-26in (61-66cm).

Alaskan Malamute

THIS POWERFUL SPITZ-TYPE BREED is one of the oldest sled-dogs. Stronger than the Siberian Husky, it could not only pull heavier loads, but was also used to carry back-packs over very long distances.

History

The Alaskan Malamute probably derives its name from the Mahlemuts, an Inuit people, and early records of the first North American settlers mention the breed. These handsome creatures possess remarkable powers of fortitude and endurance; before the snowmobile, when sturdy dogs were still necessary for travel in the far north, the Mahlemuts were much envied for their dogs by the other Inuit peoples. The Malamute was nearly lost through cross-breeding with imported dogs after Alaska was opened up to exploitation, but in 1926 steps were taken in the US to preserve the pure strain.

Temperament

This loyal animal is a good worker, a fine guard dog, and an affectionate family pet.

SIZE
Dogs 25in (63.5cm) tall; bitches 23in (58.5cm).

COAT
Densely woolly, oily undercoat with thick, hard outer coat standing out from body. Colors are light gray to black, or gold to liver, with white on the underbody, feet, parts of legs, and face. White is the only pure color permitted.

BODY
Powerfully built, with deep chest, and straight back sloping down to the hindquarters.

Alaskan Malamutes are renowned for their strength and endurance, and have often been used in Arctic and Antarctic expeditions.

TAIL
Well furred and set fairly high. Carried over its back when working, but should not be tightly curled.

Alaskan Malamute
The Inuit peoples thought highly of the breed, and used it to hunt polar bear and wolf, and to guard their herds of caribou.

This rugged breed thrives on plenty of exercise, and actually prefers to live outside.

EARS
Medium-sized, triangular, set wide apart, and held erect or folded back.

EYES
Brown, medium-sized, almond-shaped, and set obliquely.

"Smiling" lips

LEGS
Heavy, muscular forelegs; broad, powerful hind legs.

HEAD
Broad skull, with large muzzle, powerful jaws and black nose.

Wolf-like appearance

FEET
Fairly large, but compact. Toes are well arched and close-set, with hair in between. Pads are thick and tough.

FACIAL CHARACTERISTICS
Alaskan Malamute

Australian Cattle Dog

FORMERLY KNOWN AS THE Queensland Heeler, the Australian Cattle Dog is notable for its powerful bite, an essential attribute for a dog required to drive cattle over long distances in the outback. Bred to survive in a harsh environment, it is essentially an energetic, out-of-doors dog that needs plenty of exercise.

History

In the 1830s, Australian stockmen developed a tough working breed, because, in the words of an Australian breed historian, the existing cattle dogs "bit like an alligator and barked like a consumptive". Various dogs were involved in the creation of the Australian Cattle Dog; they included Dingoes, for their hardiness and silence; an obscure, rugged breed known as the Smithfield; blue merle Collies; Dalmatians; Australian Kelpies; and Old English Sheepdogs.

Temperament

An intelligent and alert animal, the Australian Cattle Dog is courageous, reliable, and very hard-working.

HEAD
Broad and strong, with top of skull parallel to top of muzzle. Powerful lower jaw.

BODY
Strong, level back, and deep, fairly broad chest.

COAT
Dense undercoat with coarse, straight, weather-resistant outer coat. Colors are blue, or mottled blue, with or without black or tan markings. Reds should be evenly speckled. Even head markings are preferred.

SIZE
Dogs 18-20in (46-51cm) tall; bitches 17-19in (43-48cm).

This breed has also been known as the Australian Heeler, or Blue Heeler. "Heeler" refers to its herding skill of snapping and biting cattle's heels.

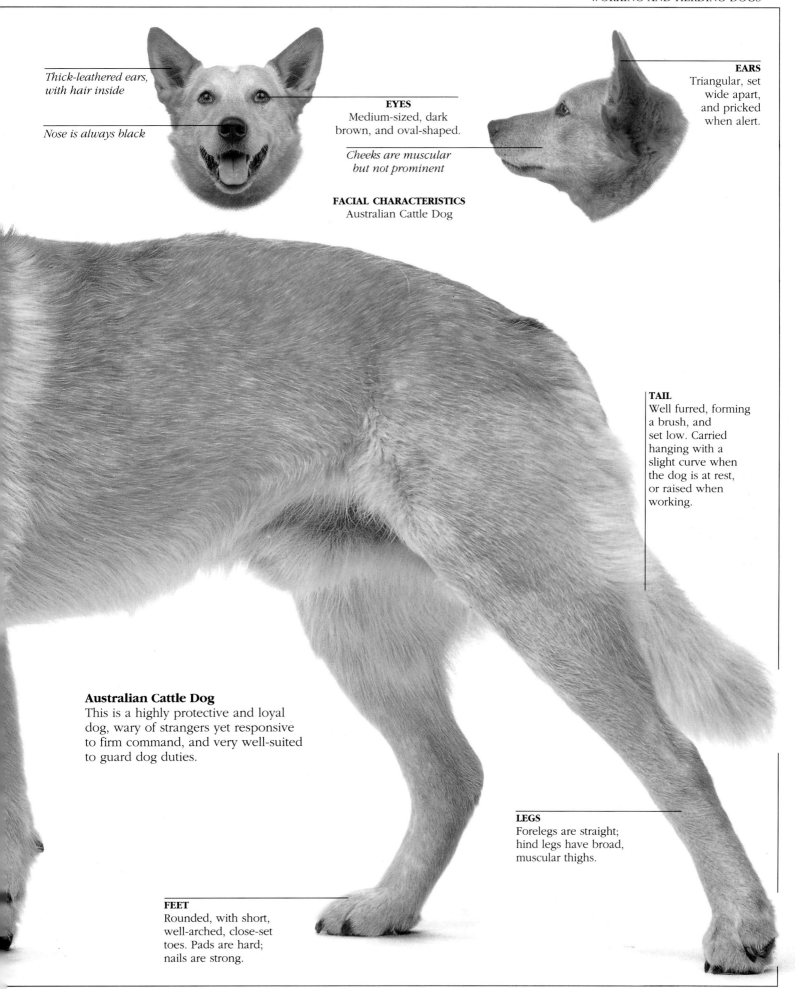

Thick-leathered ears, with hair inside

Nose is always black

EYES
Medium-sized, dark brown, and oval-shaped.

Cheeks are muscular but not prominent

FACIAL CHARACTERISTICS
Australian Cattle Dog

EARS
Triangular, set wide apart, and pricked when alert.

TAIL
Well furred, forming a brush, and set low. Carried hanging with a slight curve when the dog is at rest, or raised when working.

Australian Cattle Dog
This is a highly protective and loyal dog, wary of strangers yet responsive to firm command, and very well-suited to guard dog duties.

LEGS
Forelegs are straight; hind legs have broad, muscular thighs.

FEET
Rounded, with short, well-arched, close-set toes. Pads are hard; nails are strong.

Belgian Sheepdogs

As their name indicates, prior to the twentieth century Belgian Sheepdogs were widely used to guard flocks in and around Belgium. Nowadays their main work is as guard dogs — for the police, for the army, and even for publicans, but they also make endearing family pets.

History

Many closely related breeds of sheepdog existed in Belgium up to the late nineteenth century, but as shepherding became increasingly unnecessary, breeders refined these dogs to produce one basic type with four color and coat varieties. In most countries they are accepted as different forms of the same breed, but in the US three are recognized as separate breeds (Groenendael, also known as the Belgian Sheepdog, or Belgian Shepherd Dog; Belgian Tervuren; and Malinois). The Laekenois has yet to achieve recognition in the US.

Temperament

Belgian Sheepdogs are alert, intelligent, and very watchful. Although primarily outdoor dogs, they can adapt well to home life providing they can stretch their legs at regular intervals.

HEAD
Long and finely chiselled, with flat cheeks. Skull and muzzle are of equal length.

COAT
Long, straight outer coat, with dense undercoat. Hair is short on the head and lower legs. Colors are red, gray, fawn, to russet, with black shading on the tip of each hair. Black mask on face continuing up to the ears.

Laekenois
This is the only rough-coated variety of Belgian Sheepdog. Its hair is wiry and dry but never curled, and its coat color is a ruddy fawn, with black shading.

BODY
Athletic and muscular. Deep chest, level back, and broad, sloping rump.

TAIL
Well furred, and of medium length. Hangs with the tip curved up when the dog is resting; lifted when active.

LEG
Long, lean, and muscular.

Groenendael

Most popular of the four types of Belgian Sheepdog, the Groenendael has an abundant, long, black outer coat, and sometimes has small white markings.

Belgian Tervuren

This finely proportioned breed is full of vitality, and is constantly on the move when not relaxing.

EARS
Set high, triangular, and erect.

Black nose

EYES
Medium-sized, almond-shaped, and preferably dark brown in color.

Neck is slightly elongated

FACIAL CHARACTERISTICS
Belgian Tervuren

FEET
Forefeet are rounded; hind feet are oval. Well-arched, close-set toes, thick pads, and dark nails.

SIZE
Dogs 25-27in (63.5-69cm) tall; bitches 23-26in (58-66cm).

Bernese Mountain Dog

HEAD
Broad, flat skull, with well-defined stop, slight furrow, and straight muzzle. Nose is black.

O F THE FOUR BREEDS of Swiss mountain dog in existence, the Bernese Mountain Dog is by far the most popular. In Switzerland's Berne district, it was developed as a draft animal, pulling carts for cheesemakers and weavers.

History

It is likely that the Bernese Mountain Dog's ancestors came to Switzerland as guard dogs with the Roman legions, and were left behind to cross-breed with the local sheepdogs when the invaders departed. The result was four Swiss mountain breeds: the Bernese Mountain Dog, also known as the Bernese Sennenhund; the Great Swiss Mountain Dog; and the Apenzell and Entlebuch Sennenhunds. In the nineteenth century the Bernese Mountain Dog was in danger of extinction, but it was revived to the extent that a breed club was established in Switzerland in 1907. The breed reached the US thirty years later.

Temperament

Bernese Mountain Dogs are self-confident, cheerful, and make excellent pets for all the family.

Tip of the tail should preferably be white

The Bernese Mountain Dog still shows traces of its working past, often being used to pull children's carts at shows and fairs.

FEET
Rounded and short, with close-set toes, and white nails.

BODY
Compact and powerful, with level back, and broad, deep chest.

Bernese Mountain Dog
This highly attractive breed needs regular grooming, lots of exercise, and plenty of food.

EYES
Almond-shaped, and dark brown in color. Intelligent, gentle expression

Upper lip does not hang down too far over lower jaw

EARS
Set high, of medium size, and triangular in shape.

Ears lie flat when the dog is at rest; brought forward when alert

Scissor bite, with upper teeth closely overlapping lower teeth

FACIAL CHARACTERISTICS
Bernese Mountain Dog

TAIL
Medium-length, scimitar-shaped, and bushy. Raised when the dog is alert.

COAT
Long, thick, soft, and silky, with slight wave and high luster. Tricolored (jet black, with rich rust and white markings).

LEGS
Straight, strong forelegs; muscular hind legs. Dewclaws should be removed.

SIZE
Dogs 24$^{1}/_{2}$-27$^{1}/_{2}$in (62-70cm) tall; bitches 22-26in (56-66cm).

Bouvier Des Flandres

COAT
Thick and about 2½in (6cm) long. Dense undercoat with coarse, harsh, outer coat of tousled appearance. Colors from fawn to black, including brindle (brown with dark streaks).

FORMERLY ONE OF THE MOST skilful cattle dogs in western Europe, the shaggy Bouvier is now employed as a guide dog, guard dog, and tracker. It originated around the Franco-Belgian border, and a literal translation of its name is "Ox-drover of Flanders".

History

The exact origins of the Bouvier are unclear, but at the turn of the century Flanders boasted several types of cattle dog. Bouviers were first shown in 1910 at the Brussels International Dog Show, but a breed standard was not established until 1912. World War I brought it widespread recognition for its strength and courage in army work, carrying messages and finding wounded soldiers. Unfortunately, Belgium and north-eastern France bore the brunt of the fighting, and the Bouvier nearly died out through wartime casualties and the obliteration of its homeland. Dedicated Flemish breeders revived the Bouvier in the 1920s.

Temperament

The Bouvier is intelligent and lively, but also calm and sensible. It is capable of extreme loyalty and courage.

Briard

Not dissimilar in looks to the Bouvier, the Briard is a descendant of several ancient breeds, including perhaps the Alaunt and the Persian Sheepdog. It was once a hunting and guard dog of the French aristocracy, but after the 1789 Revolution its role became that of a general-purpose farm dog. It first took part in dog shows in France at the end of the nineteenth century, and served its country well during World War II.

SIZE
Height: 23-27in (59-68cm).

EARS
Set high, fairly wide, triangular, if cropped.

Cheeks should be flat

Bouvier des Flandres
This is an imposing dog, its body giving an impression of great power without clumsiness, and its beard adding a forbidding expression.

TAIL
Customarily docked short to the second or third joint. Should be carried jauntily when on the move.

Nose is black and well-developed, with wide nostrils

EYES
Dark, oval, medium-sized, well-spaced, and alert in expression.

FACIAL CHARACTERISTICS
Bouvier des Flandres

BODY
Deep, broad, chest, and powerfully built, compact trunk.

LEGS
Moderately long, muscular, and heavy-boned.

Crop-eared Bouvier des Flandres
It was the Bouvier's working role that was the original reason for cropping the breed's ears, which might otherwise have got in its way. These days, although the practice is still allowed in some countries, notably the US and Canada, an increasing number of dogs are left with their ears intact. Almost certainly, the numbers of crop-eared Bouviers will continue to fall.

FEET
Round and short. Toes well-arched and held close together. Thick pads, strong black nails.

Boxer

Gifted with seemingly boundless reserves of energy, the Boxer is one of the canine world's great characters. The breed only became well known in Britain and the US after World War II, but since then has gained enormous popularity both as a family pet and guard dog.

History

The Boxer's main ancestors were two German dogs of the Mastiff type — the Bullenbeiszer and the Barenbeiszer — that were used in the Middle Ages for bull-baiting and hunting boar and deer. In the nineteenth century they were crossed with other breeds, particularly the Bulldog, to create the Boxer. Despite its German origins, "Boxer" is an English name that aptly describes the dog's punchy fighting style.

Temperament

The Boxer is always keen to work and play, but can be rather boisterous, and even in old age it is still extremely athletic. Noted for courage as well as discipline, it makes an excellent guard dog. Also well suited to family life, the Boxer is very affectionate, loyal, and fond of children.

COAT
Short, smooth, shiny, and lying flat to the body. Colors are shades of fawn or brindle. Any white markings should not take up more than one-third of the coat color.

HEAD
Square, with deep, broad muzzle, and upturned nose. Lower jaw projects beyond the upper, and curves slightly upwards. Alert, intelligent expression.

Back is broad, short, and well muscled.

BODY
Deep chest, with well-arched ribs. Loins are short.

SIZE
Dogs 22½-25in (57-63.5cm) tall; bitches 21-23in (53-60cm).

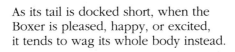

As its tail is docked short, when the Boxer is pleased, happy, or excited, it tends to wag its whole body instead.

EYES
Medium-sized, dark
brown, with dark
eye-rims.

*Nose is broad and
black, with a line
between wide nostrils*

*Neither the teeth nor the
tongue should be visible when
the mouth is closed*

FACIAL CHARACTERISTICS
Boxer

EARS
Thin, set high, and
wide apart. Lying
flat and close to the
head when the dog
is in repose; falling
forward when alert.

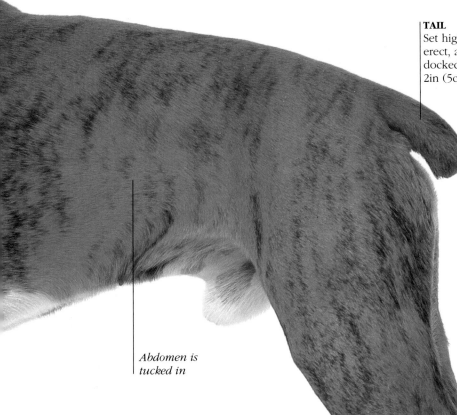

TAIL
Set high, carried
erect, and usually
docked short to
2in (5cm).

In the US and other countries (but not
the UK), it is traditional for most Boxers
to have ears that are cropped to a point.

*Abdomen is
tucked in*

Boxer
One of the more distinctive dogs in
appearance, the Boxer needs plenty of
exercise to keep it looking and feeling
its best. It is generally trustworthy, but
has a strong guarding instinct.

LEGS
Forelegs are long,
straight, and parallel;
hind legs are well
muscled, with broad,
curved thighs.

FEET
Small, with ample
pads and well-arched
toes. Hind feet are
longer than forefeet.

139

Bullmastiff

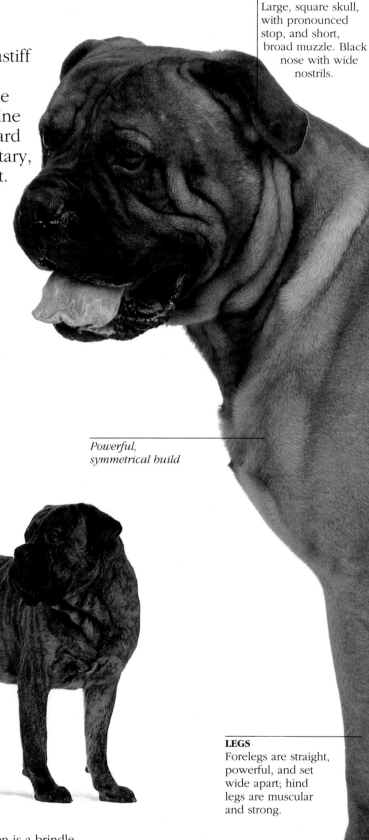

HEAD
Large, square skull,
with pronounced
stop, and short,
broad muzzle. Black
nose with wide
nostrils.

A TRUE "DESIGNER DOG", the Bullmastiff was bred in England in the nineteenth century by crossing the Bulldog with the Mastiff to combine their qualities. Now used as a guard dog by police forces and the military, it can also be a lovable family pet.

History

Poaching was often a necessary way of life in nineteenth-century England, and the heavy penalties imposed upon offenders meant that poachers were often prepared to shoot gamekeepers to escape justice. The Bullmastiff was the ideal protector and companion for a gamekeeper, for it combined the courage and ferocity of the Bulldog, with the power, speed, and nose of the Mastiff. The breed became known as the "Gamekeeper's Night Dog", and would attack on command, knocking down and pinning a poacher to the ground without mauling him. The Bullmastiff is classified as a Working Dog in the US and the UK, but as a Utility Dog in Australia.

Temperament

Once renowned for its aggression, the Bullmastiff is now an energetic and bright breed, with a calm, loyal, and affectionate nature.

*Powerful,
symmetrical build*

LEGS
Forelegs are straight,
powerful, and set
wide apart; hind
legs are muscular
and strong.

SIZE
Dogs 25-27in
(63.5-68.5cm) tall;
bitches 24-26in
(61-66cm).

This fine specimen is a brindle Bullmastiff. Other colors include shades of red or fawn, and any white markings should be on the chest only.

EYES
Medium-sized, dark or hazel in color. Set wide apart with furrows in between.

Dark eye-rims and black mask on muzzle

Upper lips do not hang below level of lower jaw

FACIAL CHARACTERISTICS
Bullmastiff

EARS
V-shaped and small. Set high, wide apart, and folded back to give a squarish look to the head; of a darker color than the body.

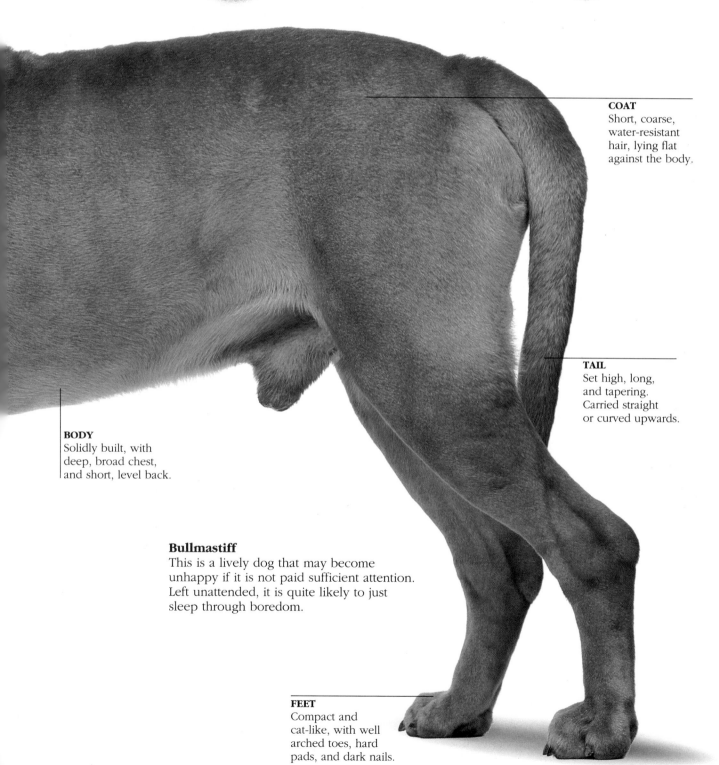

COAT
Short, coarse, water-resistant hair, lying flat against the body.

TAIL
Set high, long, and tapering. Carried straight or curved upwards.

BODY
Solidly built, with deep, broad chest, and short, level back.

Bullmastiff
This is a lively dog that may become unhappy if it is not paid sufficient attention. Left unattended, it is quite likely to just sleep through boredom.

FEET
Compact and cat-like, with well arched toes, hard pads, and dark nails.

Bearded Collie

HEAD
Broad, flat-topped, square skull with muzzle and skull of equal length.

Previously known as the Highland Collie, the Bearded Collie is an active dog that retains its enthusiasm for being out-of-doors, yet makes a perfect household companion. Similar in looks to the Old English Sheepdog, this breed is smaller, leaner, and has an undocked tail.

History
The exact origins of the collie family are unclear, but their ancestors may have been ancient breeds native to Scotland. Some authorities suggest, however, that Magyar dogs brought by Polish traders to the north of Britain in the Middle Ages may have been one of the main ancestors of the Bearded Collie. The breed almost disappeared in the early part of the twentieth century, but was rescued through mating a pair in 1944.

Temperament
Noted for its friendliness, the Bearded Collie is a lively, intelligent, and even-tempered dog. It thrives on regular exercise.

LEGS
Covered with shaggy hair all round. Straight, well-boned forelegs and well-muscled hind legs.

FEET
Oval and well covered with hair, with ample pads. Well-arched, close toes.

Border Collie
Originally from the Scottish border country, this breed is an outstanding sheepdog valued by farmers all over the world.

Bearded Collie
This is an intelligent working dog, and it should have a soft, affectionate expression. There should be no sign of nervousness or aggression.

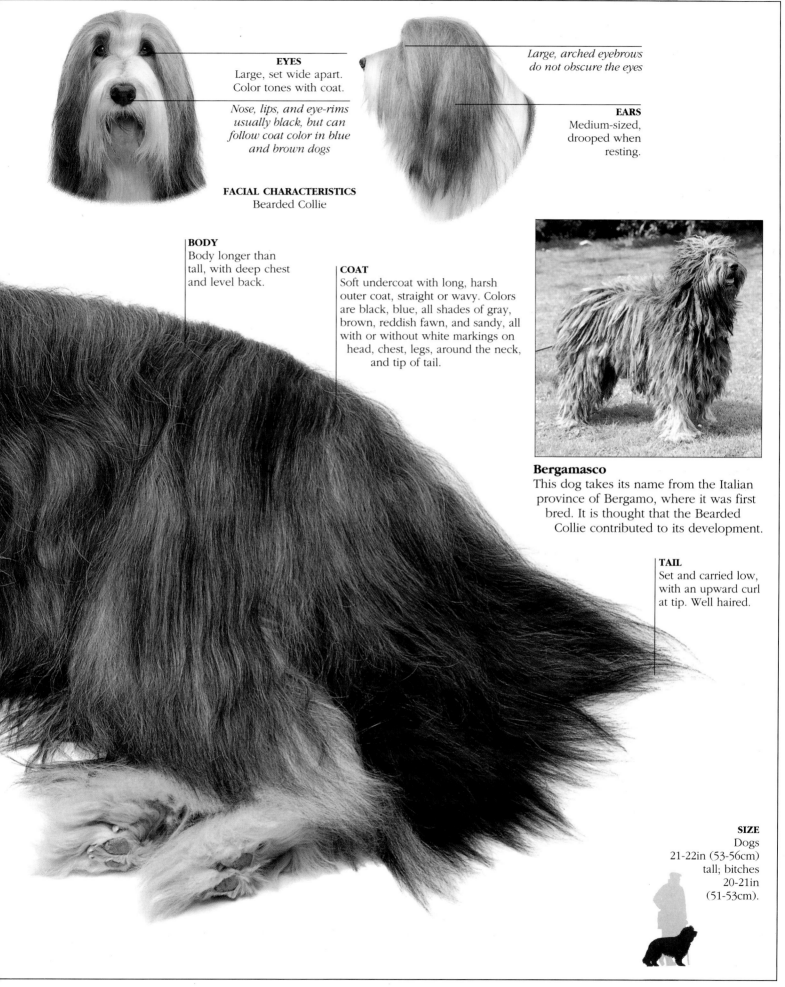

EYES
Large, set wide apart.
Color tones with coat.

*Nose, lips, and eye-rims
usually black, but can
follow coat color in blue
and brown dogs*

*Large, arched eyebrows
do not obscure the eyes*

EARS
Medium-sized,
drooped when
resting.

FACIAL CHARACTERISTICS
Bearded Collie

BODY
Body longer than
tall, with deep chest
and level back.

COAT
Soft undercoat with long, harsh
outer coat, straight or wavy. Colors
are black, blue, all shades of gray,
brown, reddish fawn, and sandy, all
with or without white markings on
head, chest, legs, around the neck,
and tip of tail.

Bergamasco
This dog takes its name from the Italian
province of Bergamo, where it was first
bred. It is thought that the Bearded
Collie contributed to its development.

TAIL
Set and carried low,
with an upward curl
at tip. Well haired.

SIZE
Dogs
21-22in (53-56cm)
tall; bitches
20-21in
(51-53cm).

Rough-Coated Collie

F OR CENTURIES the Rough-Coated Collie was hardly known outside Scotland, but it is now one of the world's most popular breeds. Descended from generations of hard-working herding dogs, it is a conscientious creature of immense intelligence.

History

Rough-Coated Collies originated in the Lowlands of Scotland, and probably take their name from a local type of black sheep known as the Colley. Like many dogs, they owe much of their popularity to Queen Victoria. She became enchanted by these attractive animals while visiting her Scottish estate at Balmoral in the 1860s, and took some Collies back home with her to Windsor Castle. It quickly became a highly sought-after show-dog in England, and, by the late 1880s, in the US too. In the 1940s the breed shot to even greater fame when it was chosen to star as "Lassie" in the much-loved series of films based on Eric Knight's classic novel *Lassie Come Home*.

Temperament

This is a good-natured, friendly dog, energetic out of doors, wary of strangers, and very affectionate to its owner and family.

HEAD
Long and tapered, with flat skull, and black nose.

Rough-Coated Collie
The Rough Collie is endowed with expressive ears — thrown back when the dog is in repose, and carried forwards and semi-erect when it is alert. They are also highly functional appendages, and can reputedly detect a shepherd's whistle, or voice, from a distance of up to one mile.

COAT
Abundant, with thick undercoat, and long, straight, harsh outer coat. Colors are sable and white, tricolor, or blue merle.

End of muzzle is blunt, not square

This gregarious creature usually shows no trace of nervousness or aggression.

Very slight stop

EYES
Almond-shaped, medium-sized, and obliquely set. Color is dark brown, or blue in blue merles.

FACIAL CHARACTERISTICS
Rough-Coated Collie

EARS
Small, and neither too close together nor too far apart.

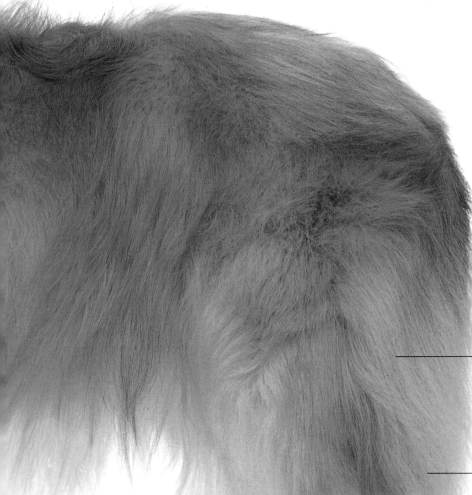

Australian Kelpie
This excellent working dog is notorious for its rather odd skill of running along sheep's backs to reach the head of the flock. It is a tough, durable breed, and can go without water for long periods.

BODY
Greater in length than height. Chest is deep, and back is slightly arched over well-muscled loins.

TAIL
Long and set low, with the tip turned upwards. Carried gaily when the dog is excited.

LEGS
Forelegs are straight and muscular; hind legs are powerful and sinewy.

FEET
Oval-shaped, with well-padded soles, and arched toes.

SIZE
Dogs 22-24in (56-61cm) tall; bitches 20-22in (51-56cm).

Doberman Pinscher

D**ESPITE ITS CURRENT POPULARITY**, the
Doberman has only existed as a
breed for a little over one hundred years.
An exceptionally powerful animal, its
principal role is that of a guard dog,
but it can also be trained for tracking,
retrieving, and even sheep herding.

History
Between 1865 and 1870 a German
tax inspector, Louis Dobermann,
endeavored to create the perfect
guard dog by crossing a variety of
breeds. His exact formula remains a
secret, but probably involved local
cattle dogs, the Rottweiler, Pinscher,
the Manchester Terrier, and maybe
even the Greyhound. Dobermans
were officially recognized by the
German Kennel Club in 1900, and
the breed then quickly reached the
US and Britain. In World War I it
served the German Army in the
front lines as a guard and patrol
dog, and has since been used by
police forces all over the world.

In the US and some
other countries, it is
traditional for the
breed to have
cropped ears.

Temperament
The Doberman is a natural guard
dog — intelligent, strong, and
aggressive when necessary.
Consequently it needs firm control,
but can still become a loyal and
even affectionate companion.

BODY
Squarely built, with
well-developed,
muscular chest,
and tucked-up belly.

TAIL
Continues the
line of the
spine, but is
carried higher
when the dog
is alert. Usually
docked at the
second joint.

HEAD
Long with blunt,
wedge-shaped
profile and
powerful jaws. Top
of skull is flat, and
parallel to top of
muzzle.

The moderate size of the Doberman belies
its surprising weight and muscular power.

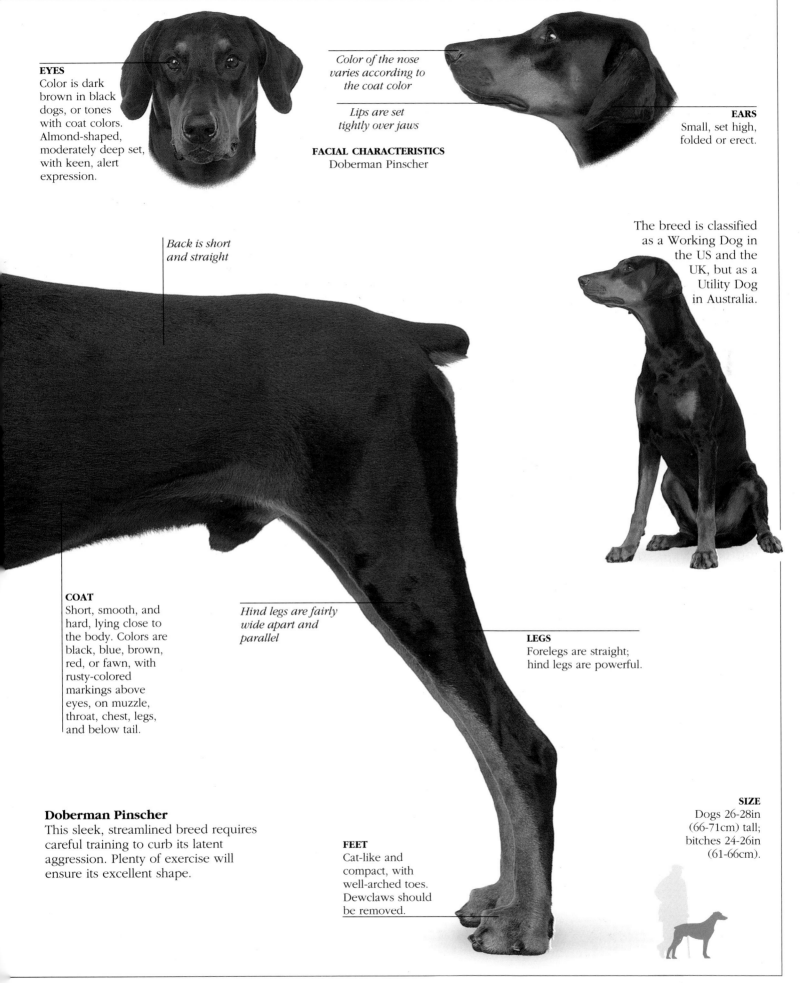

EYES
Color is dark brown in black dogs, or tones with coat colors. Almond-shaped, moderately deep set, with keen, alert expression.

Color of the nose varies according to the coat color

Lips are set tightly over jaws

FACIAL CHARACTERISTICS
Doberman Pinscher

EARS
Small, set high, folded or erect.

The breed is classified as a Working Dog in the US and the UK, but as a Utility Dog in Australia.

Back is short and straight

COAT
Short, smooth, and hard, lying close to the body. Colors are black, blue, brown, red, or fawn, with rusty-colored markings above eyes, on muzzle, throat, chest, legs, and below tail.

Hind legs are fairly wide apart and parallel

LEGS
Forelegs are straight; hind legs are powerful.

Doberman Pinscher
This sleek, streamlined breed requires careful training to curb its latent aggression. Plenty of exercise will ensure its excellent shape.

FEET
Cat-like and compact, with well-arched toes. Dewclaws should be removed.

SIZE
Dogs 26-28in (66-71cm) tall; bitches 24-26in (61-66cm).

German Shepherd Dog

ALSO KNOWN AS THE ALSATIAN, the German Shepherd is one of the most versatile working dogs ever developed. Throughout the world it is used by police forces and armies as a guard and sniffer dog, by the blind as a guide dog, and by farmers as a sheepdog. It is also a popular pet, providing personal protection and companionship.

History

The breed was established in Germany in the 1880s, although there is still some debate about its ancestry. Initially it was a farm dog, but having shown its versatility in the German army during World War I, it was soon introduced into the US and the British Commonwealth by returning Allied soldiers. Since then it has rapidly achieved widespread popularity, undoubtedly with the help of scene-stealing "character" roles such as "Rin-Tin-Tin" in the 1920s, and "Bullet", Roy Rogers' companion, in the 1950s.

Temperament

The German Shepherd is extremely intelligent and generally dependable. Given correct and early training, it can make an obedient and loyal companion for all the family.

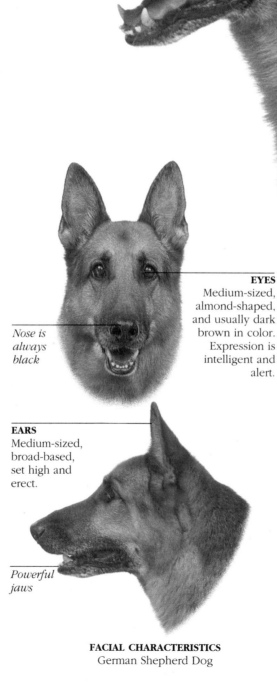

HEAD
Broad skull and wedge-shaped muzzle are of equal length.

Nose is always black

EYES
Medium-sized, almond-shaped, and usually dark brown in color. Expression is intelligent and alert.

EARS
Medium-sized, broad-based, set high and erect.

LEGS
Straight forelegs; broad and powerful thighs on the hind legs.

Powerful jaws

SIZE
Height: dogs 24-26in (61-66cm); bitches 22-24in (56-61cm).

FACIAL CHARACTERISTICS
German Shepherd Dog

German Shepherds are very active animals, both mentally and physically, and require considerable attention from their owners.

German Shepherd Dog
Once known as the Alsatian Wolf Dog, this breed is a star performer in the show-ring. It made its show debut in Hanover in 1922.

BODY
Length is greater than height. Deep chest, well-sprung ribs, straight back, and sloping hindquarters. Loins are broad and strong.

COAT
Outer coat of hard, coarse, flat hair, with a thick undercoat. Hair is somewhat longer on backs of forelegs and hind legs. Many colors are permissible, but vibrant colors are preferred. White is disqualified.

FEET
Compact, with rounded, well-arched toes. Pads are well developed; nails are short and dark. Dewclaws are usually removed.

TAIL
Medium length, bushy, and set low. Hangs down with a saber-like curve when the dog is at rest; slightly raised when moving.

Great Dane

Onᴇ ᴏꜰ ᴛʜᴇ ɢᴇɴᴛʟᴇ ɢɪᴀɴᴛs of the canine world, the Great Dane possesses enormous strength as well as a kindly nature. Although its name suggests Danish origins, the breed was actually developed in Germany, where it is known as the *Deutsche Dogge*, or German Mastiff.

History

Large mastiff-like dogs are portrayed in the artefacts of many ancient civilizations. It may have been Phoenician traders who brought these animals to Mediterranean countries, or Roman legions who brought them directly to Germany. Either way, the forebears of today's Great Dane were to be found in the households of royalty and nobles throughout Europe in the Middle Ages. Not only medieval status symbols, Great Danes showed their considerable mettle by hunting wild boar, stags, and wolves.

Temperament

The Great Dane is a very affectionate, kindly dog, capable of great loyalty. Because of its large size, however, early training is essential if an effective, but controllable guard dog is required.

HEAD
Flat, narrow skull, pronounced stop with broad, deep muzzle.

COAT
Short, thick and glossy. Colors are brindle, fawn, blue, black, and harlequin (white with black markings).

It is usual practice in the US and Canada for Great Danes to have their ears cropped between two and three months of age.

This truly "great" breed likes to be physically cosseted — it needs, and relishes, somewhere warm to sleep.

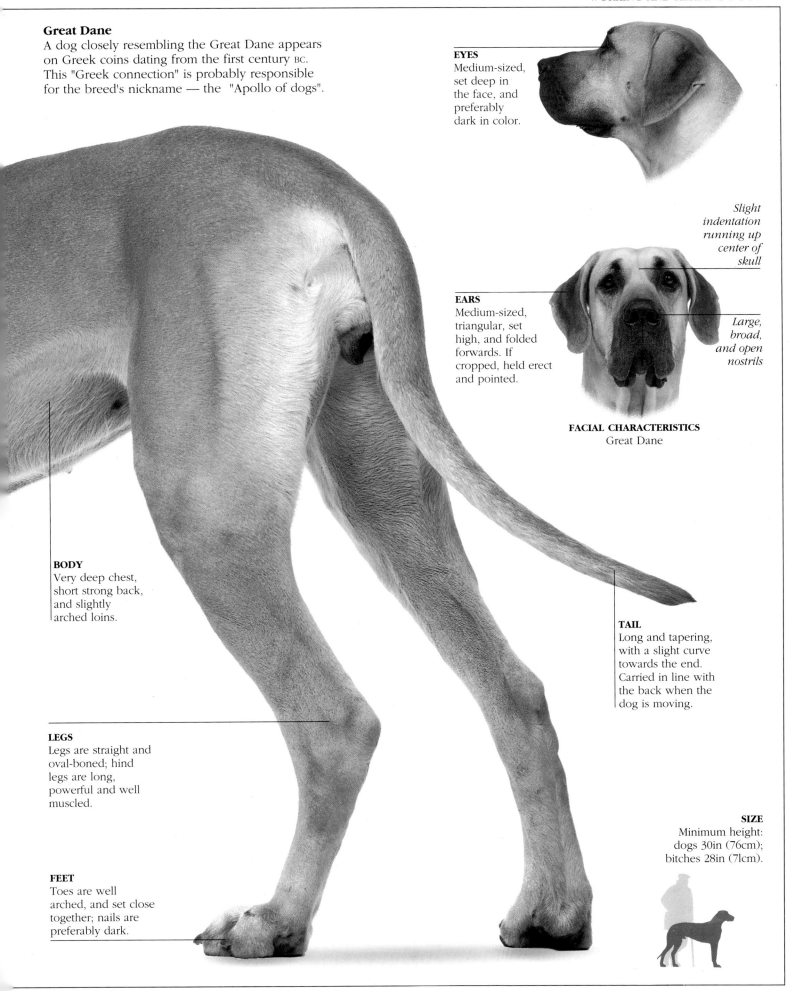

Great Dane
A dog closely resembling the Great Dane appears on Greek coins dating from the first century BC. This "Greek connection" is probably responsible for the breed's nickname — the "Apollo of dogs".

EYES
Medium-sized, set deep in the face, and preferably dark in color.

Slight indentation running up center of skull

EARS
Medium-sized, triangular, set high, and folded forwards. If cropped, held erect and pointed.

Large, broad, and open nostrils

FACIAL CHARACTERISTICS
Great Dane

BODY
Very deep chest, short strong back, and slightly arched loins.

TAIL
Long and tapering, with a slight curve towards the end. Carried in line with the back when the dog is moving.

LEGS
Legs are straight and oval-boned; hind legs are long, powerful and well muscled.

SIZE
Minimum height: dogs 30in (76cm); bitches 28in (7lcm).

FEET
Toes are well arched, and set close together; nails are preferably dark.

151

Mastiff

THE MASTIFF IS ONE of the oldest dog breeds, and despite its warrior past is nowadays another of our gentle canine giants. Although still used for guard dog duties, the Mastiff is more often simply an affectionate member of the family!

History

Mastiff-like dogs are depicted in Egyptian artefacts dating back to 3000 BC, and the breed may have been introduced into Britain by Phoenician traders, or by invading Angles and Saxons. The native Celts certainly had Mastiffs fighting with them when Julius Caesar invaded Britain in 55 BC, and they were used as dogs of war up until the seventeenth century. Their other uses were to hunt bears and wolves, and as participants in the "sports" of dog-fighting and bear-baiting. After these were banned in the nineteenth century the Mastiff's popularity waned in Britain, but the breed has been maintained in two strains, those of Lyme Hall Kennels in Cheshire, and the dogs bred by the Duke of Devonshire at Chatsworth.

Temperament

Although Mastiffs are generally even-tempered, gentle and loyal, they retain the ability to guard, and must be handled firmly.

HEAD
Massive appearance. Heavy, broad, moderately rounded skull, with short, broad muzzle.

COAT
Short, coarse and lying flat with dense undercoat. Colors are apricot-fawn, silver-fawn, or dark fawn-brindle with black facial mask.

BODY
Powerful build, with broad, deep rounded chest, and wide back and loins.

FEET
Arched toes in compact, round feet. Black nails.

LEGS
Forelegs strong, set wide apart; hindquarters muscular and set wide apart.

EYES
Medium size, set wide apart, and dark brown in color.

EARS
Small, thin, and set wide apart. Lying close to cheeks when at rest.

FACIAL CHARACTERISTICS
Mastiff

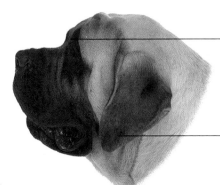

Depression in centre of forehead between eyes

Ears, nose, and muzzle should all be black

Neopolitan Mastiff
Less popular at present than the Mastiff, this dog can trace its ancestry back for over 2,500 years to the Molossus, a fighting dog of ancient Greece and Rome. A heavy, muscular breed, often employed as a formidable guard dog, it can nonetheless make a loyal and affectionate pet if properly trained.

Mastiff
A very English dog, featured in the poetry of Chaucer and present at the Battle of Agincourt in 1415. Now it is seldom seen in Britain but has flourished in the US in recent years.

SIZE
Minimum height: dogs 30in (75cm); bitches 27¹/2in (70cm).

TAIL
Long, set moderately high, and tapering. Curved when excited, but not over back.

153

Newfoundland

D EVELOPED ON THE ISLAND of Newfoundland, this bear-like dog possesses remarkable skills as a life-saver from water. One of the strongest working dogs ever developed, it is also intensely loyal, and fits superbly into family life.

History
The ancestors of this breed remain largely unknown. Some claim that the Vikings brought its forebears to Newfoundland in the tenth century, while others claim that it is a descendant of the Pyrenean Mountain Dogs that accompanied emigrating Basque fishermen. Whatever the truth, the breed evolved on Newfoundland into an outstanding sea-rescue dog and draft animal. In the eighteenth century it was imported into Britain and France and rapidly became popular with English sailors as a ship dog. The Scottish author J.M. Barrie based the dog "Nana" in *Peter Pan* on his own Newfoundland.

Temperament
It is a particularly pleasant and docile dog. Despite its considerable bulk, it is very gentle with children.

FEET
Large, broad, and cat-like, with webbing between the toes for swimming.

SIZE
Dogs 28in (71cm) tall; bitches 26in (66cm).

Newfoundland
The Newfoundland is a powerful swimmer, with a natural passion for water. It should have access to the sea, a pond, or a river.

COAT
Outer coat is coarse, straight, and flat, with an oily, water-resistant quality; undercoat is dense. Colors are black, browns, or white with black markings (known as a "Landseer").

Black and brown dogs sometimes have splashes of white on the chest, toes, and tail-tip

This densely coated dog is understandably unhappy in high temperatures.

EYES
Small, deep-set eyes, spaced wide apart. Dark brown in color.

Muzzle is covered in short, fine hair

HEAD
Broad, massive skull, with deep muzzle, rounded on top.

EARS
Small, set back, and lying close to the head.

Mouth is very soft

FACIAL CHARACTERISTICS
Newfoundland

TAIL
Thick, well covered with hair, and slightly curved. Hangs downwards when the dog is at rest; raised on the move.

LEGS
Forelegs are straight, and well feathered; hind legs are partially feathered.

BODY
Deep, broad chest, level back, and powerful loins.

155

Old English Sheepdog

ONE OF ENGLAND'S most ancient sheepdog breeds, the Old English Sheepdog has now become a much-loved, and highly distinctive, family pet. With its rolling gait, and abundantly shaggy coat, it can easily be mistaken for a bear.

History
The breed was developed in England's West Country by farmers who needed an agile cattle drover and sheep herder to take their animals to market. Its ancestors probably include the Bearded Collie and a variety of imported European herding dogs. By the nineteenth century, the Old English Sheepdog was widely used in agricultural areas. It made its British show debut in 1873.

Temperament
Several generations ago, the breed was described as fierce and untrustworthy, but these characteristics have long since disappeared. Although still capable of guarding, the Old English Sheepdog is friendly, faithful, and even-tempered, with an intelligent and boisterous manner. The breed is exceptionally good, and popular, with children.

The completely cropped tail gave the breed its nickname of "Bobtail" or "Bob".

HEAD
Square, broad skull, well-arched over the eyes. Muzzle is square, with a strong jaw.

BODY
Short and compact, with deep chest, and fairly arched loins. Should be lower at the shoulder.

LEGS
Well covered with hair. Forelegs are straight; hind legs are muscular.

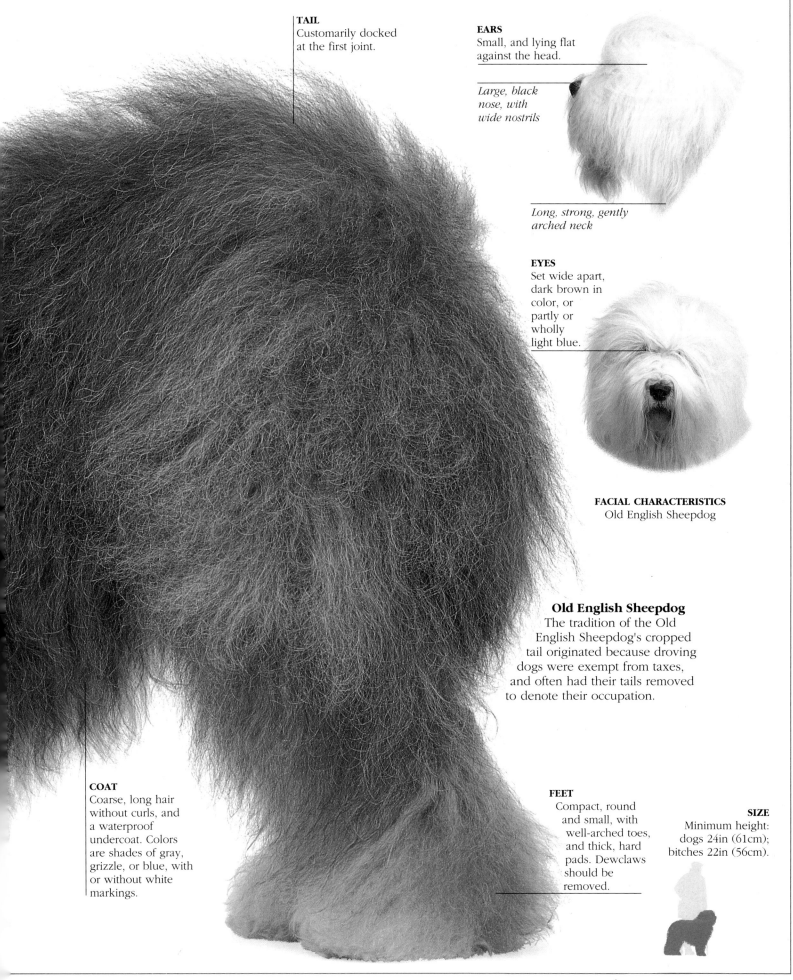

TAIL
Customarily docked at the first joint.

EARS
Small, and lying flat against the head.

Large, black nose, with wide nostrils

Long, strong, gently arched neck

EYES
Set wide apart, dark brown in color, or partly or wholly light blue.

FACIAL CHARACTERISTICS
Old English Sheepdog

Old English Sheepdog
The tradition of the Old English Sheepdog's cropped tail originated because droving dogs were exempt from taxes, and often had their tails removed to denote their occupation.

COAT
Coarse, long hair without curls, and a waterproof undercoat. Colors are shades of gray, grizzle, or blue, with or without white markings.

FEET
Compact, round and small, with well-arched toes, and thick, hard pads. Dewclaws should be removed.

SIZE
Minimum height: dogs 24in (61cm); bitches 22in (56cm).

Great Pyrenees

Pᴿᴼᴮᴬᴮᴸʸ ᴛʜᴇ ᴍᴏsᴛ ᴘᴏᴡᴇʀꜰᵁᴸ breed in existence, the Great Pyrenees fortunately carries a kindly nature within its immense frame. Though suited to family life, it is not a dog to be kept indoors.

History

For centuries these dogs were used in the Pyrenees to protect sheep flocks from marauding bears and wolf packs. Their ancestor was probably the Tibetan Mastiff, brought from Asia over a thousand years ago, but there may have been a certain amount of cross-breeding with indigenous marsh dogs present in the area since prehistoric times. In the fifteenth century they were used as guards, and became particularly fashionable during the reign of Louis XIV, after he installed one at the Louvre as a watchdog. It wasn't long before Great Pyrenees were to be found guarding chateaux all over the country. However, their popularity in France declined markedly following the Revolution of 1789.

Temperament

A kind-natured, gentle dog, obedient, loyal, and affectionate, but capable of guarding.

COAT
Abundant undercoat of fine hairs; long, thick and coarse outer coat, straight or wavy. Colors are white or white with patches of badger, wolf-gray or pale yellow.

HEAD
Large, wedge-shaped skull with deep, strong muzzle. Nose black.

Great Pyrenees
These dogs need an enormous amount of food, lots of exercise and frequent grooming to keep them happy, healthy and looking their best.

BODY
Solidly built with deep chest, and broad straight back, sloping slightly at the rump.

SIZE
Dogs 27-32in (69-81cm) tall; bitches 25-29in (63.5-74cm).

Skull and muzzle are joined by a gentle slope, with only a slight furrow between

EYES
Dark brown with dark eye-rims. Set obliquely.

The lips are black and the roof of the mouth is marked with black

FACIAL CHARACTERISTICS
Great Pyrenees

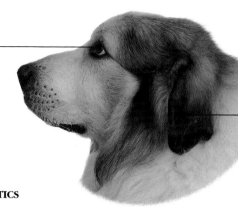

EARS
Medium-sized, triangular and set level with the eyes. Carried low, close to the head.

Maremma Sheepdog
The Maremma is to the shepherds of Italy what the Beauceron and the Collie are to their counterparts in France and Britain. Usually white, but sometimes fawn or lemon in color, this handsome dog may be related to the Kuvasz and the Great Pyrenees.

The Great Pyrenees has not always been known for its gentleness, and was at one time used in battle as a dog of war, often with iron spikes fitted to its collar.

LEGS
Straight and well feathered with double dewclaws, on hind legs.

FEET
Short and compact feet with slightly arched toes. Thick, strong nails.

TAIL
Long, tapering, well feathered, with tip slightly curled. Tail rises from low position to curl above back as dog becomes excited.

Rottweiler

ONE OF THE strongest and most powerful dogs in the world for its size, the Rottweiler, a former cattle dog, is intelligent, robust, and companionable. It is now a highly valued guard and police dog, but can also make a rewarding pet.

History

After the Roman legions retreated, their large, mastiff-type dogs were left in Southern Europe, and became known as hunters of wild boar. By the Middle Ages, in Rottweil, Germany, the Roman dogs had been crossed with local sheepdogs to create the *Rottweiler Metzgerhund*, the "Rottweil butchers' dog". Butchers were using their dogs as drovers and security guards, because livestock was only able to be moved around on foot. In the nineteenth century, with cattle driving becoming illegal in Gemany, and livestock being transported by railway, the Rottweiler suffered a decline in popularity. Enthusiasts came to the rescue about 1900, and the breed reached the US and Britain in the 1930s.

Temperament

The Rottweiler is a natural guard dog and can be aggressive towards intruders. Obedience training and firm handling may be required, but Rottweilers can, and do, make affectionate, calm-tempered pets.

HEAD
Of medium length, with broad skull and deep muzzle. Forehead is fairly arched and cheeks are well boned.

COAT
Medium length, coarse top coat, and fine undercoat on neck and thighs. Color is black, with rust to mahogany markings, not exceeding one tenth of body color. Undercoat colors are black and gray, and should not show through.

BODY
Squarely built, compact, and powerful. Deep, broad chest, straight back, and sloping rump.

Grooming the Rottweiler is an easy task, for daily brushing is adequate to keep the coat in good condition.

Skin on the head can form a wrinkle when dog is alert

EYES
Almond-shaped, dark brown in color, and medium-sized.

EARS
Small, set high, and held close to cheek.

Nose is well developed and always black

FACIAL CHARACTERISTICS
Rottweiler

TAIL
Set high, and carried horizontally. It is traditionally docked to the first joint.

Beauceron
A superb, instinctive herding dog, the Beauceron is the sheepdog star of France. Powerfully built, intelligent, and with a reputation for aggressiveness akin to that of the Rottweiler, it needs equally careful raising and training. If correctly brought up, its loyalty and protective nature can make it a loving companion. The Beauceron is not, however, a dog for the town.

Rottweiler
The talents of this breed as a guard dog have long been recognized — in the Middle Ages, rich merchants would cleverly avoid robbery by fastening their money bags round Rottweilers' necks.

LEGS
Forelegs are straight and muscular; hind legs are well angled.

FEET
Compact, with round front feet, and longer hind feet. Hard pads, short black nails, and well-arched toes, preferably with black pencil markings. The rear dewclaws must be removed.

SIZE
Dogs 25-27in (63-69cm) tall; bitches 23-25in (58-63.5cm).

St Bernard

HEAD
Large, broad, and rounded skull, with a definite stop, down to a short, deep muzzle.

DURING THREE CENTURIES of arduous mountain rescue work, the St Bernard has saved an estimated 2,500 human lives. Modern roads and transport have now made the breed's life-saving skills redundant — today it is highly prized as an intelligent and soft-hearted family dog.

History

The breed takes its name from the Hospice of the Great Saint Bernard Pass. It was founded in AD 980 by St Bernard de Menthon, as a refuge for travelers through the perilous Alpine pass between Switzerland and Italy. Early records have unfortunately been lost, but by the eighteenth century the monks of the hospice were breeding St Bernards to guide, find, and recover people in the treacherous mountain conditions. The original St Bernards had short coats, but the introduction of Newfoundland blood, to reverse the effects of inbreeding, produced a long-coated variety.

Temperament

Despite their tremendous bulk, St Bernards are extremely gentle and friendly. Very tolerant of children, they make ideal family pets as long as they have plenty of space, food, and exercise.

BODY
Moderately deep chest, powerful, straight back, and slightly sloping hindquarters.

The most successful mountain-rescue dog ever was a St Bernard named "Barry", who died in 1814 with a total of forty lives to his credit.

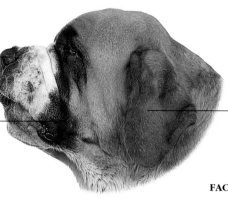

Large, black nose, with well-developed nostrils

Well-developed, high cheek bones

EYES
Dark brown in color, and medium in size.

EARS
Medium-sized, set high, and lying flat against the cheeks.

FACIAL CHARACTERISTICS
St Bernard

COAT
Both long- and smooth-haired varieties have a thick, dense, flat-lying coat. Color is white, with orange, mahogany, or red-brindle markings. The long-haired type has medium-length, slightly wavy hair over the back. The tail is bushy.

TAIL
Long, heavy, and set high. Carried low when the dog is in repose; raised during activity.

St Bernard

In mountain-rescue work, the dogs worked in teams of four. On locating a victim of avalanche or exposure, two St Bernards would lie down next to him to keep him warm, one would lick his face to revive him, and one would return to the hospice to get human help. If the victim began to recover, he could revive himself further by drinking brandy from a barrel, firmly attached to each dog's collar.

LEGS
Forelegs are straight and long; hind legs are heavy-boned, muscular, and powerful.

FEET
Very large, with well-arched toes. Dewclaws should be removed.

SIZE
Height: dogs at least 27$\frac{1}{2}$in (70cm); bitches 25$\frac{1}{2}$in (65cm).

Samoyed

THE LAVISH, SNOW-WHITE COAT and famous "Samoyed smile" ensure that this glamorous creature will turn heads and make friends wherever it goes! Elegant and agile, it is now one of the most fashionable show and companion breeds, yet has a history of hard work in severe conditions.

The erect ears, tail carried over the back, and coat standing off the body, all point towards the Samoyed's Spitz ancestry.

LEGS
Forelegs are long, straight, and well boned; hind legs are very muscular.

History

The breed's ancestors were the tough European Spitz dogs. A nomadic Siberian people, the Samoyed, gave the dogs their name, and used them to pull sleds and herd reindeer. The breed became renowned for its endurance and hardiness, and European explorers used Samoyeds in their polar expeditions. Originally "Sammy" (as the breed is affectionately known) was a multicolored dog, usually black, black and white, or black and tan, but eventually the white in the coat became dominant. In the late nineteenth century, fur traders recognized the potential profit of Sammy's glistening white coat, and started to import the breed into the US and Europe. The first Samoyeds reached Britain in 1889, and Queen Alexandra was among their many admirers.

COAT
Thick, soft undercoat, with long harsh outer coat growing through. Straight, weather-resistant outer coat should stand away from the body, and have silver tips. Colors are pure white, white and biscuit, and cream.

Temperament

The Samoyed is a lively creature, with an intelligent and independent nature. It will gladly be friendly to all, including intruders!

FEET
Long, flat, hare-like, and feathered. Toes are arched and well spaced, with protective hair growing in between.

BODY
Muscular back, strong loins, and deep, moderately broad chest.

HEAD
Wedge-shaped, slightly rounded, broad skull, and medium-length muzzle. Nose is preferably black.

Samoyed

Appearances are not deceptive in this case — the characteristic "Samoyed smile", caused by the lips being slightly curved at the corner of the mouth, does seem to reveal the breed's true character. It is even-tempered, good-natured, and generally a very happy dog, with a natural affinity for human company.

EYES
Fairly wide apart, almond-shaped, set slanted, and medium to dark brown in color. Eye-rims should be black.

EARS
Set wide, erect, and well haired.

Smiling expression

Lips are black

FACIAL CHARACTERISTICS
Samoyed

SIZE
Dogs 21-23½in (53-60cm) tall; bitches 19-21in (48-53cm).

TAIL
Long, thick, and carried over the back. When alert, carried to the side; when resting, carried dropped.

Shetland Sheepdog

A PARTICULARLY WELL-PROPORTIONED, handsome animal, the Shetland Sheepdog or "Sheltie", is easily mistaken for a small Rough-Coated Collie. Despite being bred as a sheepdog, it makes an excellent family pet and competent guard dog.

History

For centuries these little dogs were used to herd and guard the sheep flocks of the Shetlands — those rugged islands off the Scottish coast where many of the animals are rather small in stature. Their ancestors are thought to have been either the Scottish Rough Collie or the Icelandic Yakki, brought to the islands by whalers. Refinement of the breed took place mainly in the twentieth century after the export of Shelties to mainland Scotland and beyond.

Temperament

A dog of remarkable intelligence and trainability, the Sheltie has retained many of the characteristics of its working forebears. It makes a fine guard dog in the home, for it is loyal and affectionate to its owners, but wary of strangers.

Shetland Sheepdog

These animals are easily trained, which makes them ideal as working dogs, show-dogs, or pets. Shelties thrive on regular exercise, and their long coats reward frequent grooming.

BODY
Deep chest, level back, and gently sloping rump. Ribs are well sprung.

SIZE
Height is 13-16in (33-41cm).

LEGS
Forelegs are straight and well feathered; hind legs have powerful, muscular thighs.

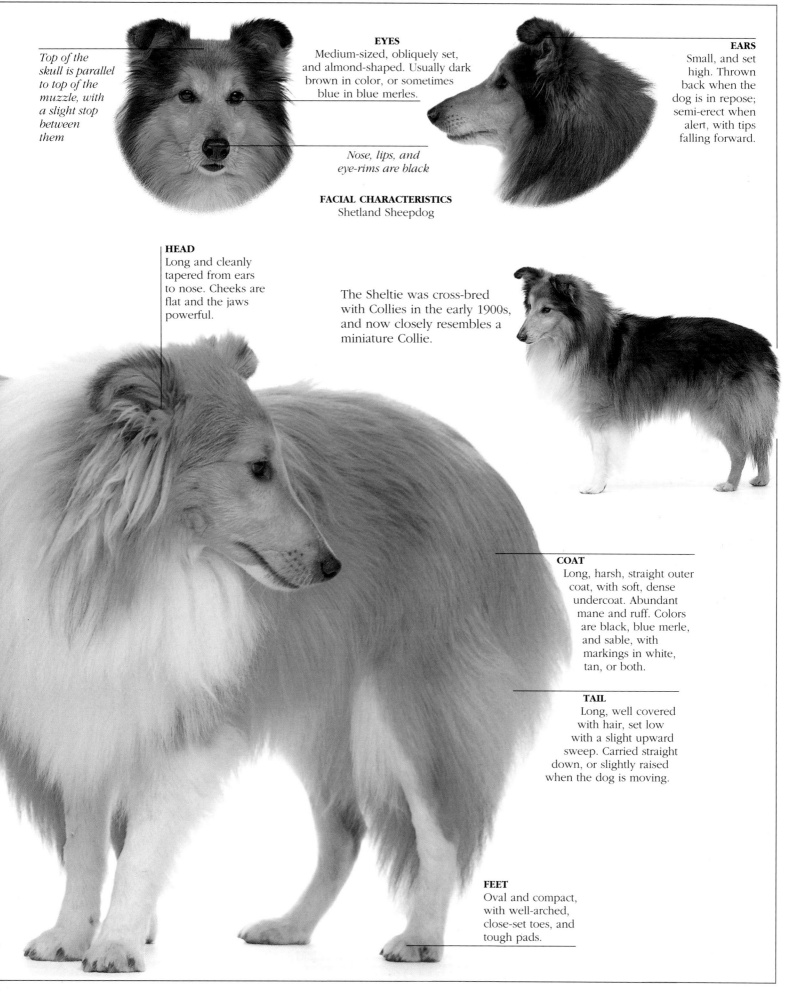

Top of the skull is parallel to top of the muzzle, with a slight stop between them

EYES
Medium-sized, obliquely set, and almond-shaped. Usually dark brown in color, or sometimes blue in blue merles.

EARS
Small, and set high. Thrown back when the dog is in repose; semi-erect when alert, with tips falling forward.

Nose, lips, and eye-rims are black

FACIAL CHARACTERISTICS
Shetland Sheepdog

HEAD
Long and cleanly tapered from ears to nose. Cheeks are flat and the jaws powerful.

The Sheltie was cross-bred with Collies in the early 1900s, and now closely resembles a miniature Collie.

COAT
Long, harsh, straight outer coat, with soft, dense undercoat. Abundant mane and ruff. Colors are black, blue merle, and sable, with markings in white, tan, or both.

TAIL
Long, well covered with hair, set low with a slight upward sweep. Carried straight down, or slightly raised when the dog is moving.

FEET
Oval and compact, with well-arched, close-set toes, and tough pads.

Siberian Husky

STRICTLY SPEAKING, this is the only breed that should be called a husky, although the term is loosely applied to many sled dogs. It has a handsome, rather wolf-like appearance, an excellent temperament, and enormous stamina.

History

Siberian Huskies were developed by the nomadic Chukchi, an Inuit people of eastern Siberia, for pulling sleds, herding reindeer, and as a watchdog. They were the perfect working dogs for the harsh Siberian conditions — hardy, able to integrate into small packs, and quite happy to work for hours on end. Huskies remained isolated in Siberia for hundreds of years, until the beginning of this century, when fur traders took them to North America. They soon became the undisputed champions of competitive sled racing, and are now popular as companion dogs.

Temperament

This breed has an extremely amiable character — docile but alert — and is always willing to work.

HEAD
Slightly rounded skull, with definite stop down to tapering muzzle. Skull and muzzle are of equal length.

COAT
Dense undercoat, with straight, soft outer coat of medium length. All colors and markings are acceptable.

BODY
Deep chest, and muscular, level back. Loins are slightly arched.

SIZE
Dogs 21-23in (53-58.5cm) tall; bitches 20-22in (51-56cm).

Despite its great strength, the Siberian Husky makes an ineffective guard dog, as its disposition is too gentle.

FEET
Compact, well furred, and oval, with strong pads, and a slight web between the toes. Dewclaws should be removed.

A characteristic of the Siberian Husky is that it usually howls rather than barks.

TAIL
Well furred, like a fox's brush, carried hanging when the dog is at rest or working; curved over the back when attentive.

Siberian Husky
This hardy breed has a beautiful, odor-free coat that needs no trimming, except around the feet.

EYES
Almond-shaped, and obliquely set. Colors are any shade of blue or brown, and sometimes one of each color.

Nose is black, liver, or flesh, toning with the coat color

EARS
Medium-sized, triangular, set close together and high. Well furred both on the insides and the outsides.

LEGS
Forelegs are straight and strong; hind legs are parallel and muscular.

Lips are black, and close-fitting

FACIAL CHARACTERISTICS
Siberian Husky

Welsh Corgis

W ELSH CORGIS PROBABLY DERIVE their name from the Welsh word *Corrci*, meaning dwarf dog. There are two closely related varieties — the Pembroke and the Cardigan. The Pembroke enjoys much more popularity than the Cardigan, perhaps because it has always had friends in high places, despite its small size! Through the ages it has been a big favorite of royalty, from Richard I to Queen Elizabeth II.

The Pembroke Welsh Corgi's water-resistant coat needs daily brushing to keep it looking trim.

History

The Pembroke Welsh Corgi (the Corgi without a tail) is thought by most to have arrived in Wales in 1107 with the Flemish weavers. Some claim that its Flemish history and fox-like head point towards Spitz ancestry, while others suspect that trading between Wales and Sweden introduced the Swedish Vallhund into the local canine stock. Both breeds enjoyed success in herding cattle. Being quick and agile, Welsh Corgis could nip their herd's heels, then nimbly elude the angry hoof! The Cardigan and the Pembroke were recognized as separate breeds in the US in 1935 and 1936 respectively.

Temperament

Welsh Corgis are loyal, affectionate, friendly, and very good with children. They tend to be wary of strangers, and therefore make good guard dogs.

TAIL
Naturally short tail is preferred, otherwise docked close.

COAT
Medium length, soft and quite dense. Colors are red, sable, fawn, or black and tan with or without white markings.

BODY
Fairly powerfully built, with deep, broad chest, and level back.

FEET
Oval, with short nails, strong pads, and well-arched toes. The two center toes are longer than the outer toes.

SIZE
Height: 10-12in (25.5-30.5cm).

LEGS
Short, well boned, and strong.

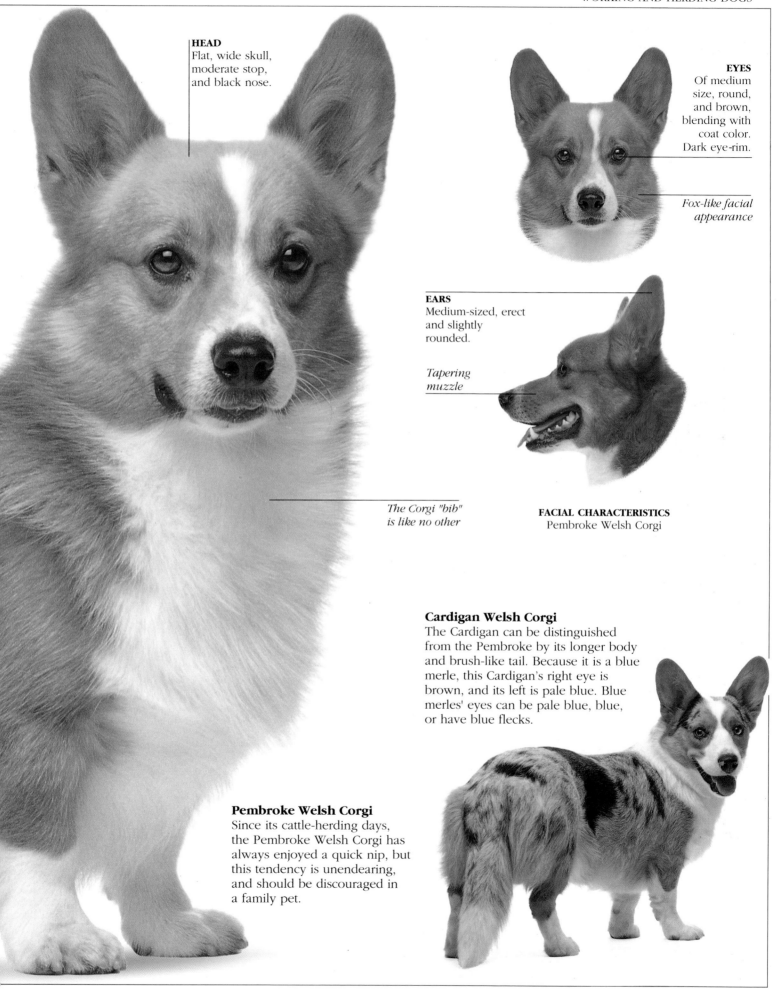

HEAD
Flat, wide skull, moderate stop, and black nose.

EYES
Of medium size, round, and brown, blending with coat color. Dark eye-rim.

Fox-like facial appearance

EARS
Medium-sized, erect and slightly rounded.

Tapering muzzle

The Corgi "bib" is like no other

FACIAL CHARACTERISTICS
Pembroke Welsh Corgi

Cardigan Welsh Corgi

The Cardigan can be distinguished from the Pembroke by its longer body and brush-like tail. Because it is a blue merle, this Cardigan's right eye is brown, and its left is pale blue. Blue merles' eyes can be pale blue, blue, or have blue flecks.

Pembroke Welsh Corgi

Since its cattle-herding days, the Pembroke Welsh Corgi has always enjoyed a quick nip, but this tendency is unendearing, and should be discouraged in a family pet.

Toy Dogs

Although in many cases they were developed from bigger working dogs through the process of miniaturization, Toy Dogs are specialists in their own particular way — as companion animals, and as small, conveniently-sized, and esthetically pleasing pets. They play a vital role in the lives of many people who live alone, and their beneficial effects on the wellbeing of the old, the ill, and the housebound, are increasingly acknowledged. Their presence has even been shown to speed recovery from sickness and to counter depression; stroking them lowers blood pressure. They dispel loneliness, give great pleasure, a lifetime's friendship and loyalty — and much more besides.

Papillon

English Toy Spaniel

The smallest of dogs
The word "toy" meaning a thing of little or no importance, a trifle or a plaything for children, is very much what they are not! Applied to dogs, as it has been since 1863, it means quite simply "diminutive". Toy Dogs are, of course, a varied and decorative group, but, no less than other breeds, they usually develop a strong protective instinct towards their human friends and the home in which they live. It is this quality that often makes them effective sentries who warn of the presence of strangers with loud barks and yelps. Some are so protective of their property, that despite their small size, they have no compunction in attacking intruders. No mere ornaments these.

A fair selection
In the main, Toy Dogs have been produced by selective breeding to give a pleasing appearance. Some, such as the Italian Greyhound and Toy Spaniels, are mini-versions of "full-sized" breeds in the Hound and Sporting groups; and the Pomeranian is the diminutive representative of the Spitz group of

Yorkshire Terrier

dogs that originated in northern lands, and which includes the Finnish Spitz, Samoyed, Akita, and Keeshond. But there are also Toys that were developed for special purposes. The Tibetan Spaniel, for example, was used to turn prayer wheels, and another crossbred kind of Toy Dog that did similar work for his masters was the Turnspit. This bandy-legged individual paddled a

Pug

Chihuahua

wheel that turned the spit on which game or sucking pig were roasted over the fire.

A long history

Toy breeds are not recent developments aimed at the show bench and designed to the arbitrary and subjective whims of modern dog fanciers or show judges. Four thousand years ago the Chinese kept "lion dogs" that were almost identical to the

Pomeranian

Pekingese of today, and "lap dogs" were popular with the Romans. As one might expect, Toy Dogs were also particular favorites of noble ladies, and these diminutive companion-animals have been associated with such royal names as Mary Queen of Scots, Queen Victoria, Queen Marie Antoinette and Madame de Pompadour of France, and the last Czarina of Russia, Alexandra. And long ago, when the Empress of China entered her court, a hundred dogs of the type that we now call Japanese Chins would stand up on their hind legs and remain so until she was seated. Men have been just as devoted to Toy Dogs, from Charles II and the little

Italian Greyhound

spaniels named after him, through Louis XV of France who adored tiny "truffle" dogs, to the Dalai Lamas of Tibet who exchanged Lhasa Apsos for Shih Tzus with visiting officials from China.

A charming tale

In medieval times it was not unusual for people to take dogs with them when they went to church for use as "foot-warmers". The amusing story is told of how once, when the Bishop of Gloucester was holding a service in Bath Abbey with a goodly sprinkling of dogs among the congregation, including some Turnspits accompanying their cooks, the first lesson happened to be from the Book of Ezekiel. The reading included the verses in the tenth chapter that refer several times to "wheels" and the "animals that control them". The Turnspits were only too familiar with the word "wheel" and what it implied, and a witness reported gleefully that "they all clapt their Tails between their Legs and ran out of the Church."!

Pekingese

Chihuahuas

THE TINIEST OF A TINY GROUP, the Chihuahua enjoys enormous popularity, out of all proportion to its size. It manages to combine the delightful appeal of a Toy with the hunting and protective instincts of a much larger dog.

History

Up until 1898, when it was imported into the US from Mexico, the history of the Chihuahua is open to conjecture. Is it a truly indigenous South American breed, descended from the dogs held sacred first by the Incas and then by the Aztecs? Was it introduced into the New World by the Conquistadors? Or did it arrive from China as recently as the nineteenth century? Evidence for the Chihuahua's antecedents include carvings in the monastry of Huejotzingo, which can be dated back to the Toltecs; remains of small dogs found on archaeological digs in Mexico; and records of a small dog such as the Chinese Crested being brought across from Asia. In all probability, the breed is not the product of just one type of dog, but of several that are both ancient and relatively modern.

Temperament

Unintimidated by other dogs whatever their size, the Chihuahua is nevertheless fussy about the company it keeps and tends to prefer its own kind.

No excess wrinkles on the face

HEAD
Graceful in appearance, well rounded, apple-domed skull. The cheeks should be cleanly chiselled, lean and flat.

COAT
The fur is long and soft in texture, either flat or slightly wavy. A large neck ruff is a desirable feature. Any color or combination of colors is accepted.

Despite its ample covering, the Long Coated Chihuahua is as prone to "the shivers" as its Smooth Coated cousin — although it is no more likely to catch a chill than any other type of breed.

SIZE
As diminutive as possible; height is 6-9in (15-23cm).

BODY
The back should be level, the shoulders lean, and the chest deep. Ribs are rounded, without being "barrel-shaped".

FEET
Small, dainty, and cushioned, with toes that are well divided but not spread apart.

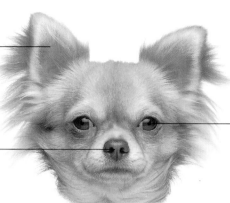

EARS
Large, flared, feathered, and set at an angle of approximately forty-five degrees.

Nose is narrow and can be any color

EYES
Large, round, and set well apart. Colors are dark or ruby, or light in light-colored dogs.

Slightly tapered muzzle

FACIAL CHARACTERISTICS
Long Coated Chihuahua

Long Coated Chihuahua

The Aztecs had no wool or cotton and so depended on dog hair to make cloth. It is more than possible that their raw material came from dogs very similar to the Chihuahua. The modern long-haired version of the breed may have arisen through crossing the Smooth Coated Chihuahua with other miniature breeds such as the Papillon, Pomeranian, and Yorkshire Terrier.

TAIL
Medium in length, set high and carried up and over the back. It should be long and plume-like.

LEGS
The forelegs should be straight and the hindquarters muscular.

Smooth Coated Chihuahua
Fur that is glossy and close-lying, and smooth and soft, is the only difference between this variety of the breed and the Long Coated. The Smooth Coated is the most popular type of Chihuahua in the US.

English Toy Spaniel

PERHAPS THE MOST ROYAL OF BREEDS, the English Toy Spaniel, known in other countries as the King Charles Spaniel, was a favorite of both Mary Queen of Scots and Charles II of England. At Mary's beheading, "one of the executioners espied her little dog which had crept under her clothes which could not be gotten forth but by force"; and Charles was so enamored with the breed that Samuel Pepys noted "the silliness of the King playing with his dog all the while and not minding his business."

History

The English Toy Spaniel probably originates from China or Japan. In the sixteenth century it crossed the English Channel from France, where it had long been established as a sporting breed. In the early nineteenth century it was still used as a "cocker" on woodcock shoots, but selective breeding produced a shorter-nosed dog, with both good looks and nature.

Temperament

It is affectionate, level-headed, good with children, and mixes well with other dogs.

SIZE
Height
10in (25.5cm).

HEAD
Well-domed, with a black, snub, turned-up nose. Deep square muzzle.

COAT
Silky in texture, long, and glossy. A slight wave is permitted. There is profuse feathering on the neck and chest.

LEGS
Short, straight, strong, and stout. Heavily feathered.

Cavalier King Charles Spaniel
Cross-breeding during the nineteenth century led to the creation of a separate type of dog, that is somewhat larger than the English Toy, with a flat skull and longer muzzle. Former President Ronald Reagan owns a Cavalier Spaniel.

Stop is well defined

Skull is large in comparison to the size of the dog

EYES
Large, dark in color, and set wide apart. The eyelids should align horizontally.

EARS
Very long, set low and hanging beside the cheeks. Heavily feathered.

FACIAL CHARACTERISTICS
English Toy Spaniel

BODY
Cobby and compact in appearance, with a short, broad back, and a deep chest.

Prince Charles and Blenheim King Charles Spaniels
A tricolored dog, the Prince Charles has a pearly white coat with black and tan markings. The Blenheim has the same white coat, but with chestnut-red patches. The two other varieties of the breed are the original Black and Tan, and the Ruby, which is a solid-colored red.

TAIL
A square "flag" shape, well feathered and carried below the level of the back.

English Toy Spaniel
It was Charles II's inordinate fondness for the dog that gave this breed its English name, the King Charles Spaniel. Such was his affection that he allowed his numerous pets access to all parts of the palace of Whitehall, and, it was rumored, on occasion neglected affairs of state in order to play with them.

FEET
Should be cat-like, compact and round, well padded and heavily feathered.

Japanese Chin

DESPITE ITS NAME, the Japanese Chin is of Chinese extraction. It shares the same family tree, rooted in the ancient Tibetan Spaniel, as the Pug and Pekingese.

History

The long and venerable history of the Japanese Chin extends back over 2,700 years, when the breed was introduced to Japan from China. At the Imperial Japanese court, Chins were often kept in gilded hanging cages, much like rare, exotic birds. In 1853, when Commodore Perry brought out several examples of the breed, the West was at last able to enjoy the company of these graceful and elegant little dogs. Although the breed was almost decimated by the distemper virus shortly after its entry into the US, numbers on both sides of the Atlantic are now healthy and increasing steadily.

Temperament

The Chin is a zestful, affectionate, and entertaining pet with excellent manners and a great sense of humor. It likes to be the center of attention, and makes a good show-dog.

HEAD
Broad skull, well rounded at the front and between the ears. Nose is black in the Black and White variety, or flesh-colored in the Red and White.

BODY
Short, square, and compact. About as long as it is tall, with a broad, deep chest.

SIZE
Weight is no more than 7lb (3.2kg).

The status of the breed became particularly elevated at one stage, when a devoted Japanese emperor decreed that it should be worshipped.

Japanese Chin

Black and White is the original and most popular variety of the breed, but various shades of red, including sable, lemon, and orange, with white are also permitted.

COAT
Should be long, lush, silky, and straight, standing out from the body without any waves or curls. There is a ruff at the neck and profuse feathering.

The wide distance between its eyes gives the Japanese Chin a bemused, slightly cross-eyed expression when it looks straight ahead. All types of Chin should have an Oriental appearance.

TAIL
Lushly feathered with long hair to form a plume that falls to one side as the tail is carried curled over the back.

EARS
V-shaped, small, set wide apart and high on the head. Should be feathered and carried slightly forward.

EYES
Large, rather prominent and dark. Set wide apart.

Muzzle is short and very wide

LEGS
Small and fine with good feathering.

FEET
Small but longish, with a slight tendency to stand on tiptoe.

FACIAL CHARACTERISTICS
Japanese Chin

Maltese

Issa, the Maltese owned by the Roman Governor of Malta in the first century received this most moving of poetic tributes: "Issa is more frolicsome than Catulla's sparrow. Issa is purer than a dove's kiss. Issa is gentler than a maiden. Issa is more precious than Indian gems. Lest the last days that she sees light should snatch him from her for ever, Publius has had her painted."

History

The Maltese may well have originated either in Malta or from the Sicilian town of Melita. It is one of the oldest breeds: statues of similar dogs have been found in Egyptian tombs of the thirteenth century BC, and the dog may have arrived in Great Britain with the Roman legions as early as 55 BC. In any event, by the Middle Ages it was a regular consort of European nobility, and from that point on its popularity has never waned.

Temperament

Loving and loyal, as well as tough, the Maltese makes a first-class pet as well as an efficient watchdog.

HEAD
Medium in size, with a slightly rounded top to the skull. The nose should be black.

Not surprisingly, the long, silky coat of the Maltese needs a great deal of care and attention to keep it in top condition. These dogs should not be exposed to extreme cold or heavy downpours of rain.

FEET
Small and round, covered with hair. Pads and nails should be black.

EYES
Fairly large, oval in shape, and dark brown with black rims. Gentle appealing expression.

Stop is moderate

Medium length muzzle, fine and tapered

EARS
Long, set low, hanging close to the head, and heavily feathered.

FACIAL CHARACTERISTICS
Maltese

COAT
Single coat, straight and silky without curls, reaching or almost reaching the ground. Pure white in color.

TAIL
Abundant, long hair forming a plume that is carried curled over the back.

Maltese
A truly ancient breed, the Maltese was one of the first dogs to be shown — in Britain in 1862, and in the US in 1877.

BODY
Low-set and compact, with a short, level back, and a fairly deep, well-sprung chest.

LEGS
Short, straight, fine forelegs and strong hind legs with muscular thighs.

SIZE
Height: 8-10in (20-25.5cm).

Miniature Pinscher

THIS LIVELY, ROBUST LITTLE DOG, with its characteristic high-stepping gait, has gained widespread popularity in the US in recent years, but was almost unknown outside Germany before 1900. Although it looks like a miniature version of the Doberman, there are no genetic ties.

HEAD
Narrow, tapering skull, with flat top.

COAT
Short, smooth, and shiny. Colors are black or chocolate with tan markings, solid red, or solid brown.

History

The small Pinscher (the word means "terrier" in German) existed in Germany and Scandinavia for centuries before the Miniature Pinscher emerged as a distinct breed. In 1895 the German Pinscher Klub (later the Pinscher Schnauzer Klub) was formed in Germany, and the Miniature Pinscher was officially recognized not long after. The dog's popularity increased in the 1920s after having been exported to the US, and in 1929 the Miniature Pinscher Club of America was founded. Only six years later, an American-bred Miniature Pinscher was awarded the accolade of Best in Toy Group at the Chicago Show.

Temperament

Alert, intelligent, and loyal, the breed is very courageous for its diminutive size. It makes a good watchdog and family pet, and is an excellent rat-catcher.

This is a distinctive little animal, with a precise hackney gait, an animated manner, and the fearless spirit of a dog twice its size.

SIZE
Ideal height:
11-11$\frac{1}{2}$in
(28-29cm).

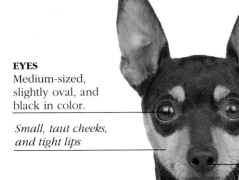

EARS
Set high, and
carried erect.

EYES
Medium-sized,
slightly oval, and
black in color.

*Scissor bite: the upper
teeth closely overlap
the lower teeth*

*Small, taut cheeks,
and tight lips*

*The color of the nose
matches the coat*

FACIAL CHARACTERISTICS
Miniature Pinscher

BODY
Squarely built,
with deep chest,
level or slightly
sloping back, and
moderately
tucked-up belly.

TAIL
Set, and carried,
fairly high.
Customarily
docked short.

The ears can be
cropped to a point
in the US and some
other countries. As
ear cropping is
illegal in the UK,
British breeders are
producing "Min
Pins" with naturally
erect ears.

LEGS
Straight forelegs;
muscular hind legs,
set wide apart.

The Miniature Pinscher is a
born show-dog, elegant and
vivacious, and its clean, close
coat is easy to groom.

*The muzzle is
strong, and in
proportion to
the head as a
whole*

Miniature Pinscher
On a typical black and tan Miniature
Pinscher, there are tan markings on the
cheeks, lips, lower jaw, throat, over the eyes,
on the chest, forelegs, hind legs, feet, and on
the area beneath the tail. There are preferably
no white markings on the chest.

FEET
Short, round, well-
arched feet, with thick
pads and short dark
nails. Dewclaws
should be removed.

Papillon

T HE FRENCH WORD for butterfly gives this delightful dog its name, at least for the prick-eared variety; the original drop-eared form of the breed is called a Phalène, meaning "moth". These canine moths and butterflies have been flitting through history since at least the sixteenth century, and there are some experts who claim that they are the oldest European breed.

History

Although little is certain about the Papillon's origins, its history after 1545, when there is a record of one being sold, is well documented. The Dwarf Spaniel is thought to be the ancestor of the breed, which may have been brought to Spain from China. By the sixteenth century it was firmly established as the favorite lap dog of the Spanish and French nobility. Indeed, like Mary Queen of Scots and her English Toy Spaniel, Marie Antoinette had her much-loved Papillon with her when she went to the scaffold. By the late nineteenth century French and Belgian breeders had developed the erect-eared type which was first shown in Britain in 1923 and which received recognition in the US in 1935.

Temperament

The Papillon is a friendly, intelligent dog that is tougher than it looks, and loves outdoor exercise. It may be very possessive of its owner and resent outsiders.

SIZE
8-11in
(20-28cm) tall.

The Papillon was once known as a Squirrel Spaniel because of the way it carries its tail over its back.

TAIL
Long and set high, curled over the back with a heavy plume.

COAT
Long, silky, and flat, with slightly wavy areas. Color is white, with patches in black or any other shade apart from liver. The blaze and noseband should be well defined.

Papillon
Heavily-fringed ears that look like open butterfly wings earned this breed its name. American and British breeders have developed a slightly smaller dog than elsewhere.

BODY
Rather longer than it is tall, not stocky, with a straight back and medium-deep chest.

HEAD
Small and medium-wide, with a slightly domed skull. Nose is round and black.

EARS
Large, set wide apart and well back. Should be abundantly fringed.

Stop is well defined

Muzzle is finely pointed

EYES
Set quite low, medium in size and round, although they should not bulge out. Color is dark with dark rims. The expression should be alert and eager.

FEET
Thin and long like those of a hare, with compact, well-arched toes covered with fine hair.

FACIAL CHARACTERISTICS
Papillon

LEGS
Fine-boned and parallel. Fringed on back of forelegs, and feathery culottes on hind legs.

Pekingese

T OY DOGS ARE RENOWNED for their royal and aristocratic connections, but the Pekingese is undoubtedly the leader of the pack, having been at one time the sacred animal of the Chinese Imperial House.

History
Regarded as manifestations of the legendary Foo Dog that drove away evil spirits, Pekingese were venerated as semi-divine by the Chinese. Commoners had to bow to them; to steal one was punishable by death; and when an emperor died his Pekingese were sacrificed so that they could go with him to give protection in the afterlife. The breed reached the West after 1860, when British troops over-ran the Summer Palace during the Second Opium War. The Imperial Guards were ordered to kill the little dogs to prevent them falling into the hands of the "foreign devils", but five survived. These were taken to England, where one was presented to Queen Victoria, who named it, appropriately, "Looty". It is from these canine spoils of war that the modern Pekingese is descended. The breed was first shown in Britain in 1893. It achieved recognition in the US in 1909.

Temperament
Pekingese are brave, combative, and loyal. They may be prone to breathing difficulties, so owners should keep an especially close watch on their health.

COAT
Very long, straight, coarse top coat over a thick undercoat with a thick mane. Ears, backs of legs, tail, and toes should be profusely feathered. All colors.

LEGS
Short; hind legs are lighter-boned, upper forelegs are bowed.

FEET
Flat and large, with front toes turned out.

HEAD
Large, broad, and flat between the ears. Nose is very snub, broad, and black.

EYES
Prominent, dark, and round. Set wide apart.

Stop is pronounced

Wide, wrinkled muzzle

EARS
Heart-shaped and drooping but not long.

Very flat profile

Ears are profusely feathered

FACIAL CHARACTERISTICS
Pekingese

Pekingese

Quintessentially Oriental, the smallest of these remarkable little dogs were carried in the wide sleeves of Chinese courtiers, making them true "sleeve dogs". Other names for them were "Lion Dog" — they do have a leonine look — and "Sun Dog", so golden-red were their coats.

BODY
Short, but well built in front, with broad chest, well-sprung ribs, and straight back. Lion-like shape.

TAIL
Set high and curled over the back to either side.

SIZE
Weight should not exceed 14lb (6.4kg).

Pomeranian

ALTHOUGH THE POMERANIAN is one of the first breeds to spring to mind when the term "toy dogs" is mentioned, it was once a larger, very hard-working dog that earned its keep by the sweat of its brow. These days, however, it is one of the most expensive breeds to buy and one that demands extensive care to keep it in top show condition.

History

A Spitz-type, the Pomeranian is almost certainly descended from the sledge-pulling dogs of the Arctic, and is probably related to the Keeshond, Norwegian Elkhound, and Samoyed. The first reliable records of dogs similar to the breed came, not surprisingly, from Pomerania, a region bordering the Baltic in what is now partly Poland and partly East Germany, where it was used to herd sheep. By the mid-eighteenth century, Pomeranians had spread to several European countries, including Italy; and it was in Florence that Queen Victoria was presented with the "Pom" that was to lead to a life-long attachment to the breed. Early Pomeranians were relatively big, mostly white, dogs, but selective breeding from the beginning of the last century has produced a diminutive animal prized for its full, flowing, colorful coat.

Temperament

At one stage, the Pomeranian had a reputation for being a snappy, volatile dog, but that has now given way to a personality that is agreed to be loyal and friendly while still lively. It makes an excellent watchdog as well as being very much at home in the show ring.

SIZE
Weight is 4.5-5.5lb (1.8-2kg) for a dog; 4-4.5lb (2-2.5kg) for a bitch.

HEAD
Fox-like, with a wide, flattish skull and a fine, wedge-shaped muzzle. The color of the nose depends on that of the coat.

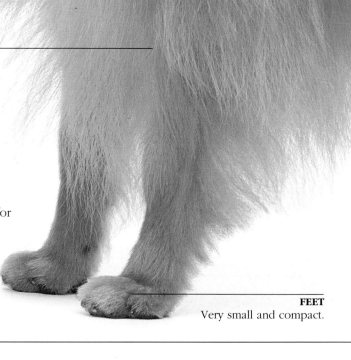

BODY
Short and compact, with a relatively deep, well-rounded chest.

Pomeranian
The "Pom" is not a breed for those who cannot make time for a regular grooming regime. Its spectacular double coat requires meticulous daily brushing.

FEET
Very small and compact.

TAIL
Turned over the back and carried flat in typical Spitz fashion. It should be covered with profuse, long hair.

Not only was the Pomeranian a favorite of Queen Victoria, who founded a kennel and exhibited the breed, but also of Napoleon's Josephine and of Mozart.

COAT
A long, hard, straight, and gleaming outer coat should overlie a soft and fluffy undercoat to give the impression of a ball of fluff from which the limbs protrude. All coat colors are allowed, including orange, brown, cream, black, blue, and particolors.

Skull is large in proportion to muzzle

Black eye rims, except self-colored in browns and blues

EYES
Medium-sized, a slight oval in shape, and dark brown in color. They should not be set too wide apart.

EARS
Should be small, not too far apart, and pricked, like those of a fox.

Fairly short neck, set well into shoulders

LEGS
Should be fine-boned, of medium length, and well feathered.

FACIAL CHARACTERISTICS
Pomeranian

Pug

THE OLD WORD for a goblin, a snub nose, or small monkey, became appended to this charming, most fastidious of dogs in the late eighteenth century.

History

The family tree of the Pug is a matter of debate. Some experts think it came from the Lowlands, brought back from the Far East by Dutch traders. It is possibly of Oriental stock, descended from a short-haired relative of the Pekingese, but another school of thought claims it to be the result of crossing small Bulldogs. Yet another theory is that it is a miniature form of the rare French mastiff called the Dogue de Bordeaux. The breed was a favorite of the artist Hogarth, who included his pet Pug "Trump" in several of his works. From the sixteenth century, it became a fashionable adornment of the European Courts, reaching its peak of popularity in Victorian times.

Temperament

The Pug is a very loving and attentive dog that doesn't need much grooming or exercise, but does demand company.

The Pug communicates by grunts, snorts, and snuffles.

HEAD
Large and round, with much wrinkling. The muzzle, or mask is black and clearly defined.

SIZE
Height: 10-11in tall.

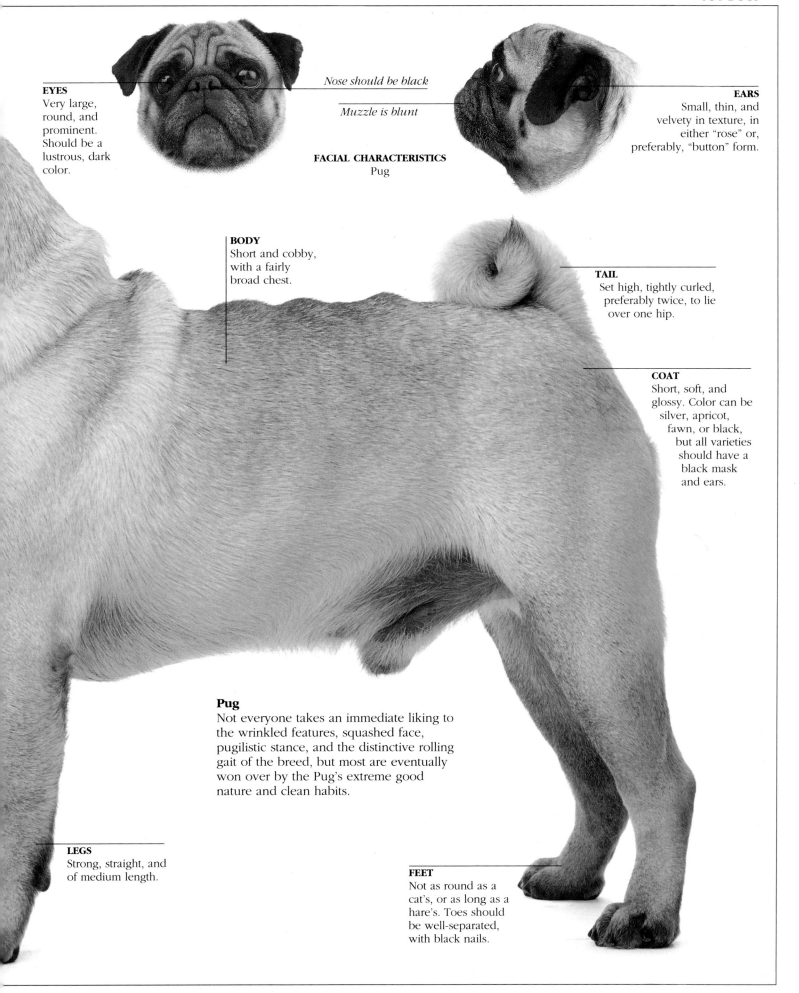

EYES
Very large, round, and prominent. Should be a lustrous, dark color.

Nose should be black

Muzzle is blunt

FACIAL CHARACTERISTICS
Pug

EARS
Small, thin, and velvety in texture, in either "rose" or, preferably, "button" form.

BODY
Short and cobby, with a fairly broad chest.

TAIL
Set high, tightly curled, preferably twice, to lie over one hip.

COAT
Short, soft, and glossy. Color can be silver, apricot, fawn, or black, but all varieties should have a black mask and ears.

Pug
Not everyone takes an immediate liking to the wrinkled features, squashed face, pugilistic stance, and the distinctive rolling gait of the breed, but most are eventually won over by the Pug's extreme good nature and clean habits.

LEGS
Strong, straight, and of medium length.

FEET
Not as round as a cat's, or as long as a hare's. Toes should be well-separated, with black nails.

Shih Tzu

THE FLOWING MANE-LIKE LOCKS of the Shih Tzu are probably responsible for its name, meaning "Lion Dog" in Chinese. Today it will happily adorn and protect the home, but its ancestors were used to rather grander surroundings, such as the palaces of the Manchu emperors in Imperial China.

History

Secrecy shrouds the exact origin of the Shih Tzu, but Lamaism, the religion of Tibet and a form of Buddhism, offers some clues. Maujusri, the Lamaist god of learning, was often accompanied by a small dog, that could transform itself into a lion. Because of its leonine looks, the Tibetan Lhasa Apso became strongly associated with this "Lion Dog". The Chinese emperors were presented with Lhasa Apsos by Tibet's ruler, the Dalai Lama, and it is likely that having reached China, these exotic-looking dogs were crossed with the Pekingese to create the breed that we know today. The Shih Tzu is classifed as a Non-Sporting Dog in Australia, as a Toy in the US, and as a Utility Dog in the UK.

Temperament

Playful and energetic, the Shih Tzu makes an appealing pet, and a very alert watchdog.

HEAD
Broad, with short, square muzzle. Nose is black in color, and tip-tilted or level, with open nostrils.

LEGS
Short and muscular, with abundant hair.

SIZE
Height not more than 9-10$\frac{1}{2}$in (23-27cm).

FEET
Round and appearing large, because of hair between pads and over feet.

COAT
Long, soft, and dense, with good undercoat. Wavy or straight, and all colors. White forehead blaze and tail-tip is desirable in particolors.

To avoid eye infections, the Shih Tzu's long crown-hair should be tied up in a "top-knot".

Due to the reluctance of the Chinese to sell or export Shih Tzus, they only reached the UK and the US in the 1930s, but have rapidly enjoyed popularity in the show-ring.

TAIL
Set high, well-plumed, and carried curved over back. Ideal height is approximately level with the skull.

BODY
Length greatly exceeds height of the dog. Level back, broad chest, and firm shoulders.

EYES
Large and well-spaced. Usually dark in color, but lighter shades are permitted in liver marked or liver dogs.

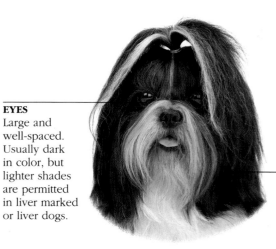

Ears appear to blend into neck

Abundant hair on the muzzle and the crown

EARS
Large and drooping, with abundant hair.

FACIAL CHARACTERISTICS
Shih Tzu

Shih Tzu
Long daily grooming sessions are necessary, else combing out the tangles can be a painful process for both dog and owner!

Silky Terrier

GIVEN THE OPPORTUNITY, it might get into the odd scrap, but the Silky Terrier has never done a scrap of work! Unlike other terriers, this cheerful little dog was not bred to do any particular hunting job, but purely, and most agreeably, to be a companion animal. Nevertheless, its terrier blood shows through in its active, assertive nature, and in the skill it displays killing vermin in its native country.

History
Sydney was the birth place of the breed, which was known at one time simply as the "Sydney Silky". Australian and Yorkshire Terriers were used as part of an intricate cross-breeding program to produce a dog that combined the best features of both types. The carefully determined result must be counted as a modern success story. The Silky Terrier was first shown in Australia in 1907, in Britain in 1930, and was recognized by the American Kennel Club in 1933.

Temperament
The Silky is a pretty, lively, and intelligent animal that is quick to warn of the presence of strangers. It makes an ideal watchdog and pet for town dwellers with small apartments, but also enjoys country strolls.

Silky Terrier
Terrier in spirit, if not in practice, the Silky is an ideal pet for those who want a small companion with a big heart.

A kissing-cousin to the Yorkshire Terrier, the Silky Terrier has a coat that is extremely similar, although not quite so long.

FEET
Small, round, and compact, like those of a cat, with thick, springy pads and dark nails.

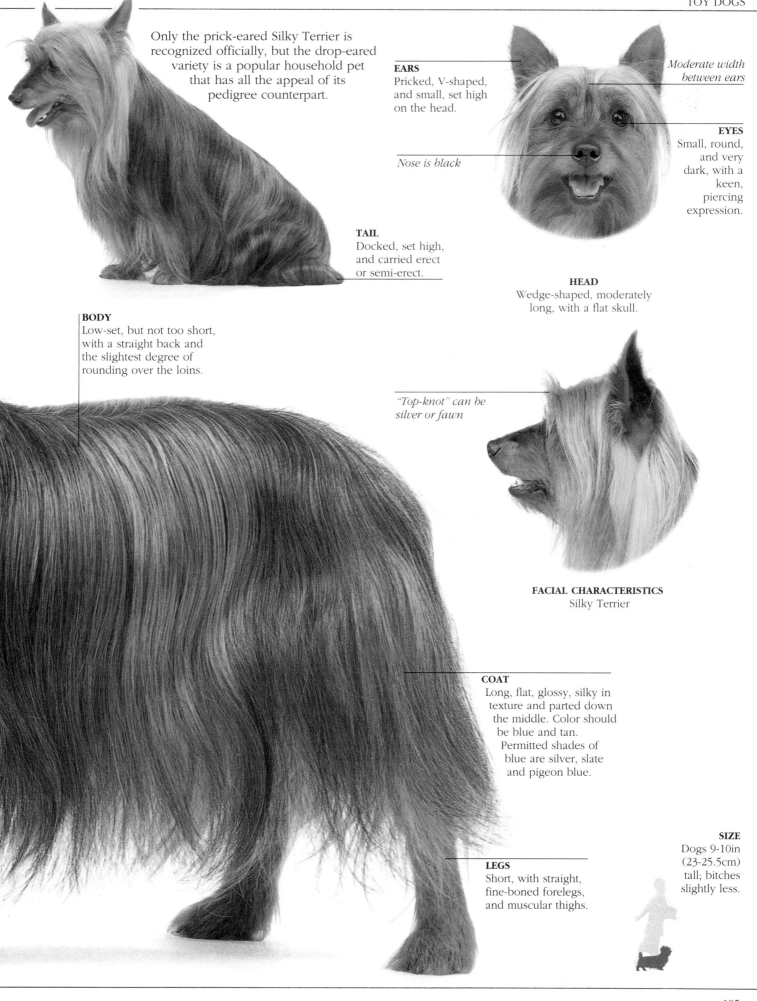

Only the prick-eared Silky Terrier is recognized officially, but the drop-eared variety is a popular household pet that has all the appeal of its pedigree counterpart.

EARS
Pricked, V-shaped, and small, set high on the head.

Moderate width between ears

Nose is black

EYES
Small, round, and very dark, with a keen, piercing expression.

TAIL
Docked, set high, and carried erect or semi-erect.

HEAD
Wedge-shaped, moderately long, with a flat skull.

BODY
Low-set, but not too short, with a straight back and the slightest degree of rounding over the loins.

"Top-knot" can be silver or fawn

FACIAL CHARACTERISTICS
Silky Terrier

COAT
Long, flat, glossy, silky in texture and parted down the middle. Color should be blue and tan. Permitted shades of blue are silver, slate and pigeon blue.

LEGS
Short, with straight, fine-boned forelegs, and muscular thighs.

SIZE
Dogs 9-10in (23-25.5cm) tall; bitches slightly less.

Yorkshire Terrier

SMALL IN STATURE — closely following the Chihuahua as the most diminutive dog of all — the Yorkshire Terrier still looms large in the popularity stakes. Often beribboned and clad in long silky fur, the breed has a "boudoir" appeal that disguises its roguish terrier spirit.

History

Although the breed is only 100 years old or so, its origins are not entirely certain, probably because the working men of the north of England who developed the Yorkshire Terrier avoided divulging the secret of their success to those who might have cashed in on a lucrative side-line. However, it seems likely that Scotsmen seeking work in the woollen mills of Yorkshire brought with them various types of terrier, including the Skye and the now-extinct Clydesdale. These were then crossed with local types, such as the long-haired Leeds Terrier. The Maltese, Black and Tan, Manchester, and Dandie Dinmont terriers may also have contributed blood-lines. At first the "Yorkie" was a much bigger animal than the one we see today, but by selectively breeding the smallest individuals, the dog was gradually miniaturized over the years.

Temperament

As befits an animal that was once used as a ratter, the Yorkshire Terrier is a spirited, sparkling character who is not intimidated by either larger dogs or intruders into the house. Besides being a good guard dog, the breed makes a particularly loving pet.

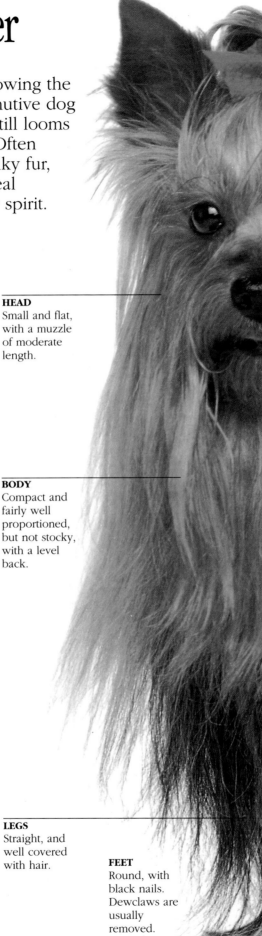

HEAD
Small and flat, with a muzzle of moderate length.

BODY
Compact and fairly well proportioned, but not stocky, with a level back.

SIZE
Height: 8-9in (20-23cm).

LEGS
Straight, and well covered with hair.

FEET
Round, with black nails. Dewclaws are usually removed.

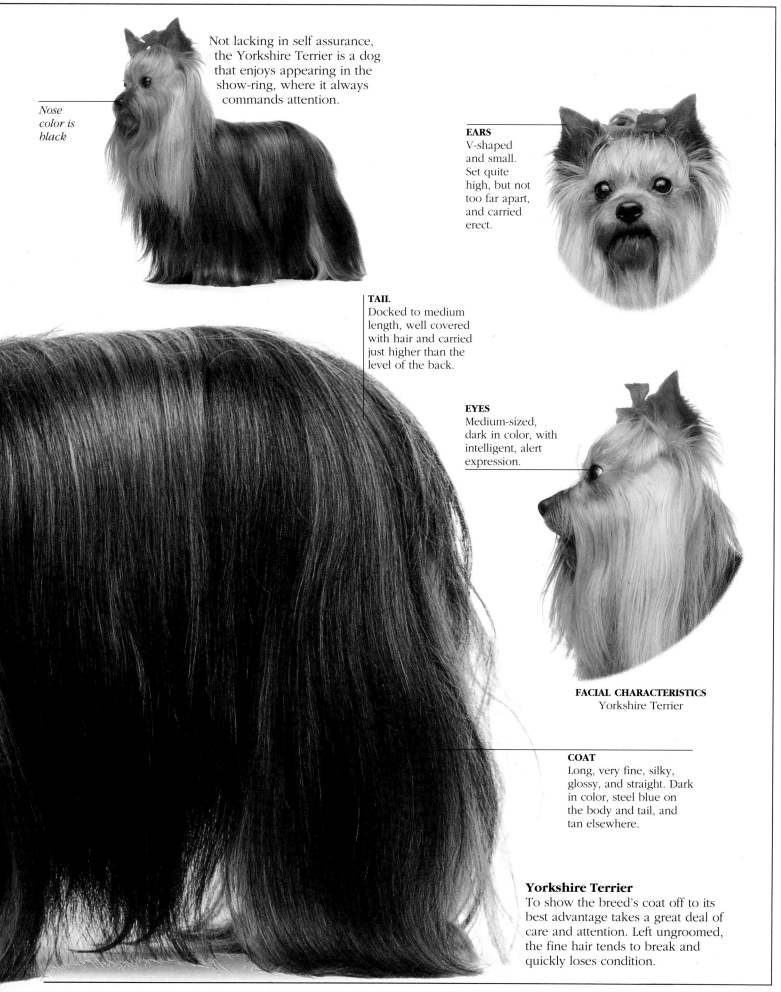

Not lacking in self assurance, the Yorkshire Terrier is a dog that enjoys appearing in the show-ring, where it always commands attention.

Nose color is black

EARS
V-shaped and small. Set quite high, but not too far apart, and carried erect.

TAIL
Docked to medium length, well covered with hair and carried just higher than the level of the back.

EYES
Medium-sized, dark in color, with intelligent, alert expression.

FACIAL CHARACTERISTICS
Yorkshire Terrier

COAT
Long, very fine, silky, glossy, and straight. Dark in color, steel blue on the body and tail, and tan elsewhere.

Yorkshire Terrier
To show the breed's coat off to its best advantage takes a great deal of care and attention. Left ungroomed, the fine hair tends to break and quickly loses condition.

Mongrels

Nᴇᴀʀʟʏ ᴀʟʟ ᴛʜᴇ ᴘᴜʀᴇʙʀᴇᴅ ᴅᴏɢs in this book have been produced originally by mating together different kinds of dogs, and therefore it could be said that they too are mongrels! So, if you are not particularly interested in showing a beautifully coiffured and beribboned canine specimen, and instead seek companionship, friendship, and loyalty, make your way to an animal shelter or humane society, and you will find a dog as good as any in the world.

Characteristics

All domestic dogs belong to the species *Canis familiaris*, and mongrels are at least as rich in qualities as the most aristocratic of purebred dogs. Some might argue that in some cases mongrels are even richer in endearing attributes. Apart from the sheer charm of a "ragamuffin", cross-breeds are endowed with plenty of "hybrid vigor", and are often tougher, better-tempered, less disease-prone, and considerably more adaptable than their pedigree counterparts.

The typical mongrel

If all the purebred dogs in the world were turned loose to interbreed, the laws of survival of the fittest, and natural selection would gradually shape the dog of the future. It would be a happy medium of a dog, without any extremes of physical form or function.

Coat is neither too long, nor too short

Ears are pert, and expressive

Legs are strong, and well proportioned

Mongrels

Most of today's mongrels display moderation in all things. Natural, rather than artificial, selection has ensured that the hardiest, healthiest, and happiest animals survive.

Very good bone structure

Nose is fairly well developed

Back is not over-stretched

Eyes are bright, with an alert, and lively expression

Neck is muscular, and of good length

FACIAL CHARACTERISTICS
Mongrels

Body outline is shapely, and well defined

SIZE
All sizes are possible.

Tail is of medium length

Keeping a Dog

Even more than cats, dogs require *keeping*. Yes, there are regular chores to be done, and efforts to be made, if you are to discover the best in your dog. To keep it hale, hearty, and happy through a long life, you must be prepared to provide intelligent care and attention.

In fact, looking after a dog properly need not take too much time, and should be enjoyable for both animal and owner. Keeping a dog fit helps keep you fit. Making a dog look good helps keep it healthy. The more time you spend attending to your dog, the more fascinating aspects of *Canis familiaris* are revealed to you.

Dogs can be appreciated and valued on many levels. To some they are the sincerest, the truest of friends, and the best of companions. To others they are skilled workers and assistants, substituting efficiently for men or machines. If you become involved in showing or breeding dogs they can become an enthralling hobby or even a full-time business, in which case canine esthetics in all their complexity are bound to be a lifelong preoccupation.

The following section covers briefly the main aspects of the proper care and understanding of the domestic dog, mongrel no less than purebred. Further information on this fascinating subject is best obtained by talking to breeders and veterinarians, or by reading specialized books on the particular breeds. Whatever kind of dog you have, it will appreciate being looked after – and you're sure to have more fun too!

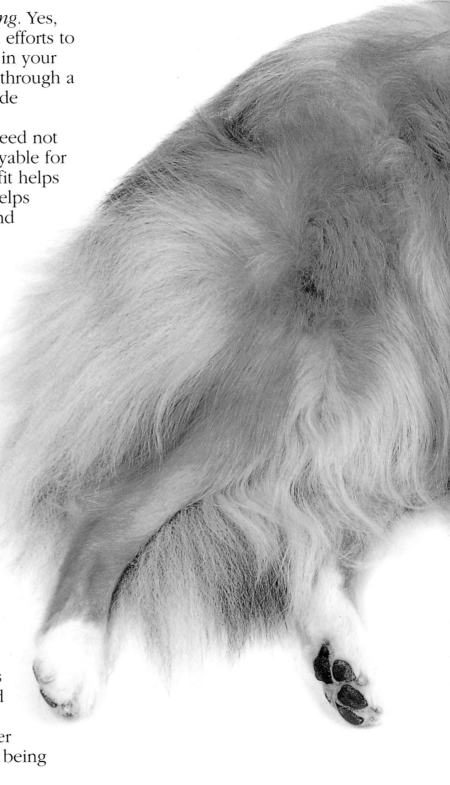

Your New Dog

All the care and consideration that goes into picking that dumbest of family pets, the car, needs to be brought into play when planning to acquire a dog. As when buying a vehicle, you need to ask yourself certain questions. What do I want it to do? How much fuel will it use? What about garaging? Can I afford to have it serviced regularly? Am I capable of driving (exercising) the model I have in mind? And another question has to be asked that does not arise when buying a car: can I make a lifelong commitment (about twelve years on average) to a dog?

What kind of dog?

Try to match your own lifestyle to the physical characteristics, temperament, and particular requirements of the dog. Having done that you must then decide on age, size, and sex, and then whether to go for a mongrel or purebred dog.

German Shepherds and Borzois are not for apartments on the sixteenth floor, Great Danes eat as much meat as a two-year-old lion, and Afghan Hounds demand constant grooming. Think first. Think hard.

If you haven't the space or the inclination to jog with your dog, or if

An older dog that has been well looked after may suit you better than a puppy, which will need a lot of care and attention.

there isn't an abundance of cash around, then think small – a Toy or a small breed. Small dogs have the advantage over larger breeds of greater life expectancy; Toys, however, do not generally live quite as long as regular small breeds.

If it's a companion, friend, or a watchdog you need, why go for a purebred anyway? Mongrels are cheap, come in all sizes, give and take as much affection as any blue-blood, are less prone to hereditary disease, and may well have that inbuilt healthiness that scientists call "hybrid vigor".

Puppy or adult?

Puppies are great fun, particularly if there are children around, but if you want a companion that you can take out with you straightaway, a young adult dog may be best. Old people can find an energetic puppy a bit of a handful, but may be able to give refuge to a homeless older dog. Make sure that any adult dog you buy is house-trained – a dog that has spent a long time in kennels might not be.

A puppy will need someone to take the place of its mother, to look after it, feed it, house-train it, and generally spend time with it to build a good relationship. So if you are away from home all day, do not even consider getting one.

Beds
The traditional wicker basket has many advantages, but is difficult to clean. Make sure that your dog does not get into the habit of chewing it, as wicker fragments can be harmful to dogs.

plastic puppy bowl

wicker basket with washable cushion

Dog or bitch?

It may not be easy to decide which sex you want. Obviously one of the main drawbacks of bitches, unless you are keen to breed, is their twice-yearly reproductive cycle. During her heat a bitch is attractive to dogs and may try to escape to go courting. Some people object to the messiness of their vaginal discharge, and some bitches can be prone to false pregnancy, which can be worrying. Surgical neutering or the periodic use of contraceptive drugs can also add significantly to the cost of owning a dog.

Some people consider dogs to have a more even temperament than bitches. However, they cannot resist wandering in search of romance if a bitch is in heat in the neighborhood.

Collars and leads

Your dog should wear an identity tag with your name and address on it. A leather collar is probably best for everyday wear. The lead can be of leather or nylon.

You will need a certain amount of basic equipment for your new dog. Choose carefully from the range at the pet shop, and, if in doubt, ask your vet for advice.

Toys

Play is very important for dogs, especially puppies, and there is a wide range of toys available. Tug of war is always a popular game, and the dog pull allows both animal and owner to get a good grip. The fun ring can be used in this way too, and also as an object to be thrown and retrieved. Do not use sticks and stones for games of fetch; special toys such as rubber bones and large balls are much safer for the dog.

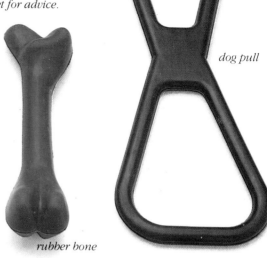

dog pull

rubber bone

leather collar with identity tag

fun ring

rubber ball

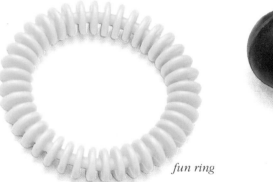

nylon lead

earthenware bowl

stainless steel bowl

Grooming kit

The basic equipment for grooming is a brush and a comb. Clean and dry these after use and do not let the dog chew them.

double-sided pin and bristle brush

wide-toothed comb

fine-toothed comb

Feeding and water bowls

Bowls come in three different materials. An earthenware bowl is heavy, and difficult to knock over, but will eventually chip or break. Stainless steel bowls are the least stable, and plastic bowls are cheap but can get chewed. Special deep bowls for long-eared breeds are also available; these prevent the dog dangling its ears in the food.

Purebred or mongrel?

Purebreds may well have the shape, proportions, and color that breeders intend and admire, but they are also heir to some unwelcome hereditary problems that go along with their aristocracy as surely as hemophilia ran through some of the royal houses of Europe. The long backs of Basset Hounds and Dachshunds are just asking for slipped-disc troubles; German Shepherds can have hereditary hip-joint disease; Irish Setters get problems in the retinas of their eyes more frequently than do many other breeds; the Bulldog is prone to skin disease between its loose folds of facial skin; the higher humidity of the floppy ears of spaniels can predispose them to canker infection; and there can be whelping difficulties in such flat-nosed breeds as the Pug. All of these complaints, of course, can and do crop up occasionally in mongrels, but they are just not as likely.

If you would be happy with a mongrel, look for advertisements in the pets' column of a newspaper or magazine, or contact the nearest dog welfare or rescue organization. Avoid pet shops or the sort of puppy farm that churns out animals like a sausage machine; they are so often reservoirs of serious disease. If it's a purebred you're after, look into the special needs and problems of the breed. Ask local vets about any particular health problems in local strains. Although a vet won't tell you anything about a breeder who happens to be one of his clients without his client's permission, he may well be able to point you in the right direction!

Try to make as many inquiries as you can before going to see a litter of puppies, and take along someone who has experience with that particular breed before making the purchase. Remember, it's not likely that you'll be given a champion, no matter what you pay. It is difficult with young puppies for anyone, even an expert, to spot a future star. Why you need your experienced companion is to make sure that you aren't palmed off with the runt of the litter, an animal with an imperfect set of teeth, or one that shows faulty congenital features such as white spots on a variety that should be all-black. True, the Poodle with one pale blue and one dark brown eye may have the cutest expression and it'll still make an attractive, robust pet, but you shouldn't be paying the price that a show-quality individual would fetch.

Ask to see the mother – she should give you an idea of how the puppies will develop. Never ignore the hereditary defects to which some breeds are prone. It is most important that you ask the breeder for written guarantees against any hereditary defects known in the breed.

What to look for

The main thing, assuming that you are not rescuing a homeless animal, is to ensure that the dog is fit. Make an agreement that you can return the puppy to the breeder if it is not healthy. Whatever you do, let the vet examine it as soon as possible (preferably before taking it home

EXAMINING A PUPPY

2 Lift the ear flaps to inspect the ear canals, which should be dry, clean, and free from crusty, scaly, or sticky deposits and discharges.

1 A healthy puppy with a good temperament is happy to be picked up. Its body should feel firm but relaxed, and it should show no sign of pain.

3 Gently part the lips to examine the tongue, gums, and teeth. The tongue and gums should be pink. The "bite" (relative position of upper and lower front teeth) is important, particularly in purebred dogs for showing. Consult an expert if in doubt.

The correct way to carry a puppy comfortably.

to meet the family, just in case...). When selecting a pup look for:
- lively, energetic behavior
- a firm, well-covered body, and no signs of pain when it is picked up
- clean nose, eyes, and ears with no signs of discharge – a clear drop of "water" from the nostrils is OK
- pink gums, tongue, and area inside the eyelids
- no sign of diarrhea – look at the stools if possible and make sure that the area around the anus and the hair of the legs is not fouled with loose droppings
- no spots, sores, or scales in the coat or on the hairless part of the stomach
- no cough.

If the vendor gives an excuse, such as: "He's just getting over a bit of a cold, but it's nothing," or "Don't worry about that tummy rash, you always get that in Tripehounds," prick up your ears. No matter how eminent the breeder, have the "cold" or "rash" checked out at once by the vet. Better still, postpone buying the puppy until the allegedly trivial ailment has cleared up.

If the dog is sold as having been vaccinated, make sure that you receive a certificate to that effect, signed by a registered vet. If there is any doubt about whether the animal has been vaccinated, have it done again to be sure. At two months old, dogs should be vaccinated against distemper, parvovirus, leptospirosis, hepatitis, kennel cough, and, at about five months old, rabies.

Of course, if you are taking in a stray or unwanted animal, things are slightly different. You may have to deal with an already sick or infirm individual. But you will be going into this relationship with your eyes open, and the vet will be able to advise you at the outset as to what problems you may have to face.

This pedigree Dachshund (left) may suffer from slipped discs; a mongrel (above) may be a naturally healthier proposition.

4 The eyes should be clear, bright, and free from discharges, tears, cloudiness, or opacity. The dog should be able to keep its eyes wide open, without excessive blinking. Avoid a puppy that paws at its eyes.

5 Run your hand against the grain of the coat and inspect the skin for sores, scaliness, or the black dust that betrays the presence of fleas.

6 Look under the puppy's tail to ensure that the anal area is not stained by liquid stools; this is clear evidence of diarrhea.

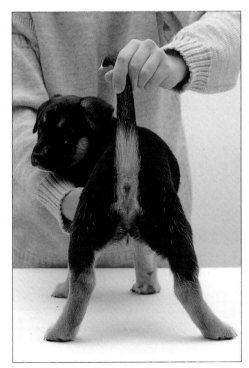

Diet

It would be a mistake to regard the dog family as narrow-minded carnivores. Foxes have a catholic taste that ranges through grubs, rodents, snakes, crayfish, mushrooms, acorns, and various sorts of fruit. The jackal augments its diet with vegetables, fruit, and sugar-cane. The bat-eared fox or fennec likes termites, and the Chilean Wild Dog eats shellfish.

Nutritional needs

Like its wild cousins, the domestic dog needs more than meat in its dish to keep it going. The principal nutritional requirements are:
• protein for body-building and repair
• carbohydrates for energy
• fats for energy and good health of skin and hair
• vitamins and minerals for certain essential chemical reactions in the body
• bulk for good digestive and bowel action
• water for all processes occurring everywhere in the body.

As a rule of thumb we can say that a dog needs the following amounts of calories daily at the different stages in its life:
• puppy 100 calories per lb (910kJ per kg) body weight
• adult 60 calories per lb (550kJ per kg) body weight
• geriatric 25 calories per lb (230kJ per kg) body weight.

These figures are calculated for moderately active animals.

Apart from age, degree of activity, environment, pregnancy, lactation, and disease, any of which markedly alters an animal's needs, we must never forget that all dogs are

chocolate-coated biscuits / beef and chicken treats / donut treats / bone-shaped biscuits

Experiment with a wide variety of treats and biscuits to see which your dog prefers.

individuals, and vary in their efficiency at processing foods. It is most important not to overfeed, and to reduce the size of meals at the first sign of obesity.

FOODS FOR DOGS

Dogs can eat all of the following foods, but, within reason, allowances can be made for your pet's personal taste.

Meat

Meat is low in calcium and rich in phosphorus. An all-lean-meat diet is

Snacks come in many flavors and shapes.

too low in fat and would be nutritionally unbalanced. Liver should not exceed five per cent of the total diet.

Fish

Packed with protein, minerals, and, in some cases, fats. Best fed cooked, and with the main bones removed.

Cheese and milk products

Rich in protein, fat, and minerals. Some dogs cannot digest lactose (milk sugar)

due to the absence of an enzyme in their body. This produces diarrhea and occasionally vomiting, but is not serious: simply take milk off the diet.

Cereals

Either as dog-meal or in biscuit form, these are an inexpensive source of energy, bulk, minerals, and some vitamins. Cooked rice is an excellent substitute for cereals.

Vegetables

Vegetables such as cabbage, carrots, and other root vegetables are valuable, either cooked or shredded raw, and also cooked potatoes.

Fruit

Dogs make their own vitamin C internally, but moderate quantities of fruit, if they like it, are beneficial from time to time.

Eggs

Whole egg should be fed cooked to avoid the effect of an anti-vitamin B factor present in raw egg-white.

Others

Nuts, edible seeds, and honey are all excellent additions to the diet. And if your dog insists on chewing and swallowing grass and herbs, let it, even if it vomits shortly afterwards. This is perfectly natural behavior. A word about

dry complete food

canned meat and dog-meal

semi-moist complete food

Three types of dog food; also available is a canned complete food that does not need dog-meal added to it.

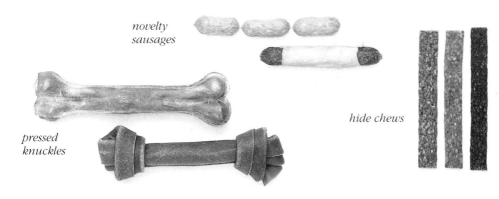

novelty sausages

hide chews

pressed knuckles

Dog-chews are better than bones for keeping teeth clean and free from tartar.

bones: no, they don't clean the teeth. They can cause problems such as constipation, or obstruction or perforation of the digestive tract. Give only uncooked bones of the broad, marrow-bone type.

WAYS OF FEEDING

Whether you buy dog food or make it up yourself, your dog must have a nutritionally balanced diet.

Do-it-yourself
The meat, scraps, and biscuit system is still popular, gives variety and may be economical. The daily intake of meat should be about $1/2$ oz per lb (30g per kg) body weight per day for young animals and $1/3$ oz per lb (20g per kg) for adults. Bear in mind that cooked scraps, including vegetables, may lack vitamins, which are destroyed by heat.

Commercial foods
Modern dog foods are generally very good, and you cannot go far wrong if you follow the feeding instructions.

Canned food
This is of two types, the wholly meaty kind that contains very little carbohydrate, and the complete diet that consists of meat, carbohydrates, fat, minerals, and vitamins in correct balance. The first kind is essentially conveniently packed, sterile meat with added vitamins, and to make a complete diet, dog-meal or biscuits must be added to it (see right).

The complete diet foods have been produced after careful nutritional research by the big pet-food companies, and you don't need to add anything to them to feed your dog properly.

Dry complete food
These pellets or biscuits of dried food contain meat and/or fish products together with carbohydrates, minerals, and vitamins. They are easy to store and the most economical of convenience foods. They are not to be confused with simple dog-meals or biscuits that are largely cereal in content and do not provide a complete diet. As ever, a plentiful supply of fresh water is essential.

Semi-moist complete food
This modern, highly processed food makes up a perfectly balanced diet. As value for money it falls between the dry and canned foods, but does not store as long as either.

Which diet to choose?
All diets have their advantages. There is no reason why you should not switch from one to the other according to your pet's fads and fancies. If you find that one type is well received by the dog and has no drawbacks, by all means stick to it. Remember always to prepare food freshly and to serve it in thoroughly cleaned dishes. Clean, fresh water should always be available.

The best idea is to split the daily requirement into two parts and feed twice. Nutrition isn't everything; why shouldn't your dog start the day with a full stomach and go to bed likewise? It is probably best to give the second meal at least an hour before bedtime.

HOW MUCH TO FEED?				
Dog weight	Canned meat*	Canned complete food	Dry complete food	Semi-moist complete food
11lb (5kg) Pekingese	8oz (225g)	14oz (400g)	5oz (150g)	6oz (170g)
22lb (10kg) Bedlington Terrier	13oz (370g)	27oz (760g)	9oz (250g)	10oz (285g)
44lb (20kg) Springer Spaniel	21oz (600g)	44oz (1250g)	14oz (400g)	16oz (450g)
88lb (40kg) German Shepherd	27oz (760g)	66oz (1875g)	23oz (650g)	27oz (760g)

NB *These figures are intended as an approximate guide only. Refer also to manufacturers' instructions on the packaging.*

Dog-meal or biscuits must be added to the canned meat in the ratio of 1:1 for small breeds, and up to 2:1 for large breeds.

Grooming

Grooming is necessary, not just to make your dog look good, but also as an important aid to skin health and hygiene, and in order to control parasites. Done regularly, it enhances your relationship with your dog, and although it takes time, patience, and sometimes a little effort, it should be a pleasurable experience for both groomer and groomed.

Begin grooming a pup at five to six weeks of age. Wiry-coated breeds can be trimmed lightly around head and tail from about four months. First baths may be given, if necessary, at three months of age or when puppies arrive from kennels.

The hair of the dog

A dog's coat comprises two main kinds of hair, the coarser primary or "guard" hairs of the outer coat, and the softer, shorter, secondary hairs of the undercoat. The hairs are rooted in skin follicles to which are connected sebaceous glands, which produce oil to give the coat its gloss and some degree of waterproofing and insulation.

The five main types of dog coat are: long; silky; smooth; non-shedding curly; and wiry. There are also some oddities such as the almost hairless Mexican Hairless Dog and the Hungarian Puli, which has a dense coat twisted into cords.

A coat hair grows to its optimum length, stops growing, and then is finally pushed out by a newly growing hair and lost. This process goes on continuously all over the dog's body, a natural balance of hairs in the three different phases being maintained.

Most breeds (but not Poodles, Kerry Blues, or Bedlington Terriers) change their coats twice a year, usually in spring and autumn. During this process a more pronounced loss of hair occurs, under the influence of changes in environmental temperature and length of daylight acting through the hormone-producing glands of the dog's body. Sometimes a dog will shed almost

Combs and brushes

Q-tips

double-sided pin and bristle brush

hound glove

toothbrush

wide-toothed comb

fine-toothed comb

slicker brush

permanently and this may be due to its body being deceived by artificial factors such as indoor heating and lighting. Diet and hormone irregularities may also be involved.

COAT TYPES

Long coats such as those of collies, Old English Sheepdogs, Newfoundlands, and Spitz-type dogs. Brush and comb the coat forwards towards the head and shoulders and then comb it back. Brush the flanks following the hair grain. These coats need extra combing when the dog is shedding. Bathing should be done in spring and autumn at least, with additional shampoos (wet or dry) during the year if necessary.

Silky coats such as those of Afghan Hounds, Maltese Terriers, Yorkshire Terriers, Lhasa Apsos, spaniels, setters, and Pekingese. These breeds demand a lot of attention. Afghans, spaniels, and setters must be stripped of dead hair and bathed regularly. Spaniels and setters also require regular trimming. Trim excess hair on spaniels' ears and paws, to keep them free of mud and foreign bodies such as grass seeds.

Smooth coats such as those of Boxers, Whippets, Smooth-haired Dachshunds, and Labradors. These are the easiest breeds to groom. A hound glove is all you need for the short coats (Whippet, Boxer, and Smooth-haired Dachshund), and the others require little more than a comb and a bristle brush. Don't bathe these dogs too often. After a bath it takes around six weeks for the natural oil in the coat to be replaced.

Non-shedding curly coats such as those of Bedlington Terriers, Poodles, and Kerry Blues. Although these dogs do not shed, they need a clip and a bath every two months or so. Check the ears frequently and pluck out excess hair growing in the ear canal (do not use scissors). Clipping of these breeds should first take place at fourteen to fifteen weeks old.

Wiry coats such as those of the Wire-haired Dachshund, Schnauzers, and most terriers. Give these dogs lots of regular combing to avoid matting. Strip and pluck the coat, and then bathe every three to four months. An alternative is to machine clip every six to eight weeks. Trim excess hair around the eyes and ears with blunt-ended scissors.

Unusual coats found on some exotic breeds need specialized attention – consult the breeder or your vet for advice. The coat of the Hungarian Puli (illustrated here) hangs in cord-like strands, and should not be combed if the dog is to be shown. Even virtually hairless breeds such as the Mexican Hairless Dog require regular gentle brushing.

Trimming equipment

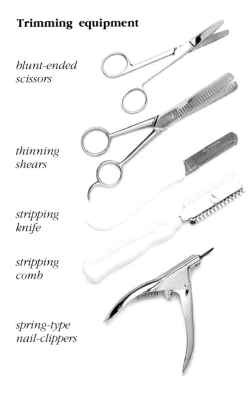

blunt-ended scissors

thinning shears

stripping knife

stripping comb

spring-type nail-clippers

Equipment

You must have a brush and comb at least, but a full grooming kit might consist of a pin brush, bristle brush, slicker brush, rubber brush, fine- and wide-toothed metal combs, a hound glove, a carder, blunt-ended scissors, nail-clippers, thinning shears, stripping comb, stripping knife, and a hairdrier. Q-tips for cleaning excess wax from the ears and a toothbrush for dental care are useful additions to the kit – see the section on Health Care for how to use them properly.

GROOMING A COCKER SPANIEL

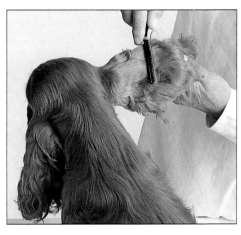

1 Break up the coat and untangle matted areas using a wide-toothed comb. Spaniels need special attention to the long, silky hair on their ears.

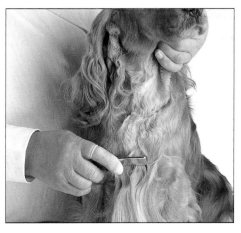

2 Use a fine comb under chin and tail and behind the ears. Carefully tidy up around paws and under tail with blunt-ended scissors.

3 Brush as appropriate for the breed. Follow the "hair grain" – lines of hair growth that run from the head down the back and sides to the legs and feet.

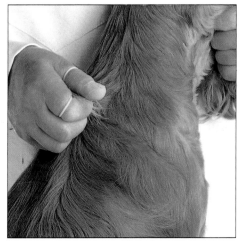

4 On silky and wiry coats, gently pluck out dead hairs from neck and back. Rubber finger cots as shown here help protect the fingers.

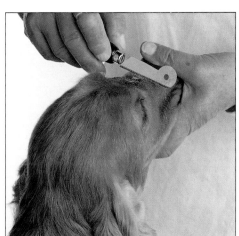

5 Professional groomers may use a stripping comb or stripping knife as shown here. They may also thin the coat if necessary, using thinning shears, before giving the dog a bath.

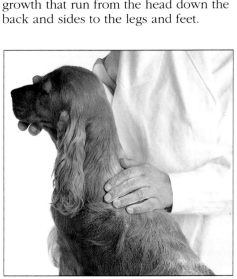

6 Bathe the dog (see following page) or use a dry shampoo, as shown here. Rub the powder into the dog's coat a section at a time and then brush out. Do the head last.

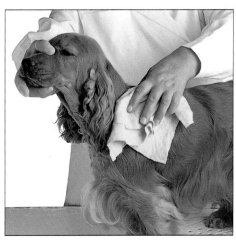

7 Give a final brush, rub down the coat with a damp chamois leather and then polish with a piece of silk or velvet. A special spray can be used to give a finishing sparkle for showing.

BATHING A DOG

When a dog is dirty or smelly it needs bathing, but this should not be done too often. Some dogs, such as Scotties, have a tendency to dandruff, and may need a bath once a month. Other breeds may only need bathing once or twice a year. Always groom the dog before bathing, and use special dog or baby shampoo, never household soap.

A dry shampoo is ideal for a quick clean-up if the coat is not badly fouled or smelly. It is a powder that is thoroughly dusted into the coat and then brushed out. Oily coats in particular benefit from the occasional dry shampoo.

1 Ensure that the water is warm but not hot before lifting the dog into the bathtub. You may need help to hold the dog still as you pour water liberally over its back and sides. Hold the dog around the muzzle in order to steady it.

2 Apply some shampoo along the back and work it well into the coat, moving down over the sides and legs. Wash the head last, taking care to keep shampoo out of the dog's eyes. The dog is most likely to shake when its head gets wet.

3 The next stage is to rinse out the shampoo, starting with the head and working backwards. Use plenty of water to rinse through the coat, and then go over the dog again, squeezing out the excess to leave it as dry as possible.

4 Lift the dog out of the bathtub and stand it on a bath-mat. You can either towel-dry it or use a hairdrier. If the dog is not used to hairdriers, it may take fright, so start from the front, where it can see what you're doing.

NAIL-CLIPPING

You may prefer to leave clipping of the dog's nails to the vet or a professional groomer, but if you are going to do it yourself, ask your vet to show you how. It is best to use the special spring-type clippers rather than the human "pliers" design. To avoid causing pain and bleeding, cut at least one-tenth of an inch (2mm) in front of the pink area (the quick) lying inside the nail. If in doubt be cautious, and leave more rather than less nail on the toe.

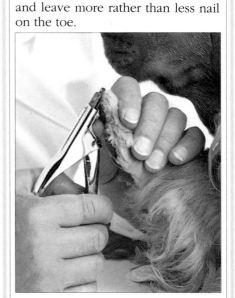

A puppy's nails should be clipped at 2-3 weeks old, to avoid them scratching the mother's belly skin with the "kneading" movements the feet make while the puppy suckles. It saves a lot of hard work later on if you accustom the dog to nail-clipping as a puppy.

BATHTIME KIT

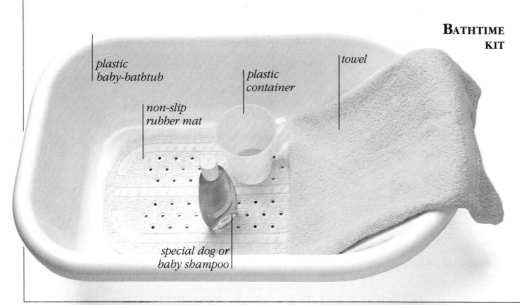

plastic baby-bathtub

non-slip rubber mat

plastic container

towel

special dog or baby shampoo

Traveling

The best way to avoid travel sickness is to accustom your dog to travel from puppyhood. Regular car journeys with something pleasant at the end of them, such as a long walk, generally condition the dog to enjoy the ride.

Car journeys

Large dogs are best in the back of a station wagon behind a dog grill or guard. Small dogs can go in special wire or fiberglass carrying crates, and cardboard carriers are useful for infrequent journeys. Puppies travel well in an ordinary cardboard box that is well padded and furnished with a hot-water bottle.

If sickness is a problem, ask your vet for travel-sickness pills. Sedatives are not a good idea as they can interfere with a dog's heat regulation. Very nervous and agitated animals can, however, be tranquilized with special drugs available from your vet.

Do not leave a dog alone in a car for a long time, especially in hot weather. Heatstroke, which is often fatal, can occur surprisingly easily. If the dog is not in a container, adjustable guards that fit inside the open windows are useful in preventing it from getting loose while assisting ventilation on warm days.

Before starting any journey, give the dog a chance to urinate and defecate.

Most dogs enjoy car journeys. The safest way to carry a large dog is behind a dog grill.

The animal should also have a drink and a snack about two hours before departure. Stop every two or three hours to give the dog an opportunity to have a drink and relieve itself. On very long trips, give a little more food after four or five hours.

Air travel

Over longer distances, air travel has advantages, since it is relatively cheap and its speed keeps the period of distress to a minimum. As with other travel, give the dog a small drink and a snack a couple of hours before departure. All dogs must travel in a container that complies with the regulations laid down by the International Air Transport Association (IATA). Some airlines have their own rules; avoid delays by finding out about such regulations and those of the countries between which the dog will be traveling well before departure.

Other IATA recommendations are:
• Snub-nosed dogs (Boxers, Bulldogs, Pekingese, and Pugs) must be free from respiratory troubles before traveling. Their containers must have open bars from top to bottom at the front end.
• Air travel is not recommended for bitches in heat.
• Nursing bitches and unweaned puppies are not acceptable for carriage.
• Weaned puppies younger than eight weeks should not be transported.
• Puppies may travel well together, although some countries insist that each animal is crated individually.
• A familiar article placed in the container helps to comfort a dog.
• The dog's name must be marked on the outside of the container.

International travel

If you intend to take your dog abroad, you must first find out about any regulations governing the importation of animals into the country of destination. There may be vaccination or quarantine requirements, and there will certainly be documentation needed including veterinary certification in the country of origin. It is your responsibility to obtain all necessary information and documentation from the appropriate embassies, consulates, or government departments, well before the date of travel.

CONTAINER SPECIFICATIONS

Containers for dogs traveling by air must conform to standards laid down by the IATA. Their minimum dimensions must be related to those of the dog as illustrated.

The container must display a "This Way Up" sticker as well as an IATA "Live Animals" label.

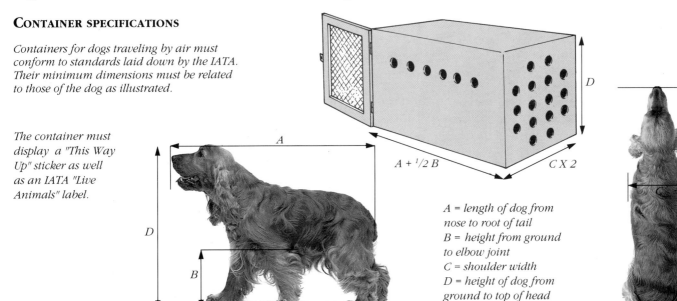

A = length of dog from nose to root of tail
B = height from ground to elbow joint
C = shoulder width
D = height of dog from ground to top of head

Training

Even if you do not aspire to having a pet with the skills of a seeing-eye dog or a champion sheepdog, you must accept that all dogs, like their owners, require a certain amount of training if they are to be civilized.

House-training

First, of course, there is the business of house-training a puppy. This should begin as soon as it starts on solid food, at around six weeks old. If you are at home for most of the day and the pup can easily be taken outside, do so when it wakes, after every meal, after every period of activity, when it hasn't urinated for some time, and, crucially, when it shows signs of wanting to. Don't carry it out – let it follow you to learn the route. At night put down newspapers by the outside door.

If you live in an apartment or are out for long periods during the day, confine the pup to one room where the floor can be covered with paper. The pup will soon pick one area that it prefers. Then remove the rest of the paper. Gradually move the paper until it is by the door. When the weather is fine, move the paper outside, and finally discard it altogether.

Clear up at once any accidental mess the puppy makes and spray the spot with a neutralizing aerosol. This prevents it from being attracted back to the same place and "triggered off" by lingering aromas to do the deed once more. Be patient – never punish a puppy for slowness in learning or for unfortunate lapses. On the other hand, make a great fuss of it whenever it performs correctly.

General training

If you are interested in specialized dog training as a hobby or as part of your work, there are many training clubs or organizations that you can join. But there are certain desirable things that all owners should teach their dogs to do. The best idea is to join a dog-training club or class, where dogs and owners can all learn together from an expert. You will find that this considerably enhances the relationship between you and your pet.

Begin training when the dog is between three and four months old. The puppy should be accustomed to behaving calmly and obediently when out and about with you. Don't stop for other dogs. Don't let it sniff lamp-posts. Only gradually introduce it to places with crowds and noisy traffic. Always use pleasant, reassuring, clear tones when talking to the dog.

It should be taught to heel by holding the lead firmly then shortening it so that the animal comes into position with its right shoulder beside your left leg. This is first practiced while you stand still. Then you do it at the walk, going in a straight line, and saying "heel" firmly when you start. Next come right turns, moving away from the dog so that the novice cannot become entangled with your legs, and finally left turns.

After learning to walk and heel correctly, the dog should be trained to sit on command, and also every time you come to a halt on a walk, for example, at the edge of a curb before crossing a road. During a walk in quiet surroundings, stop and press the dog gently but firmly into a sitting position with your hand on its back, just in front of the pelvis. As you do this say "sit". It will soon get the idea.

WALKING TO HEEL

With the lead held in your left hand, and the dog beside your left leg, start walking straight ahead. When the dog pulls in front, jerk the lead sharply back and say "heel" firmly. Praise the dog all the time it is in the correct position. The next stage is to practice first right-hand and then left-hand turns. Do not train for long periods without a rest for play and praise.

SIT

Teach the dog to sit when you come to a halt. Transfer the lead to your right hand, stroke your left hand down the dog's back, and push down on the rump to make it sit. Say "sit" and praise the dog when it obeys.

WAIT AND COME

SIT AND STAY

With the dog sitting, give the command "stay", and, keeping the lead taut, walk around the dog. If it tries to move, jerk the lead, and re-settle the dog. Give the command "sit – stay" with the signal shown, and walk in a wider circle. Over several training sessions you can continue to increase the distance until you are eventually out of sight. Always praise the dog when you return.

Sit and stay

Once the dog will sit on command, introduce the idea of "staying". Walk with it to heel and then make it sit. Hold the lead taut and vertical, command "stay", and walk round the dog. If it attempts to move give it a gentle yet firm jerk of the lead. As the dog begins to understand, slacken the lead and walk in a wider circle. Now give the command "sit – stay" without the lead, again gradually moving further away from the dog. Reinforce the verbal command with a clear visual signal by stretching out one arm towards the animal, palm of the hand outwards. Over successive training sessions you can progress to the next stages, which are to slacken the lead, to let it go altogether, to turn and walk away, and eventually to go out of sight. Always praise the dog lavishly when you return.

Teaching the dog to "wait and come" is best done using an extendable lead or by adding 10-15yd (10-15m) of nylon cord to an ordinary lead. The dog learns to wait the same way it learns to stay. When it sits correctly, command "wait", and turn and walk away. A few yards away, turn around and call the dog by name, with emphasis on the additional command word "come".

Other important techniques you may learn in a dog-training class are how to make the dog stop and lie down on command (which can be a matter of life or death if it is running towards a road), and how to make it defecate on command. If all dog-owners taught their charges these two techniques, the anti-dog lobby would have less cause for complaint, and much less public support.

When training, always keep a dog on the lead until it understands the commands, and never try to train a dog if you are in a bad mood. Do not let the dog get bored by training for too long without a break. Use a firm but gentle tone to give commands to a dog, and use the dog's name to gain its attention before giving the command. Remember that if a dog does not obey you, it is almost always because it has not been taught what is required of it. Hitting the dog will not help in any way.

In all training, bribery with tidbits should be used sparingly and not as a general rule. Praise and a short session of play is a much better reward for an obedient dog.

Using a long lead, get the dog to sit, then command "wait", and turn and walk away. A few yards away, turn, say "wait" again, and give the hand signal shown.

Call the dog to you by using its name and the additional command word "come". Guide it towards you with an open hand extended down towards the dog.

Shorten the lead as the dog approaches. Bring it to the correct position at your feet by drawing your hands up to waist level and giving the command "sit".

Showing

Showing dogs can be great fun and is a fascinating, though seldom financially rewarding hobby. For the serious amateur or professional breeder it is essential to prove the excellence of his or her stock.

The first proper dog show was held in 1859 at Newcastle-upon-Tyne in England and was open only to pointers and setters. Mr Cruft organized his first show in 1886, for terriers only, and his first general show was held in London in 1891. In the US, it all started in 1877 with the prestigious Westminster Dog Show of New York.

There are two types of dog show in the US, match shows and point shows.

Both are organized in a similar way. Wins at matches, however, carry no championship points.

Shows can also be benched or unbenched. Most shows today are unbenched, meaning that a dog is only required to be present while being judged. At a benched show, dogs have to remain in the individual stalls for a prescribed number of hours.

Champion dogs

Dogs and bitches are judged separately, except for Champions. Only dogs and bitches that have successfully completed their championship requirements are eligible to compete

Do not expect to win a trophy at your first show; only experience will bring success.

Train your dog to accept handling by strangers – the judge will appreciate it.

Competing in a large dog event can be a daunting and nerve-racking experience for both owner and dog – the secret is to relax and enjoy the show.

Some breeds need particular care over their grooming and preparation for a show. This Old English Sheepdog has had its whiskers and bangs tied back to keep them clean and dry.

Practice trotting with your dog at the speed that shows it off to best advantage.

Contestants at a local dog show get their Whippets into standing position ready for the judge's tour of inspection.

in this class, along with the overall winning dog and bitch from all the other classes.

To win a championship a dog must be awarded a total of fifteen points, under at least two different judges, with two of the wins each carrying three or more points. The number of points awarded for a win increases with the number of dogs competing in the show.

Classes offered at most shows are: Puppy, Novice, Bred by Exhibitor, American-Bred, and Open. Winners of these classes in each sex compete for Winners Dog and Winners Bitch. These two are the ones awarded points in each breed at a show.

Show procedure

Dog shows were originally established to determine the worth of a dog for breeding purposes. Today a show is as much a beauty contest as a test of a dog's quality. In order to win, a dog must be clean, thoroughly groomed, and looking its best.

Alteration of a dog, for example by tampering with the "bite" (set of the teeth), or surgically changing any part, except for ear and tail cropping as specified in the breed standards, suffers the penalty of disqualification.

Most match shows can be entered on the day of the match. Point shows must be pre-entered on forms provided by the club holding the show. About a week before the show you will receive your confirmation by mail, consisting of a judging schedule, ring number, and your entry slip.

You must take the entry slip with you to the show, as well as a show lead, grooming equipment, food (for you and the dog), feeding bowl, water (from the dog's usual supply), a chair for yourself, and some way of restraining the dog while you are waiting. Most exhibitors use wire, wood, fiberglass, or aluminum crates in which their dogs can rest and travel comfortably. At benched shows crates are permitted in the stalls, although some

exhibitors of the larger breeds prefer to use benching chains.

Before entering a show you should practice "gaiting" - trotting with your dog on a lead in order to show off its movement to the judges. It should also be used to standing in a show pose, and keeping still while it is handled.

SHOW CHECKLIST

- entry slip
- show lead
- crate (or benching chain for larger breeds)
- grooming equipment
- chair
- water (from dog's normal supply, in glass bottle)
- feeding bowl and food (for long days)

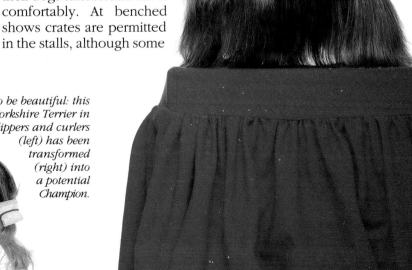

Suffering to be beautiful: this dowdy Yorkshire Terrier in slippers and curlers (left) has been transformed (right) into a potential Champion.

Health Care

An intricate machine needs a skilled mechanic. Do not tinker with your dog. The aim in this section of the book will be to explain some of the common symptoms, and what you should do about them, as well as giving tips on simple, useful first aid. Seek veterinary help for all but the mildest and briefest conditions. The basic principles behind the commoner diseases of dogs will also be outlined, together with the ways in which the vet treats these afflictions.

COMMON AILMENTS

Most common illnesses are easy to treat as long as they are diagnosed in time. It is important to keep an eye on your dog for signs of unusual behavior or signs of ill-health, and to contact the vet if these persist.

The mouth

Symptoms associated with mouth problems are salivating (slavering), pawing at the mouth, exaggerated chewing motions, signs of tenderness when chewing, and bad breath.

You can help prevent trouble by inspecting your dog's mouth regularly and cleaning the teeth once or twice a week with a soft toothbrush or cotton wad dipped in salt water (or special

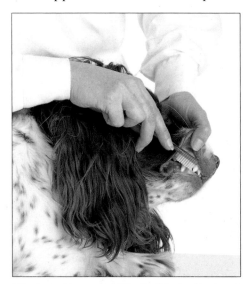

The best way to avoid the build-up of tartar on the teeth is to clean them once a week. Use a soft toothbrush or a cotton wad dipped in salt water (or special toothpaste for dogs).

doggy toothpaste), to prevent the build-up of troublesome tartar. This is a yellowy-brown, cement-like substance that accumulates on the teeth. It damages the edges of the gums, lets bacteria in to infect the tooth sockets, and thus loosens the teeth. Tartar always causes some gum inflammation and, frequently, bad breath. Giving your animal "dog chews" made out of processed hide can also help to keep tartar down to an acceptable level.

If your pet suddenly displays some of the symptoms described, open its mouth and look for a foreign body stuck between its teeth. With patience, you can usually flick such objects out with a teaspoon handle or similar blunt instrument.

Bright red edging to the gums where they meet the teeth is a sign of gingivitis. Tap each tooth with your finger or a pencil. If there are any signs of looseness or tenderness, wash out the mouth with warm, salty water, and give an aspirin. There is little else that you can do without calling for professional help.

Canine dentistry is easily tackled by the vet. Using tranquilizers or short-acting general anesthetics, he can remove tartar from teeth with special scrapers or ultrasonic scaling machines. Bad teeth must be taken out to prevent root abscesses and socket infection from causing problems – blood poisoning, sinusitis, or even kidney disease – elsewhere in the body. Fillings are rarely necessary.

Mouth ulcers, tumors, and tonsillitis also cause some of the symptoms listed above, and these will need veterinary diagnosis and treatment.

The eyes

Problems are indicated by sore, watering, or "mattery" eyes (producing a sticky discharge), and when a blue or white "film" appears over the eye.

If only one eye is involved and the only symptom is watering or sticky discharge, try washing the eye with warm human-type eyewash every few hours. A little antiseptic eye ointment can also be applied inside the lower

1 If the eye is sore or watering, irrigate it every 2-3 hours with warm, human-type eyewash or warm water squeezed from a cotton wad.

2 When administering eye-drops, steady your hand by resting it on the dog, and always approach from behind and above the eye. Keep the eye-dropper parallel to the surface of the eye, as shown.

lid. For safety's sake keep the tube parallel to the eye's surface at all times.

Particularly in young dogs, two mattery eyes may indicate the serious viral disease, distemper. Persistent watering of one or both eyes can be due to a slight infolding of the eyelid (entropion) or to blocked tear ducts. A blue or white film over one or both eyes is normally a sign of inflammation of the cornea (keratitis); it is not a cataract but requires immediate veterinary attention. Opacity of the lens (cataract) is a blue or white "film" much deeper in the eye. It usually occurs in older animals.

If any symptom in or around the eye lasts longer than a day, take the patient to the vet. Inflammations of the eye are treated in a variety of ways. Drugs are

It's true that a wet nose like this is a sign of a healthy dog, but a persistently runny nose can be a sign of trouble.

used to reduce inflammation and surgical methods to tackle ulcerated eyes under local anesthesia. Many problems can be treated surgically nowadays; these include infolding or deformed eyelids, foreign bodies embedded in the eyeball, and even some cataracts.

The nose

Common symptoms of an unhealthy nose are a cracked, sore, dry nose-tip or running, mattery nostrils and the appearance of having the human common cold. The dog with a "cold", particularly if both eyes and nose are mattery, may well have distemper.

To relieve the symptoms you can help prevent the nostrils getting caked and clogged up. Bathe them thoroughly with warm water and anoint the nose pad with a little petroleum jelly. If there is the "common cold" symptom, seek veterinary advice at once.

The ears

Symptoms associated with ear problems are shaking the head, scratching the ear, a bad smell or discharge from the ear, tilting the head to one side, ballooning of the ear flap, and the dog showing signs of pain or discomfort when the ear is touched.

Where symptoms suddenly appear, an effective and soothing emergency treatment is to swab the ear with a mixture of alcohol and water. Do not use so-called canker powders; these can cause annoying accumulations that act as foreign bodies, and may even worsen the irritation.

See the vet immediately if your dog develops ear trouble. Chronic ear complaints can be very difficult to cure and need early treatment.

Clean your dog's ears often, once a week if it is prone to ear trouble. Using twists of cotton moistened in warm water and alcohol or a commercial ear rinse, clean the part of the ear that you can see with a twisting action to remove excess brown ear wax. If it is a breed with hair growing in the ear canal (such as a Poodle or a Kerry Blue), pluck out the hair between finger and thumb. Do not cut it. (Ask your vet to show you how to do this.)

Ear irritation may be due to various things that find their way into the ear canal. Grass seeds, for example, may need professional help to remove them. Small, barely visible white ear mites that live in dog's ears cause itching and allow bacteria to set up secondary infections. Sweaty, dirty conditions, particularly in the badly ventilated ears of breeds such as the spaniels, provide an ideal opportunity for germs to multiply. The vet will decide whether mites, bacteria, fungi, or other causes are the main source of inflammation and will prescribe accordingly. Where chronically inflamed ears are badly in need of drainage, surgery under anesthetic is often necessary.

Although tilting of the head may be due simply to severe irritation on one side, it can indicate that the middle ear is involved. Middle-ear disease does not necessarily result from outer-ear infection, but may arise from trouble in the Eustachian tube that links the middle ear to the throat. It always needs rigorous veterinary attention, involving the use of antibiotics, anti-inflammatory drugs, and, in rare cases, deep drainage operations.

The ballooning of an ear flap looks dramatic but isn't. It is really a big blood blister, caused by a rupture of a blood vessel in the ear flap. It generally follows a bite from another dog or over-vigorous scratching of an itchy ear. Surgical treatment is necessary.

EAR CARE

1 To avoid ear problems, remove excess wax regularly. Use a cotton wad or Q-tips moistened in warm water and alcohol. Do not probe the ear - clean only the part that you can see.

2 If ear trouble suddenly erupts, contact the vet. A soothing temporary remedy is to swab the ear with a mixture of water and alcohol. It is sometimes easier to use a dropper or syringe rather than a swab.

3 Replace the flap and massage gently to work the soothing liquid into the deeper recesses of the ear. Inspect the ear again and clean up any wax that comes to the surface with a cotton wad or Q-tips.

The chest

The signs of chest problems include coughing, wheezing, and labored breathing. Dogs can suffer from bronchitis, pleurisy, pneumonia, heart disease, and other chest conditions. Coughing and sneezing, the signs of a "head cold", possibly together with mattery eyes, diarrhea, and listlessness, may indicate distemper. Dogs sometimes do recover from this, though the outlook is grave if there are symptoms such as fits, uncontrollable limb twitching (chorea), or paralysis, which are signs that the nervous system is affected. These may not appear until many weeks after the virus first invades the body, and can be, in some cases, the only visible symptoms.

In order to avoid problems, have your dog vaccinated against distemper and other important infectious canine diseases at the first opportunity, and make sure it gets annual booster doses.

At the first signs of illness contact the vet. Keep the animal warm, give it plenty of fluids and provide easily digestible and nourishing food. If it is too weak to eat, try spoon-feeding it human baby food, or a solution of glucose and water.

The vet can confirm or deny the presence of distemper or other infectious disease. Since it is caused by a virus, distemper is difficult to treat. Antibiotics and other drugs are useful in suppressing secondary bacterial

Vaccination of puppies against distemper is safe and effective, with side-effects being rare. The first shot should be given at 6-9 weeks, with a second 2-4 weeks later, and an annual booster to keep immunity high.

infections. Distemper antiserum, although now widely available, is rarely useful as a cure; its main value is in helping to protect animals that have been in contact with the disease and are at risk of infection.

Other types of chest disease can be investigated by the vet using stethoscope, X-rays, laboratory tests, and electrocardiographs. Heart disease is common in elderly dogs and often responds well to drug treatment.

The stomach and intestines

The commonest symptoms of stomach and intestine trouble are vomiting, diarrhea, constipation, and blood in the droppings. There are many possible causes, and any symptom persisting longer than twelve hours despite

sensible first-aid treatment needs veterinary attention.

Vomiting may be due to a mild infection of the stomach (gastritis) or to simple food poisoning. If severe, persistent, or accompanied by other major signs, it can indicate the presence of serious conditions such as distemper, leptospirosis, contagious canine hepatitis, heavy worm infestation, or obstruction of the intestine.

Diarrhea may be nothing more than a mild bowel upset. It may be serious and profuse if bacteria or serious viruses are present, also in certain types of poisoning and some allergies.

Constipation can be due to age, to a faulty diet that includes too much crunched-up bone (which sets like cement in the bowel), or to obstruction.

Blood in the stools can arise from a variety of minor and major causes: from nothing more serious than a bone splinter scraping the rectal lining to a dangerous infection.

GIVING MEDICINE

There are several techniques for giving pills to a dog:
• gently pry open the mouth by lifting the upper jaw, holding the dog's lips over its teeth to prevent it biting; place the pill as far back on the tongue as possible, then close the mouth and massage the throat to encourage the dog to swallow it
• cover the pill in honey, butter, or some other sticky, tasty substance to make it more palatable
• cut a slit in a piece of meat and insert the pill before giving it to the dog
• crush the pill in flavored milk and give to the dog as a liquid medicine (see right). (Note that some pills must be given whole; check with your vet.)

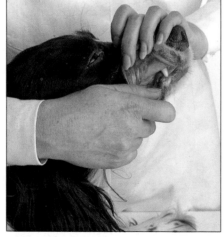

1 To administer liquid medicine, lift the dog's chin up, and gently part a pouch at the side of its mouth.

2 Pour the medicine into the pouch. It may be easier to use a dropper, syringe, or bottle, rather than a spoon.

"BLOAT" — GASTRIC DILATION AND TORSION

This is a major emergency caused by a sudden accumulation of gas or fluid in the stomach. The stomach distends and may twist, cutting off inlet and outlet passages, and the blood supply to the stomach and spleen. The only course of action is to contact the vet

The symptoms of bloat are a sudden swelling of the stomach in the flank, accompanied by severe pain and collapse. The dog will die of shock if a vet does not intervene at once.

and get the dog to the vet's clinic as fast as possible. Bloat occurs typically in large, deep-chested breeds over two years old that are allowed to exercise immediately after eating. Research into this problem continues, but possible precautions against bloat are to feed the same amount of food divided up into smaller portions two or three times a day, and to avoid exercising the dog or any vigorous play immediately before and for 2-3 hours after a meal.

All you can do in the event of stomach trouble is to try to alleviate the symptoms. With both vomiting and diarrhea, it is important to replace liquids lost by the body. Cut out solid food, milk, and fatty things. Give small and frequent doses of fluid – best of all are glucose and water or weak bouillon-cube broth. Ice-cubes can be supplied for licking. Keep the animal warm and indoors. For vomiting give 1-3 teaspoonsful (5-15ml), depending on the dog's size, of a human-type antacid dyspepsia emulsion every three hours. For diarrhea give 2-8 teaspoonsful (10-40ml) of a human-type kaolin mixture every three hours.

Give constipated animals 2-8 teaspoonsful (10-40ml) of mineral oil. If an animal is otherwise well but you know or suspect it to be clogged up with something like bone, it is safe to administer one of the small, disposable, ready-loaded, human-type enemas available at the drugstore.

Abdominal conditions in general need veterinary attention; if symptoms persist contact the vet no later than the following day. Diseases such as parvovirus infection, contagious canine hepatitis, and corona virus require intensive medical treatment with antibiotics, transfusions to replace fluids, vitamins, and minerals, and careful monitoring of progress by blood and urine tests.

Surgical techniques to remove obstructions and foreign bodies and to remedy other stomach complaints are now highly sophisticated. The vet and his team use modern anesthetics and operate in surgical theaters equipped with most of the hi-tech apparatus of a human hospital.

Anal glands

Two little glands, one on each side just within the anus, cause a lot of irritation for dogs. Owners complain of their dogs rubbing their bottoms along the floor (known as "scooting") or suddenly chasing their rear ends as if stung by a bee. Worms are often blamed, but are rarely the cause. The anal glands are at the root of the problem, since they tend to get blocked up and impacted. If they become infected, anal abscesses can result. This means antibiotic therapy and, in chronic cases, surgical removal of the glands.

It may help to avoid problems if the dog exercises the glands by producing bulky motions. Add fiber in the form of vegetables or bran to the diet. Learn from the vet how to clean out the glands by squeezing them with a pad of cotton (see below).

EMPTYING ANAL GLANDS

The dog has two anal glands, located one on each side of the anus. Their purpose is to add a scented fluid to the dog's stools to help them in marking out their territory. Now the dog is domesticated they are no longer needed for survival, but they can cause problems. Swollen glands need to be emptied; they can be felt bulging below the surface of the skin. Ask your vet to show you how to do this before you attempt it yourself. The dog may need to be muzzled, and possibly restrained by an assistant. A foul-smelling fluid should be ejected from the anus. If this does not happen, or the glands are very swollen or obviously infected, take the dog to the vet.

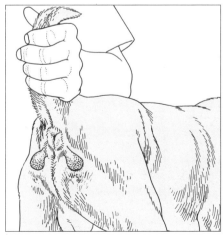

1 Hold the tail up out of the way. Wear rubber gloves and hold a large pad of cotton in the palm of your hand to catch the fluid.

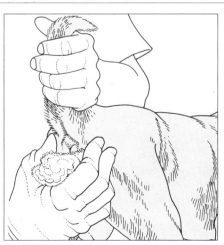

2 Place your thumb and forefinger in the nine and three o'clock positions as shown, and gently but firmly squeeze together and inwards.

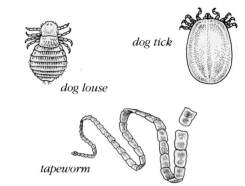

dog tick

dog louse

tapeworm

TAKING THE TEMPERATURE

The best method is to obtain an electronic thermometer and to follow the directions that come with it. Failing that, use a conventional thermometer with a stubby bulb.

• Shake the mercury down to 98.6°F (37°C) and lubricate the bulb with mineral oil or petroleum jelly.

• Holding the base of the dog's tail firmly to prevent it sitting down, insert one-third of the thermometer's length into the dog's rectum.

• Remove after three minutes, wipe clean, and read the temperature.

Normal temperature in dogs, measured in this way, is around 101°F (38.5°C). (Note that if the thermometer should break, do not attempt to remove the broken section from the rectum; contact your vet immediately.)

Urinary system

Common signs of urinary problems are difficulty in passing urine, excessive drinking and frequent urination, loss of weight and appetite, and blood in the urine.

As soon as you notice something may be wrong with your dog's waterworks, contact the vet. Inflammation of the bladder (cystitis), stones in the bladder or associated tubes, and kidney disease are all too common, and need immediate professional advice. Whatever you do, don't withhold water from an animal with a urinary problem. Fresh water should always be available to all dogs, sick or healthy, and the water bowl should be cleaned regularly.

Cystitis, diagnosed early, responds well to treatment with antibiotics. A diagnosis of stones in the urinary system can be confirmed by X-ray, and in most cases they can be easily removed by a surgical operation.

Kidney disease needs careful management and supervision of diet. Chronic kidney disease patients can live to a ripe old age if the water, protein, and mineral content of the diet is regulated, bacterial infection controlled, protein loss minimized, and stress of any sort avoided.

Genitalia

The male has genital problems from time to time (testicle tumors etc.), but the most important and common problems are found in the female; they include persistent heat, heavy bleeding, and vaginal discharge.

Any discharge apart from just prior to whelping or ordinary bleeding while in heat calls for immediate veterinary attention. In non-pregnant bitches the discharge, though looking like pus, is rarely caused by infection. It is usually one of the signs of a hormonal womb inflammation known as pyometra; see the vet at once. He may recommend medical treatment in the short term, but eventually surgical removal of the womb (hysterectomy) will be advisable. This major operation has a high success rate, but to avoid such emergencies, have the bitch spayed as soon as you decide that you do not want her to have any more puppies.

Mammary glands

From time to time turn your bitch over and run your hands along her underside. If you feel any hard lumps in the substance of the breast tissue, within the teats, or just under the skin, see the vet at once. Breast tumors, once established, spread quickly to other parts of the body. Caught early they can be removed surgically.

Inflamed, hard breasts when a bitch is producing milk may indicate the onset of mastitis, which can be treated with anti-inflammatory and anti-bacterial drugs. Sometimes the vet will stop the supply of milk by prescribing hormone tablets.

The skin

There are many kinds of skin diseases in dogs. Diagnosis needs examination and often sample analysis by the vet. Common symptoms include thin or bald patches in the coat, scratching, and wet, dry, or crusty sores. Mange, caused by an invisible mite, can cause crusty, hairless sores, and fleas, lice, and ticks can also cause damage to the coat. The presence of just one flea on a dog – terribly difficult to track down – may set up widespread skin irritation as an allergic reaction to the flea's saliva. Dietary faults such as a shortage of certain fats can also produce a poor, unhealthy-looking coat.

If you see or suspect the presence of any of the skin

Examine your bitch's breasts at least once a month for lumps that may indicate tumors. Tell your vet if you find any swellings larger than a quarter of an inch (0.5cm) across.

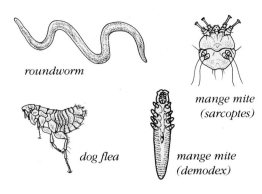

roundworm

dog flea

mange mite (sarcoptes)

mange mite (demodex)

parasites – mange mites, fleas, ticks, or lice – obtain one of the anti-parasite aerosols, powders, or baths from a pet shop, drugstore, or vet. In the case of mange, there are several types, so let the vet advise on treatment.

Ringworm is a subtle ailment and may need ultraviolet light examination or fungus culture from a hair specimen. Special drugs given by mouth or applied to the skin are needed; and care must be taken to ensure that humans do not pick up the disease from pets.

With all anti-parasite treatments, follow the instructions on the label of the preparation being used. With fleas, remember that the flea eggs are to be found not only on the animal's coat but also in its environment. Dog baskets, bedding, kennels etc. must be sprayed with anti-parasite aerosol at the same time as the animal is treated.

Skin disease caused by dietary deficiencies is easily avoided by providing balanced meals. Sore, wet "hot spots" that develop suddenly in summer or autumn may be caused by

an allergy to plant pollen and other substances. Clip the hair over and around the affected area level with the skin and apply topical medication as prescribed by your vet. Such cases will probably require treatment involving antihistamine or corticosteroid creams, injections, or tablets. Though the sores look dramatic, they are quickly cured.

Roundworms

These can cause looseness of the bowel and upsets, particularly in puppies. They can spread to humans and harm babies severely.

Rid your dog of roundworms by giving one of the modern worming drugs available from the vet or pet shop at regular three-month intervals throughout its life.

Tapeworms

These worms do not usually cause much trouble to dogs but can sometimes spread to humans. They spend part of their life-cycle in fleas, which is how they get into dogs.

Avoid tapeworm problems by keeping your dog free of fleas. Tapeworm segments look like grains of boiled rice or off-white bits of flat tape up to half an inch (1cm) long, and may move a little. If you see them in the stools or stuck to the hair round the anus, give the dog a dose of one of the modern tapeworm drugs available from the vet or pet shop.

RESTRAINING A DOG

If there is any danger of the dog biting, it should be muzzled before anyone attempts to treat it. Use the technique shown at right. Even when muzzled, the dog will probably need restraining as well, and the correct way to do this varies according to the size of dog. A small dog can be grasped firmly by the collar and scruff of the neck. A medium-sized dog should be held as at left, with head gripped in the crook of the arm and foreleg raised off the ground. Use your body weight to lean on a larger dog, using the same technique; you may also need the help of an assistant to hold the hindquarters.

MUZZLING A DOG

Any dog that is frightened or in pain may bite. This muzzling technique allows you to use a length of tape, bandage, or almost any type of material to make the dog safe.

1 Make a loop in the material and place it over the dog's muzzle.

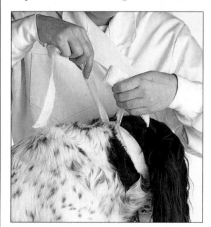

2 Cross the ends of the material under the dog's chin and secure in a knot behind the head.

3 The dog's jaws are now effectively and painlessly immobilized.

ACCIDENTS & EMERGENCIES

An injured, frightened dog may bite. Muzzling is the quickest, easiest way to avoid anyone else getting hurt. After that, get the victim away from danger and into a warm, quiet place indoors. Slip a sheet underneath the dog and carry it as in a hammock, or, failing that, by the scruff of the neck. Do not waste time; shock is your principal adversary. Lay the dog comfortably on a blanket and place a warm hot-water bottle next to it. Do not give alcoholic stimulants. Do not give aspirin. You may try to spoon-feed a few teaspoonsful of warm, sweet tea. Place a thick pad of cotton or a folded towel on any areas of heavy bleeding and press firmly – if necessary until the vet arrives. Do not try splinting limbs or experimenting with tourniquets.

Remember that it saves time to be doing all this in a car on the way to the vet's clinic, rather than waiting for the vet to come to you.

Bites and wounds

As soon as you detect a wound, clip the hair around its edges down to the skin with scissors. Bathe the area thoroughly in a strong (saturated) solution of Epsom salts (magnesium sulphate) in warm water. Apply some antiseptic cream or powder to any minor injury that does not appear to

All old dogs can benefit from daily multivitamin supplements; these can be given in pill, powder, or liquid form.

need professional attention. With a bite, however, a long-acting shot of antibiotic from the vet is a prudent measure. Minor wounds should be left open to the air, without any dressing.

Cut paw pads are troublesome but not serious. They heal slowly and are often not stitchable. Cover the paw with a child's cotton sock after cleaning the cut and applying antiseptic ointment. Do not tie on a waterproof dressing such as a plastic bag, and never fix a foot dressing with a rubber band. The dressing must allow air through, and should be held by a strip of adhesive tape or by a few turns of narrow bandage.

THE OLD DOG

Like their owners, dogs are living longer nowadays, but few pass seventeen (equivalent to eighty-four human years). Special consideration needs to be given to the care of dogs when they enter their teens, and all older animals will probably benefit from a daily multivitamin supplement.

Signs to watch for

Overweight animals won't live as long as they might. Obesity leads to heart trouble, liver inefficiency and diabetes. It is wise when contemplating the slimming of an extremely overweight animal to consult the vet first. He may recommend a special obesity diet.

Some older dogs go the other way and lose weight. A common cause is failing kidneys that "leak" body protein away into the urine. You will need veterinary advice in caring for such a dog, but special diets are available.

The kidneys are often among the first organs to show the effects of old age in the dog. There are many reasons for this, but the risk of kidney disease may well be reduced if a dog's health is carefully maintained throughout its life, and especially if its immunity to infectious diseases is kept high with regular vaccinations.

True rheumatism is uncommon in animals, but arthritis frequently occurs in various forms. As with humans there is no absolute cure, but much can be done to relieve pain, keep the joints moving, and reduce lameness. At the first signs of "bad running", let the vet examine your dog. A whole range of anti-arthritic medicine, from gold injections to corticosteroids, from acupuncture to anti-inflammatory chemicals, is now being used to tackle the problem in dogs.

MOVING AN INJURED DOG

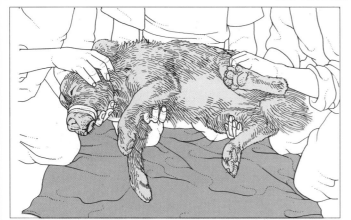

1 After an accident, the first priority is to move the dog away from immediate danger. Use a flat piece of board, if possible, as a stretcher, or, failing that, a towel, blanket, or coat. Get other people to assist you to help support the dog and to avoid bending its spine, and take care to be as gentle as possible.

2 The dog will receive treatment more quickly if you notify the vet and take the dog to the clinic yourself, rather than calling out the vet. When lifting the dog into a vehicle, make sure someone gets in first to steady the stretcher and avoid jolting the dog or bending its spine.

Owners should reduce their dog's food intake at the first sign of obesity. Over-feeding seriously reduces a dog's life expectancy.

Bowels

In later years the bowels may become sluggish, unpredictable, or loose. Make sure that you provide plenty of bulk in the diet: fibrous vegetables and wholewheat bread, for example. Do not give much liver, and do not give any bones at all.

EUTHANASIA

When the time comes, you may be lucky enough to have your pet die quietly in its sleep. If not, as a responsible, loving owner, you must be prepared to give it a dignified end. You should discuss euthanasia with your vet when an animal is in pain that cannot be easily relieved, or when it is incapacitated or in any way prevented from leading a normal life.

The best method of euthanasia is by overdosage of one of the anesthetic chemicals, usually barbiturates, administered by your vet. This is a peaceful end; once the dog is unconscious, its pain and infirmities are blotted out forever.

All the above applies equally to even the youngest puppy.

Smells

Old dogs may become somewhat odorous. The commonest source is the mouth. Don't waste your money on deodorant tablets that contain chlorophyll, and which are only a temporary cure, but take the dog to the vet, who can check the mouth and clean up the gums and teeth.

Other sources of smell in old animals are ears and rear ends. Look out for infection, particularly in breeds with floppy ears such as spaniels. When a dog is getting forgetful as to how to pass a stool neatly, see that its hindquarters are kept free of long hair that might become soiled.

A general deterioration in the coat of the elderly dog, with the production of more scurf and grease, may be the cause of the characteristic "old dog" smell. In that case bathe the dog every couple of weeks in a human-type shampoo that contains selenium.

A VETERINARY EXAMINATION

The vet will visually, and by handling, appraise the dog's condition, weight, and demeanor, and will check for points of tenderness or pain. He or she may also:

• take the temperature anally.

• feel the dog's abdomen to assess the size, position, and condition of certain major internal organs.

• examine heart and lungs using a stethoscope, and also perhaps by tapping the chest wall with the fingertips.

• inspect other special areas such as feet, anus, genitalia, and stomach skin.

• look in the outer ears for evidence of disease.

• visually examine eyes, nose, and mouth, pulling the eyelid down to check the color of the eye membrane, and opening the mouth to inspect the teeth, gums, tongue, and throat.

If further investigation is needed, the vet may suggest special tests or diagnostic techniques.

Reproduction

One of the greatest pleasures for some dog-lovers is to have their bitch give birth to a litter of puppies. Even if you don't intend to breed from your dog, you should know something about dog reproduction.

The canid family as a whole are seasonal breeders, and generally have one litter a year following a pregnancy period that ranges from seven weeks in the bat-eared fox, or fennec, to nine weeks in the domestic dog, and up to a possible eleven weeks in the African Wild Dog. The latter species also delivers the largest litters (up to sixteen young at a time) known in any carnivorous mammal.

Domestic dogs differ from wild dogs in that the females usually come into heat twice a year. They are also generally promiscuous, although there is evidence that the Beagle shows a degree of mate preference. Wolves, jackals, and coyotes, on the other hand, show strong mate preference and fidelity, and rarely indulge in promiscuity under normal, free-living conditions.

It was by manipulation of the reproductive processes of the dog, and with the benefit of pregnancy and maturation periods that are not very long compared to some other mammals, that man engineered the development of the wide variety of dog breeds we see today. With selective breeding now largely angled towards the esthetic preferences of the show judge, it may well be that the great days of dog breeding are over.

Sex and Heredity

Breeding for showing depends on the workings of the fundamental mechanisms of heredity. Living bodies are composed of cells and within each cell lies a nucleus. The nucleus contains, among other things, a number of structures called chromosomes. These resemble microscopic strings of beads, the beads being called genes. Each gene on a chromosome string carries details of the design, size or function of some particular part of the body, printed in the form of a remarkable chemical called DNA. Physical characteristics, such as eye color, ear shape, and coat length, are determined by genes.

The chromosome blueprint

The genes are arranged in a certain order along the length of the chromosomes, which together form a blueprint of the total make-up of an individual creature. The chromosomes are arranged in pairs in the nucleus. Each cell nucleus contains the same set of chromosome blueprints, so that, whether it be a cell from the liver, a tooth, or a paw pad, it has within it a complete plan of the whole body. Domestic dogs carry seventy-eight chromosomes arranged in pairs of thirty-nine, compared with pairs of nineteen chromosomes in the cat and pairs of twenty-three in the human.

When dog cells multiply by splitting into two, the seventy-eight chromosomes produce seventy-eight identical copies of themselves by dividing lengthways. Thus the genetic information is passed on from generation to generation.

Thirty-eight of the thirty-nine pairs of chromosomes in a cell nucleus are virtually identical pairs, but one may differ slightly. This is the pair that determines the sex of the individual. Females carry a pair of "XX" chromosomes, while males carry one "X" and one "Y" chromosome. The reproductive germ cells of the body, the eggs in the female and the

MATING

The best time to mate is generally on the tenth day of the bitch's heat period, and again on the twelfth day, although this varies from bitch to bitch. Things go better if at least one of the mating pair has some experience.

1 Let the dogs get acquainted if they are strangers - here the bitch is playfully nipping the dog's legs to indicate her interest in mating.

2 After some exploratory sniffing and licking by the dog, the bitch signals her readiness to mate by standing with her tail held to one side.

5 If the bitch is not steadied by her owner, she may damage the dog with her struggles. This is the correct position for the tie, back to back.

6 After about 20 minutes, on average, the tie is broken, the dogs part, and both retire to lick themselves clean.

spermatozoa in the male, are unique among all the cells of the body in having only one set of chromosomes (thirty-nine) instead of pairs. This means that when they fuse together at the moment of conception, standard chromosome pairs are formed, each pair consisting of one chromosome from the male and one from the female. All the sex chromosomes of a female are "X", whereas the sex chromosomes of a male can be "X" or "Y". Thus the sex of a puppy is dependent on whether an "X" or "Y" sperm is the first to penetrate the egg of the female.

The fertilized egg contains the genes of both mother and father in equal amounts but arranged in a slightly different order along the chromosome string. It is this new arrangement that gives each fertilized egg its individuality and makes the puppy that grows from it unique.

Mutations

Occasionally outside factors can alter the fundamental characters of genes within a cell nucleus. Atomic radiation, X-rays, and certain chemicals can do this, and the changes they cause in the body that develops from the cell are called mutations. This is why sex organs have to be specially protected against, for example, excessive ionizing radiation. Sometimes, though very rarely, a gene mutation occurs apparently spontaneously. These events lie at the very core of the evolutionary process and result in the sudden emergence of new breeds, colors, and types of dog.

Apart from mutations, non-genetic, non-hereditary processes can influence development of the embryo after its conception. Cells arrange themselves in the growing tissues in a slightly imprecise fashion and this type of congenital but non-hereditary variability results in modifications such as the unpredictable distribution of white patches on a particolor or pied coat. Again certain chemicals and forms of radiation may affect the arrangement of growing cells in the embryo, and this is why pregnant bitches should only be given medicines under the supervision of a vet.

3 The dog mounts the bitch, clasping her around the loins with his forelegs. He makes thrusting motions and releases his semen within a minute.

4 After ejaculation of the semen, the dog's penis expands to lodge itself in the vagina. This is the "tie", and the bitch may try to escape.

7 After a thorough clean-up, the dogs may join each other to play together, or just rest peacefully.

Pregnancy and Birth

The bitch usually becomes sexually mature somewhere between eight and twelve months old. It may be as early as six months in some cases, or be delayed until eighteen months. If a bitch has not had her first heat period by twenty months old, consult a vet.

Coming into heat

A heat is generally eighteen to twenty-one days long although the bitch will only accept the dog and conceive during a few days around the middle of the heat period. The first stage of heat is indicated by puffiness of the lips of the vulva. Soon, bleeding begins (this is not equivalent to the menstrual period in human females). While she is bleeding, which may last from four to fourteen days (ten days on average), the bitch is highly attractive to dogs but will not accept their advances.

Following this stage, the bleeding diminishes or ceases altogether, the vulva attains maximum enlargement, and the bitch will accept the dog. This is the fertile period, and it lasts from five to twelve days, with sexual desire at its height during the first two or three days. This is the time to let mating take place if you are planning to have puppies. Mating should be repeated two days later to increase the chance of a successful fertilization. If a bitch conceives, the heat period tends to end sooner than otherwise.

In the domestic dog, heat normally occurs twice a year, except in Basenjis, which, like the wild dogs, wolves and foxes, have only one sexual cycle per year. Most bitches have a spring heat in January-March, with the autumn heat in August-September. Exceptions frequently occur, however, and some bitches may have longer or shorter intervals between heats.

Hormones, given by mouth or injection, can be used to halt a heat, to postpone it, or to suppress the sexual cycle altogether. Be guided by your vet's advice if you are considering using hormones in this way on your bitch.

Pregnancy

Before being bred, a bitch should be checked by a vet to ensure that she is free of all external and internal parasites, and up-to-date on all vaccinations. The length of pregnancy averages around sixty-three days. Swelling of the abdomen becomes more noticeable from the fifth week onwards, though if only one or two pups are being carried, or the bitch is plump anyway, this sign of approaching maternity may be difficult to spot.

The breasts enlarge and the teats become larger and pinker from about the thirty-fifth day of pregnancy. A watery secretion can be drawn from the teats three or four days before the pups are born. In bitches that have had several litters, enlargement of the breasts may not begin until the last week of pregnancy, and true milk can often be produced as early as five or six days before the start of labor.

During a bitch's pregnancy you should feed her extra quantities of high-quality food, add multivitamins and calcium supplements to the diet as recommended by your vet, and exercise her gently right up to the end.

Get things ready for the arrival of the puppies. The whelping and nursing

4 The puppy is born, covered in the membrane of the water sac.

3 The water sac containing the fetus appears at the vulva. This puppy is arriving rear end first; just visible in the sac is its tail, and one of its paws.

2 The bitch strains when the fetus enters the pelvis; the puppy will soon be born.

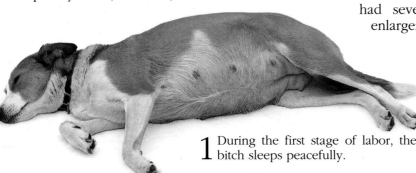

1 During the first stage of labor, the bitch sleeps peacefully.

5 The bitch strips off the membrane and bites through the umbilical cord.

6 By licking the puppy clean, the mother stimulates it to take its first few breaths.

7 The bitch rests between births and supervises her puppies suckling.

mom will need a quiet, clean refuge, such as a box, basket, or kennel, with lots of old newspapers on hand for disposable bedding. If you are new at the game, have a chat with a reliable breeder or your vet before the big day.

Whelping

If you are certain of the date of the last possible mating, don't worry if your bitch goes over the prescribed sixty-three days by a few days, provided that she is eating and is generally well, has no colored discharge from the vulva, and has not been seen to strain on any occasion other than when passing a stool. But if any of these rules are broken and pups have not appeared within two hours, consult your vet immediately.

When birth is imminent, the bitch's temperature drops by a couple of degrees. She becomes restless, may go off her food, pants fitfully, and prepares her bed. This means that she wanders about, sometimes chooses a site quite different from the one you had chosen, may paw fretfully at the bedding, and turns round and round in circles before lying down, only to be up again in a short while. This state of pre-labor usually lasts about twelve hours, but it can be much briefer or continue for a day or two, sometimes with intervals of normal behavior. If there is no straining, no colored discharge from the vulva, and the bitch is otherwise well in herself, all is in order.

Labor proper can be regarded as beginning when you see the first strain by the bitch or the appearance of a colored (often bottle-green) discharge. Count from now. Within one hour the first pup should be born. A water sac appears first, and is sometimes ruptured by the licking of the bitch. Then follows the puppy, wrapped partly or entirely in the membrane of the water sac. Puppies are often born back feet first; this is not a breech birth and is nothing to get alarmed about.

Once delivered, the puppy remains attached to the afterbirth by a cord until the mother severs it with her teeth. If this doesn't occur, and particularly if the puppy's face is covered by membrane, you can help. Clear the membrane away from the nostrils and face and break the umbilical cord. Don't use scissors. Pull the cord apart between the fingers of your two hands. Make the break about 1½in (4cm) from the navel. Return the puppy to the mother without delay.

Between the birth of each successive pup the bitch may rest for minutes or for hours. The intervals tend to get shorter as labor progresses, but may well be irregular.

Emergencies

The maximum time limit for the birth of any one pup, counting from the first strain, is two hours. Remember that this is two hours from the beginning of labor for that pup, not from the beginning of whelping. After the two hours is up, with the pup still undelivered, contact the vet. The total time for whelping an average litter of four to eight pups is up to six hours.

The afterbirths will be expelled either after each pup or irregularly, coming in clumps at intervals or at the end of whelping. It is normal for the bitch to want to eat them; do not let her have many, as she may get diarrhea.

Most bitches have no trouble giving birth; where problems do arise the vet may help the animal manually, use drugs, or advise a Cesarean operation. A Cesarean is usually recommended in cases where labor has lasted more than twelve hours. It does not rule out future breeding and normal labor in subsequent whelpings.

You should only assist in labor when a puppy is half in and half out of the vulva and progressing slowly. With scrubbed hands, grasp the baby firmly and pull smoothly and gently, with a slight screwing action, at the same time pushing against the bitch's body. Try to pull at the same time as the natural strainings of the bitch.

8 A newborn puppy only minutes old.

Maternal Behavior

Bitches make good mothers, and you can generally leave the care of the pups to them. You should be there to supervise, however, and to assist in case anything goes wrong.

The bitch's biological role can lead to problems even when she is not carrying or caring for pups. The responsible owner should know about these and how best to cope with them.

False pregnancy
It is quite common for a bitch that has not been mated to show signs of pregnancy. Eight or nine weeks after her heat, she will exhibit the restlessness, bed-making, and fullness of the breasts that occur in truly pregnant bitches. Milk may run from the teats and an old slipper or child's toy may be carefully guarded and tended in the place she has selected as her nursery.

The bitch is not consciously or unconsciously wanting to have puppies when this happens. It will not result in ovary or womb disease. It may or may not occur after each heat.

The cause is the ovary, which, having shed eggs during the heat period, carelessly assumes that fertilization must have ensued as night follows day. It therefore produces the hormones that prepare the body for the arrival of the phantom pups. Treatment is easy. Either let the phenomenon run its full course (only a couple of weeks or so) or contact your vet. He may well prescribe a course of contraceptive pills, which have the additional function of suppressing false pregnancies.

After the meal, the bitch licks the puppies' faces and genital areas, and cleans up any mess they make.

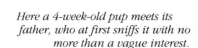

These 1-day-old pups are already expert at suckling, and, although deaf and blind, each finds its way to a nipple.

Spaying
Neutering, sterilizing, spaying: these are all other names used for the ovariectomy operation that prevents bitches from having unwanted pups. This involves major surgery and the procedure is irreversible. It is performed under general anesthetic by a veterinary surgeon and involves making a surgical incision either along the mid-line of the bitch's stomach or on one flank. It can be done at any age from twelve weeks onwards, but is best delayed until after the first heat period.

Spayed bitches are not more prone to troublesome false pregnancies but less so. Their chances of breast cancer

PATERNAL BEHAVIOR

It is rare for puppies to meet their fathers. In theory both dogs should behave as strangers, and establish their respectively subordinate and dominant positions in the canine hierarchy.

Here a 4-week-old pup meets its father, who at first sniffs it with no more than a vague interest.

The bitch and puppies relax after the meal and settle down for some sleep.

The puppies are now 26 days old (below), and the bitch finds it easier to feed them standing up. She needs about three times her normal amount of food at this stage.

are also reduced if the operation is performed before they are two years of age. Some do get fatter after the operation, but this is probably because their owners over-indulge and under-exercise them.

Spaying is the surest method of preventing unwanted pups. It also has the major benefit of preventing pyometra, the common and serious disease of bitches that occurs in middle and old age.

Although not a cheap operation, spaying is an important once-and-for-all contribution to the well-being and longevity of your pet – if you're sure that you'll never want to breed from her. If in doubt, use the contraceptive pill for a while. Spaying can be done later when you decide, or when the bitch has had a litter or two of puppies.

Care of newborn pups

You must provide the mother with a comfortable nursing box, daily changes of bedding, and extra high-quality food. It is almost impossible to overfeed a nursing bitch, and her nutritional requirements peak at about three times normal. She will have been eating more than usual in the last weeks of pregnancy, and her appetite will drop off sharply as the puppies are weaned.

Newborn puppies from a healthy litter find their way to their mother's teats soon after being born. The milk the mother produces in the first day or two (colostrum) provides a puppy with enough antibodies to protect it against most diseases for its first six to ten weeks. It is therefore important that all puppies in the litter suckle properly for the first few weeks at least.

If the bitch does not feed her pups for some reason or appears to have a shortage of milk, consult the vet. In many cases, a simple injection of pituitary hormone can produce an immediate flow.

Gradually the father progresses to circling the pup in a playful manner, and even licks its head in a tentative attempt at grooming.

The father is finally overwhelmed by other members of the litter, and abandons himself to play.

Puppy Development

At 7 days the puppy can still only sleep and suckle.

At 14 days the puppy's eyes are opening and it may be able to hear.

At 3 weeks old the puppy can focus its eyes and move around.

Puppies are born both blind and deaf. Their eyes open when they are ten to fourteen days old, but it takes them another week to focus properly. The ear canals open at around thirteen to seventeen days.

For the first week of their life, puppies do virtually nothing but sleep and suckle. They become steadily more active, and at three weeks old will be exploring their whelping box. But right up to the age of three months puppies will alternate bursts of boisterous activity with periods of deep sleep.

Keeping puppies warm

The outside world is cold compared with the constant 101.3°F (38.5°C) of the bitch's womb. The puppy arrives in the world wet, and prone to chills. It may not show any signs for up to forty-eight hours, by which time a serious and possibly lethal infection may have established itself.

Until they are seven to ten days old puppies are unable to regulate their body temperature. You must therefore provide extra heat in the form of room heaters, hot-water bottles, heating pads or infra-red lamps for at least the first two weeks, even if the puppies are in the whelping box. You will need to keep them warm even longer than that if they are orphan, rejected, or hand-reared puppies.

The room temperature should be kept at around 86-91°F (30-33°C), although puppies can tolerate slight variations on this for short periods. Alternatively you can keep the room temperature at a minimum of 68°F (20°C) and provide supplementary heat for the bitch's box. Every two weeks you can drop the room temperature by 5°F (3°C) until it returns to normal. Take care not to burn puppies with any supplementary heat source. Direct heat can damage their delicate skin.

**SPECIMEN MENU
FOR PUPPIES OF 6–12 WEEKS**

BREAKFAST
Bowl of puppy meal, baby cereal or breakfast cereal with milk.

LUNCH
Cooked ground beef, chopped canned dog food, semi-moist complete food or dry complete food.

SNACK
As for lunch, plus one drop of multivitamin syrup, if it has been prescribed by the vet.

SUPPER
As for lunch, plus puppy meal or cereal with milk.

At 12 weeks old, drop either lunch or the snack. At 6 months old, feed twice a day.

Bitches are very good mothers, and cater to most of their litter's needs, but humans can help the growing puppies in a number of ways.

At 30 days the puppy is beginning to play with its litter-mates.

At 6 weeks the puppy has all its milk teeth, and is ready for weaning.

Puppies should not be separated from mothers until 8 weeks old.

Healthy or sick?

You can tell healthy puppies because they are warm and dry to the touch and their skin has an elastic quality. They wriggle when you pick them up, and, though tiny, have a muscular, spring-like feel. The sound of a healthy litter is a gentle murmuring, with enthusiastic squeaks at feeding time. Weak puppies are limp to the touch and their skin does not spring back into place when you pick up and release a fold. They crawl around restlessly, emitting thin, plaintive wails. Eventually they give up and lie passively in a corner – often well away from the mother. Their bodies are quick to chill. Watch also for puppies that aren't getting enough milk, because a puppy that misses several feeds becomes too weak to suckle. It will probably have to be removed from the litter and reared by hand. Ask your vet for advice on this and any other puppy health problem you may encounter.

Between 6 and 12 weeks old, puppies learn the social skills necessary for survival.

CARE POINTS

• Most breeds (but not all) should have the dewclaws at the "wrist" and the "ankle" removed by a vet at 5-7 days old.

• Tail-docking should be done at the same time, but only if the breed standards demand it and you intend to show the dog.

• At 2-3 weeks old it may be necessary to trim the puppies' claws to prevent them scratching the bitch's belly skin.

• Follow your vet's advice about worming puppies. He or she may want to examine a stool sample for the presence of parasites before prescribing the appropriate medication.

• As soon as puppies have teeth, at around 3-5 weeks, they should be gradually introduced to solid foods such as puppy meal or cereal with milk. Do not rush changes to the diet.

These 18-day-old puppies are huddled together for warmth.

• The first vaccination against serious dog diseases should be given at around 6-8 weeks, with a second dose 2-4 weeks later. Keep puppies away from other dogs and public places until 2 weeks after the first shot.

• At 6 weeks puppies should begin the weaning process in earnest, and this should be completed by 10 weeks old.

• In the fourth month the growth of the puppy's permanent teeth may give rise to "teething troubles" similar to those suffered by human babies.

• At 6 months old ask your vet to check the puppies again for worms. Repeat this at 12 months old.

Raising and Fostering

In some cases, such as when a puppy is weak or a bitch does not have enough milk, you may have to consider artificial rearing. If the puppy or puppies are healthy and the problem lies in the milk supply, fostering on another lactating bitch is sometimes possible.

Artificial rearing of puppies is much more than simply buying a bottle and nipples and making up some formula milk. You have certain other maternal functions to perform by proxy, although in some cases it is possible to return the babies to their mother between feeds. However, certain highly strung bitches will reject their puppies totally once a human takes over the feeding. Others will clean and nibble the puppies in such a frenzy, so keen are they to rid their offspring of your scent, that they may actually cause harm. But many bitches do seem to relish their human friends becoming involved in the nursing process and don't mind a bit not having to breast-feed.

Whatever the attitude of the bitch, it is important to handle puppies that are kept with their mothers as little as possible, and to do so after washing the hands with an unperfumed soap and then stroking the bitch with both hands so that her scent masks your own to some extent. Premature puppies and puppies of bitches that are at first reluctant to "let down" milk are best kept with their mothers and only removed for feeding. Their presence will usually stimulate an increase in the milk flow.

Bottle-feeding puppies

If artificial feeding is indicated, do try to let the puppy have at least a few drops of the first milk (colostrum) from the bitch, if necessary by gently milking her teats.

It is very important for puppies to develop social skills by playing together, and by meeting other animals and humans.

With a little loving care, puppies raised apart from their mother can develop quite normally.

This milk provides the puppy with precious antibodies.

Get a special pet feeding bottle or premature baby bottle from a pet shop or the vet. Between feeds, clean and sterilize bottle and nipples in boiling water or disinfectant solution.

Feed newborn pups at two-hourly intervals at first and then three-hourly. The amount given depends on appetite. Hold the puppy gently but firmly around its chest and guide the nipple into its mouth. Let the legs move freely so that they can make their natural kneading or "paddling" action while feeding.

Check that the puppies are putting on weight by weighing each one at regular intervals.

The food itself is made up in a similar fashion to that of a human baby, usually by adding warm water to one of the standard bitch milk powders. Follow preparation instructions on the product label. If in doubt as to which brand to use for your puppies, ask your vet. Again, as with human babies, some pups thrive better on one brand than another. Make up a fresh supply of the artificial milk every day and keep it in the refrigerator. Feed it at blood-heat, around 100°F (38°C).

An alternative method is to make up your own substitute milk using easily obtained ingredients. The formula is as follows:

- 28 fl. oz (800ml) homogenized milk
- 7 fl. oz (200ml) cream
- 1 egg yolk
- 1 teaspoonful (6g) sterilized bone flour
- 1 teaspoonful (4g) citric acid powder
- 2-3 baby (human) vitamin drops.

A good variety of toys helps the puppy develop its physical skills.

BOTTLE-FEEDING A PUPPY

1 Leave the feet free to make the natural "paddling" movements.

2 Rub the genitals with a warm, damp cloth to stimulate defecation.

3 After each feed, clean the puppy's fur with another damp cloth.

Weak puppies may need a lighter feed. For the first few feeds give them cow's milk, diluted with one-third the volume of water and with 2½ teaspoonsful (10g) glucose added per 17 fl. oz (500ml). In order to compensate partially for the missing colostrum, add two drops of a pediatric vitamin mixture per 17 fl. oz (500ml).

Heat the mixture to around 100°F (38°C) and feed at least every two hours. (Very weak puppies may take tiny amounts as often as half-hourly until they improve.)

A puppy that won't or can't feed will quickly fade and die. Give it two hours to recover from the birth and meanwhile try to drip a little milk into its mouth. If this fails, consult the vet, who may start tube feeding. Forcing milk into a puppy is dangerous – a few drops of milk going accidentally down the windpipe can cause a rapidly fatal pneumonia.

Cleaning up

After each feed you must do what the natural mother would do by licking – clean the puppy. This has the additional function of stimulating normal bowel and bladder action. Clean the face with a warm damp cloth and then use it gently to massage the tummy and anus. Afterwards apply a little petroleum jelly around the anus.

Sometimes artificial diets cause constipation. You can try to alleviate this by putting a drop of mineral oil into the feed or directly into the mouth, and also by lubricating the anus by means of a stubby-bulb thermometer dipped into petroleum jelly and gently introduced into the rectum – no more than half an inch (1cm) deep. If a puppy develops diarrhea, try diluting the artificial feed to half-strength. Should diarrhea persist for twenty-four hours, contact the vet.

This maiden bitch was quite happy to provide warmth and cleaning and grooming services to these orphaned 4-week-old fox cubs.

Breed List

The names and groups of the American Kennel Club's breed registry.

Sporting Dogs
Brittany
Pointer
Pointer (German Short-haired)
Pointer (German Wire-haired)
Retriever (Chesapeake Bay)
Retriever (Curly-coated)
Retriever (Flat-coated)
Retriever (Golden)
Retriever (Labrador)
Setter (English)
Setter (Gordon)
Setter (Irish)
Spaniel (American Water)
Spaniel (Clumber)
Spaniel (Cocker)
Spaniel (English Cocker)
Spaniel (English Springer)
Spaniel (Field)
Spaniel (Irish Water)
Spaniel (Sussex)
Spaniel (Welsh Springer)
Vizsla
Weimaraner
Wire-haired Pointing Griffon

Hounds
Afghan Hound
Basenji
Basset Hound
Beagle
Bloodhound
Borzoi
Black and Tan Coonhound
Dachshund (Long-haired)
Dachshund (Short-haired)
Dachshund (Wire-haired)
Foxhound (American)

Foxhound (English)
Greyhound
Harrier
Ibizan Hound
Irish Wolfhound
Norwegian Elkhound
Otterhound
Pharaoh Hound
Rhodesian Ridgeback
Saluki
Scottish Deerhound
Whippet

Working Dogs
Akita
Alaskan Malamute
Bernese Mountain Dog
Boxer
Bullmastiff
Doberman Pinscher
Great Dane
Great Pyrenees
Komondor
Kuvasz
Mastiff
Newfoundland
Portuguese Water Dog
Rottweiler
St Bernard
Samoyed
Schnauzer (Giant)
Schnauzer (Standard)
Siberian Husky

Terriers
Airedale Terrier
American Staffordshire
 Terrier

Australian Terrier
Bedlington Terrier
Border Terrier
Bull Terrier
Bull Terrier (Staffordshire)
Cairn Terrier
Dandie Dinmont Terrier
Fox Terrier (Smooth)
Fox Terrier (Wire)
Irish Terrier
Kerry Blue Terrier
Lakeland Terrier
Manchester Terrier (Standard)
Norfolk Terrier
Norwich Terrier
Schnauzer (Miniature)
Scottish Terrier
Sealyham Terrier
Skye Terrier
Soft-coated Wheaten Terrier
Welsh Terrier
West Highland White Terrier

Toy Dogs
Affenpinscher
Brussels Griffon
Chihuahua (Long Coated)
Chihuahua (Smooth Coated)
English Toy Spaniel
Italian Greyhound
Japanese Chin
Maltese
Manchester Terrier (Toy)
Miniature Pinscher
Papillon
Pekingese
Pomeranian
Poodle (Toy)

Pug
Shih Tzu
Silky Terrier
Yorkshire Terrier

Non-Sporting Dogs
Bichon Frise
Boston Terrier
Bulldog
Bulldog (French)
Chow Chow
Dalmatian
Finnish Spitz
Keeshond
Lhasa Apso
Poodle (Miniature)
Poodle (Standard)
Schipperke
Tibetan Spaniel
Tibetan Terrier

Herding Dogs
Australian Cattle Dog
Belgian Malinois
Belgian Sheepdog
Belgian Tervuren
Bouvier des Flandres
Briard
Collie
Collie (Bearded)
German Shepherd Dog
Old English Sheepdog
Puli
Shetland Sheepdog
Welsh Corgi (Cardigan)
Welsh Corgi (Pembroke)

Index

Acknowledgments

Studio Dogs

pp16-17
Akita
Telsdale Acer
Jack Russell Terrier
Chip
Weimaraner
Brancaster Maximillian
Border Collie
Larkins Little Inch
owned by Mr John Fisher

pp20-21
Afghan Hound
Amudarya Shafi
owned by Linda Llewelyn

pp22-23
Basenjis
Zizunga Beguiling Whim
Zizunga Satin Doll
owned by Mrs Irene Terry

pp24-25
Basset Hound
Kentley Blind Date
owned by Mrs Humphries

pp26-27
Beagle
Rivenlea Gangster
owned by Angela Haddy

pp28-29
Bloodhounds
Nineveh's Miracle of Brighton
owned by Mrs Ickeringill
Nineveh's Mimosa of Chasedown
owned by Mr and Mrs D Richards

pp30-31
Borzoi
Vronsky Zapata
owned by Rosemarie Downes

pp32-33
Smooth-haired Dachshunds
Yatesbury Big Bang
Yatesbury Evening Star
owned by Mrs Pam Sydney

Miniature long-haired Dachshunds
Southcliff Starsky
Starsky of Springbok
owned by Mr Alan Sharman

pp34-35
Norwegian Elkhounds
Llychlyn Morgan
Kestos Adheryn
owned by Mr R Lee

pp36-37
Foxhounds
The Berks and Bucks Draghounds

pp38-39
Greyhound
Singing the Blues of Solstrand
owned by Mrs Dagmar Kenis

Segugio Italiano
Ira's Girl of Chahala
owned by Jenny Startup

Italian Greyhound
Philtre Foulla
owned by Mrs Carter

pp40-41
Irish Wolfhounds
Finneagle Frederick
Finneagle Forever True
owned by Alexandra Bennett

pp42-43
Rhodesian Ridgebacks
Bruet the Gentleman
Bruet the Countryman
owned by Peter and Cilla Edwards

pp44-45
Salukis
Al Caliphs Damn Flight
Al Caliphs Joel
owned by Mr Tom Fryer

pp46-47
Whippets
Hammonds Sebastian
Norwell Barley at Hammonds
owned by Angela Randall

pp50-51
German Short-haired Pointer
Jennaline Kentish Krumpet
owned by Jenny Jennings

pp52-53
Bracco Italiano
Lory
owned by Jonathan and Liz Shaw

pp54-55
Golden Retrievers
Melfricka Wassailer of Saintcloud
Alphinbrook Lodestar of Saintcloud
Sequantus Valkyr of Saintcloud
owned by Shirley Skinner

pp56-57
Grand Basset Griffon Vendéen
Ambassador at Dehra
owned by Mr Frost

Spinone
Kevardhu Fyn
owned by Mrs Andrea Bullock

pp58-59
Labrador Retriever
Donacre High Climber
owned by Mr, Mrs and Ms Heyward

pp60-61
Irish Setter
Caskeys Jezamy
owned by Mrs Heron

pp62-63
Cocker Spaniel
Ashweald Shoo Shoo Baby
owned by Carol Jarvis

pp64-65
English Cocker Spaniels
Donlawn Partners Choice of Bidston
Misty of Bidston
owned by Mrs Hillary Bidston

pp66-67
Vizslas
Russet Mantle Quiver
Russet Mantle October
owned by G Gottlieb

pp68-69
Weimaraner
Wilhelm Maximillian
owned by Ms B von Dwingezo-Luïten

pp72-73
Airedale Terrier
Bradus Quicksilver
owned by Mrs Wild

Welsh Terrier
Kadabra Go To Work Onan Ogg
owned by Mrs Edge

pp74-75
Bedlington Terrier
Dalip Limited Edition
owned by Mr Kitchen

pp76-77
Border Terriers
Moonline Dedication
Thoraldby Tolomeo
Halstow First Lady
owned by Mrs Moonie

pp78-79
Bull Terrier
Kerby's Tipple
owned by Mrs Youatt

pp80-81
Cairn Terrier
Deneland Super Trooper
owned by Mrs Towers

Australian Terrier
Elve Cruella de Ville
owned by Mr Michael Crawley

pp82-83
Dandie Dinmont Terrier
Josal Jester of Margham
owned by Margaret Hamilton

pp84-85
Wire Fox Terrier
Flyntwyre Flyntlock
owned by Hazel Bradford

pp86-87
Jack Russell Terriers
Ryemill Fudge
Rymill Mighty Mouse
owned by Mrs Edge

pp88-89
Kerry Blue Terrier
Deedilly Didilly Dee of Downsview
owned by Mrs Campbell

pp90-91
Manchester Terriers
Plutarch the Wise of Tyburn
L de Lavis-Trafford
owned by Mr Crawley

pp92-93
Norwich Terrier
Elve the Sorcerer
owned by Mr Michael Crawley

pp94-95
Miniature Schnauzer
Courtaud Carefree Casey
owned by Mr and Mrs S Court

pp96-97
Sealyham Terrier
Stephelcher Snow Wizard
owned by Mr Stephen Woodcock and
Mr Richard Belcher

pp98-99
Soft-Coated Wheaten Terrier
Berkley Brockbuster
owned by Lesley and Neil Smith

pp100-101
West Highland White Terrier
Cedarfell Movie Star
owned by Karen Tanner

Scottish Terriers
Anniversary of Kennelgarth
Cherry Brandy of Clemegarn
owned by Mrs Hills

pp104-105
Bichon Frise
Kynismar Heaven Sent
owned by Mrs Myra Atkins

pp106-107
Boston Terrier
Chilka Kirsty
owned by Mr and Mrs Barker

pp108-109
Bulldog
Mipoochi Delilah
owned by Mrs Leah Edwards

pp110-111
Chow Chow
Benchow the Chinaman
owned by Mrs M Bennett

pp112-113
Dalmatian
Elaridge Endeavour
owned by Mrs Stokes

pp114-115
Keeshond
Neradmik Jupiter
owned by Mrs Sharp-Bale

pp116-117
Lhasa Apsos
Chobrang Misha
Chobrang Le-Shi
owned by Irene Chamberlain

pp118-119
Toy Poodle
Philora Silver Warlord
owned by Sandra Martin

Miniature Poodle
Glayuar Galactica
owned by June Clark

pp120-121
Schipperke
Keyna's Artful Rogue
owned by Ms C Hart

pp122-123
Shar Pei
Bao Shou-Shi of Jentiki
owned by Jenny Baker

pp126-127
Akita
Overhills Cherokee Lite Fut
owned by Meg Purnell-Carpenter

pp128-129
Alaskan Malamute
Highnoons Nansamund
owned by Mr and Mrs Croly

pp130-131
Australian Cattle Dogs
Formakin Kulta
Formakin Minky
owned by Mr John Holmes

pp132-133
Belgian Sheepdogs
Heritiere du Pays des Flandres of Questenberg
Questenberg Oklahoma Kid
owned by Karen Watson

pp134-135
Bernese Mountain Dog
Sir Stanley from Meadowpark
owned by G and B Rayson

pp136-137
Bouvier des Flandres
Mr Bo Jangles at Aiulys
owned by Sue Garner

pp138-139
Boxer
Bitza Shout and Roar
owned by Mr and Mrs A Varney

pp140-141
Bullmastiffs
Dajean Loganberry
Dajean Rocky Won
owned by Ms S Wood

pp142-143
Bearded Collie
Desborough Dulcinea of Snowmead
owned by Mrs Waldren

pp144-145
Rough Collie
Leighvale Oliver Twist
owned by Les and Viv Norris

pp146-147
Doberman Pinscher
Sallate's Ferris
owned by Mr and Mrs Bevan

pp148-149
German Shepherd Dogs
Charvorne Dielander
Charvorne Lolita
owned by Mr and Mrs P Charteris

pp150-151
Great Dane
Daneton Kiri of Maricol
owned by Colin and Marie Stevens

pp152-153
Mastiffs
Tresylyan Bitter Sweet
Brookview Lucy Lastic of Tresylyan
owned by Mr and Mrs K Taylor

Neopolitan Mastiff
Kwintra Imra
owned by Mr John Turner and Dr Jean
Clark

pp154-155
Newfoundland
Seebar von Drachenfels of Yaffles
owned by Rosemary Miller

pp156-157
Old English Sheepdog
Kalaju Resident Rascal
owned by June Wilkinson

pp158-159
Pyrenean Mountain Dog
Clarance Brynhafod Barkin-Side
owned by Mr and Mrs S Clark

pp160-161
Rottweiler
Potterspride Pure 'n' Free
owned by Violet Slade

pp162-163
St Bernard
Groveacre Sophie's Choice
owned by Mr and Mrs Garey

pp164-165
Samoyeds
Krishe Khloe of Nikara
Nikara Special Edition
owned by Mrs Val Freer

pp166-167
Shetland Sheepdogs
Willow Tarn Telstar
Willow Tarn Trueman
Willow Tarn Tokaji
Trinket of Willow Tarn
owned by Mrs Rosalind Crossley

pp168-169
Siberian Huskies
Leejo's Tumak Musinka
Snowolf's Brecon
owned by Mr Ray Ball

pp170-171
Pembroke Welsh Corgi
Kaytop Dice of Rossacre
Cardigan Welsh Corgi
Deavitte Blue Fox of Rossacre
owned by Mrs Alli Boughton

pp174-175
Long Coated Chihuahua
Natimuk Wilf
owned by Dr Geoffrey Curr

pp176-177
English Toy Spaniels
Simannie Corny's Pride and Joy
owned by Barry and Sheila Byers
Grenajay Julie's Boy of Curtana
owned by Mrs Julia Huggins

pp178-179
Japanese Chins
Sangria Eclipse
Sangria Imperial Dragon
owned by Mr Bryan Bond and Mr George
Farmer

pp180-181
Maltese
Caramalta Sweet Melody of Ellwin
owned by M Lewin

pp182-183
Miniature Pinscher
Tygorsaf Tendertrap for Torilea
owned by Mrs P Powers

pp184-185
Papillons
Ju John Miss Ash at Ringlands
Ringlands Stella Star
owned by Mrs Norula

pp186-187
Pekingese
Chophoy Have a Nice Day
Chophoy Pittsburgh Stealer
owned by Mrs S Stag

pp188-189
Pomeranian
Taurusdale Intan Merah
owned by Mr Kee

pp190-191
Pugs
Puggleberry Pippa
Puggleberry Pingpong
owned by Mr and Mrs Hicks

pp192-193
Shih Tzu
Magique Magpie of Chelhama
owned by Mrs Goodwin

pp194-195
Silky Terrier
Marshdae Tumberlong
owned by Ms Anne Marshall

pp196-197
Yorkshire Terrier
*Bananas du Domaine de
Monderlay at Gaysteps*
owned by Mrs Anne Fisher

pp198-199
Mongrels
Nipper
owned by Mrs Westrope
Barney
owned by Mrs Burke
Tizzy
owned by Mrs Gardener

pp224-225
Golden Retriever
Gemma and puppies
owned by Carolyn Partridge

Author's acknowledgments
A book like *The Ultimate Dog* is, more than any other, the fruits of a co-operative effort by people with a wide variety of skills and background experience. To select any one individual above another would be invidious. I have been, yet again, admirably served, advised, and cosseted by my publishers, Dorling Kindersley, who provided an incomparable team of professionals to work with me. Among them I owe so much to the Managing Editor, Vicky Davenport, and to Gill Shaw, who led *The Ultimate Dog* brigade. I am especially grateful to the production team of Richard Williams, Sharon Lucas, Sally Hibbard, Maria Pal, and Eunice Paterson.
And, of course, I wag my tail most enthusiastically at all those canine friends who posed so glamorously and gaily for the photographer. Lastly, many thanks to my colleague, Dr John Lewis, who co-wrote large chunks of the text.

Dorling Kindersley would like to thank:
Nick Harris for support and guidance; Jillian Somerscales and Jane Mason for editorial assistance; Sandra Schneider and Lester Cheeseman for design help; Margaret Little for typing the manuscript; Ella Skene for the index, Anne Lyons for picture research; Debbie Harris for printing and initializing the disks; those dedicated dog handlers, Karen Tanner, John Fisher, and

Vivienne Braddon; Gerry and Cathy of Intellectual Animals; Hazel Taylor for handling, rearing, and helping the puppies to happen; and Teresa E Slowick, of the Kennel Club of Great Britain, for all her expert advice.

Picture credits
KEY:
b bottom, *c* centre, *l* left, *r* right, *t* top

p 8 anti-clockwise round map: Bernard Gerard/ Hutchinson Library; Syndication International; Stephen J Krasemann/Bruce Coleman

p 9 clockwise round map: Henry Ausloos/NHPA; Stephen J Krasemann/NHPA; Jen & Des Bartlett/ Bruce Coleman; Steve Krongard/Image Bank

Cabon/Vloo/Animal Photography: p 52 *bl*;
A H de Raad /Animal Photography: p 68
Bernard Rebouleau/Vloo/
Animal Photography: p 53 *b*; Sally Anne
Thompson/Animal Photography:
pp 32 *t*, 50 *c*, 51 *b*, 55 *bl*, 59 *cr*, 62 *l*, 63 *r*, 64 *l*, 79
tl, *br*, 82 *b*, 84 *l*, 92 *bl*, 118 *tr*,
132 *l*, 136 *l*, 137 *br*, 142 *bl*, 143 *r*, 146 *c*, 159 *lc*,
161 *bl*, 175 *br*, 176 *bl*, 208 *br*, 223 *t*;
R Willbie/Animal Photography: pp 58 *bl*, 60 *bl*,
109 *br*

Paddy Cutts/Animals Unlimited: pp l5 *br*, 61 *br*,
65 *tl*, 214 *tl*, *bl*, 215 *t*

J P Ferrero/Ardea: pp 10 *bl*, 145 *br*

Jan Baldwin: p 211 *t*

Jane Burton: pp 10-11 *t*, 14, 15 *t*, 204-205 except
204 *t*, 220 *t*, 226-235

Hans Reinhard/Bruce Coleman: pp 95 *tl*, 183 *cr*,
Norbern Rosing/ Bruce Coleman: p 11*br*

L Fried/Image Bank: p 214 *cr*, Peter M Miller/
Image Bank: p 11 *bl*; Sobel/Klonsky/Image Bank:
p 15 *bl*

Gerard Lacz/NHPA: p 139 *r*, l50 *c*

Stephen Oliver: pp 202-203 except 202 *t*, 206-207,
208 *tr*, 209 *tl*, 210 *bl*, 223 *b*

Robert Piercy/Animals Animals/OSF: p 36 *tr*

Syndication International: p 214 *tr*

Zefa: pp 10 *br*, 115 *t*; D J Fisher/Zefa: p 94 *c*;
M Schneider/Zefa: p 133 *t*

All other photography by Dave King